Alfred Ingham

Altrincham & Bowdon

With historical reminiscences of Ashton-on-Mersey, Sale, and surrounding townships

Alfred Ingham

Altrincham & Bowdon
With historical reminiscences of Ashton-on-Mersey, Sale, and surrounding townships

ISBN/EAN: 9783337191689

Printed in Europe, USA, Canada, Australia, Japan

Cover: Foto ©Andreas Hilbeck / pixelio.de

More available books at **www.hansebooks.com**

ALTRINCHAM & BOWDON,

WITH HISTORICAL REMINISCENCES OF

ASHTON-ON-MERSEY, SALE, AND SURROUNDING TOWNSHIPS.

BY

ALFRED INGHAM.

"Jumping o'er times,
Turning th' accomplishment of many years
Into an hour glass."
Shakespeare.

"Peruse with heed, then friendlie judge,
And blaming rashe refraine;
So maist thou reade unto thy goode,
And shall requite my paine."
Whitney's "Emblemes."

LONDON
65, WATLING STREET, E.C.
MANCHESTER:
CARTWRIGHT & RATTRAY LTD., 12, BROWN STREET.

PREFACE TO THE SECOND EDITION.

ALTHOUGH spoken of as a second edition, the present volume is to all intents and purposes a new work, embracing a large district surrounding Altrincham and Bowdon, and including the rapidly rising townships of Sale and Ashton-on-Mersey, which have increased enormously both in population and wealth during the past 20 years. It also marks a connecting link between what may be termed new and old styles, for the art of printing has made enormous strides, and by means of modern processes illustrations can now be given in greater number and variety, the cost of which was formerly prohibitive. And in the latter connection I have to express my hearty obligations to Mr. T. Colley, of Altrincham, a local artist. I may mention especially the sketch showing the Scotch rebels entering the Altrincham Market Place in 1745, also that of Lord Strange crossing the Mersey on his way to besiege Manchester; a pretty view of the Firs in the old coaching days, after William Hull, and the old church of Ringway, &c. The sketch of the vertebrate fauna of the district, which has been kindly supplied by Mr. T. A. Coward, of Bowdon, will be found most interesting to naturalists. I must also thank Mr. John Ingham, of Sale, for several excellent photographic views which he kindly placed at my disposal; Mr. Josiah Drinkwater, of Altrincham, for a capital photo. of the Free Library and Technical Schools; to Mr. W. Owen, A.I.B.A., for a view of the new Cemetery Chapel at Hale; as also to others who have in any way assisted to make the work both interesting and complete.

It was a source of the deepest pleasure to see the manner in which the "History of Altrincham and Bowdon" was received by the public, and that pleasure has since been enhanced by the remembrance that a record of the traditions and customs of the ancient boro' of Altrincham would, inevitably, have been lost but for the record which it was my good fortune to be able to make. I trust that my present effort may have as kindly a reception, and meet with the same good-natured and friendly criticism. I have endeavoured throughout to record facts and not opinions merely, and I am in hopes it will attain the object set forth in the first edition, and form not only "a book of reference, but also a local history in which the progress of the district is depicted from the earliest period to the present day."

A

CONTENTS.

	PAGE

CHAPTER I.

Bowdon, a peep at the past, geological, historical, and romantic—Boaden Downs—Watling Street, signs of Roman occupation—The tumulus in the Park—An old Saxon coin—The Barons of Dunham, their position and power—The Crusader's Cedar—The legend of the Seven Sisters—" The last of the Barons "... 1

CHAPTER II.

The Parish Church, its claims to antiquity—The yew trees, a relic of Saxon Christianity—The wakes, their origin and use—An old bead roll and its record—Description of the old church—Value of the living six centuries ago—The ringers' orders—A law suit—Another bead roll and its record—Memorials of old families—The Brereton monument—The Dunham Chapel, etc. 16

CHAPTER III.

Description of the old church, continued—The tales told by the tombstones and the tablets—A curious old stone, etc. 29

CHAPTER IV.

The Parish Church, its restoration—Reminders and relics of antiquity—Description of restored edifice—Tablets to the Ven. Archdeacon Pollock, and to the first Vicar of St. Margaret's—The stained glass windows and their donors—A run through the registers—Curious and interesting extracts—The Bowdon proverb—Notices of Vicars, with list—The ancient rating valuation, or mize, list of benefactions, etc. 38

CHAPTER V.

Altrincham 600 years ago—The ancient charter—Sanjam Fair—Election of Mayor, form of an oath and proclamation—The Court of Pye Powder—Importance of the Bellman—A Mayor's wisdom—The Earl's Christmas box—Sayings regarding the Mayor—Election of Burgesses—Progress of the trust and its disposal—Government enquiries and their result—List of Mayors—Abolition of Sanjam Fair 60

CONTENTS. vii.

PAGE

CHAPTER VI.

A retrospect—Sundry lawsuits—The first Booth of Dunham Massey; his supposed death at the Battle of Blore Heath—A Booth knighted by Queen Elizabeth—Interesting wills—Dame Booth's Charity—Contributions to the defence of the Kingdom—Dr. Dee's reference to Sir Geo. Booth—Purchase of the town of Warrington; the instructions thereon—Death of William Booth... 85

CHAPTER VII.

Birth of Sir George Booth, first Lord Delamer—Description of Sir William Brereton—Indictment against Sir George; his part in attempting to pacify the county—Its failure—The siege of Nantwich--Spirited defence—Defeat of the Royalists—Sir George elected member for Cheshire; his exclusion by Colonel Pride's purge—Royalist attempts at a Restoration—Sir George's celebrated rising—The Battle of Winnington—His betrayal and arrest; his committal to the Tower—Release and re-election—His improvements at Dunham—Description of the old mansion—His death ... 98

CHAPTER VIII.

The second Lord Delamer; his popularity; his advocacy of the people's rights—Court jealousy—His committal to the Tower on three occasions; his remarkable trial at Westminster Hall; his eloquent defence and justification; his retirement to his seat in Cheshire; his support of the Prince of Orange; his subsequent honourable career and death 107

CHAPTER IX.

The house of Dunham, continued—The Second Earl of Warrington; his character and literary attainments—The union of the House of Dunham with that of Stamford—The Honourable Booth Grey—"Domestic happiness, a family picture"—The revival of the lapsed titles of Baron Delamer and Earl of Warrington—An Africander Earl—A romance of the peerage 120

CHAPTER X.

The Maceys of Altrincham—A rebellious subject—The Bowdon family—Disposal of lands—Some old district names—Bowdon free school—Bull and bear baiting—Guy Faux at Altrincham—A witty Bowdon Curate—The advance on Manchester by Lord Strange—The Unicorn Hotel 300 years ago—An Altrincham landlord and landlady of the olden time—Sir Peter Leycester's description of the town in 1666—The story of the "Bloody Field"—Adam Martindale at Dunham; his duties there—Bowdon Dissenters troublesome—Dick Turpin; his exploits at Newbridge Hollow and Hoo Green—Prince Charlie's Troops at Altrincham 127

A 3

CONTENTS.

CHAPTER XI.

Indications of growth and enterprise—The cutting of the Bridgewater Canal—A few figures—Manufacture of woollen and cotton yarn—Obsolete punishments: penance, cucking stool, scold's bridle, public whippings at the Altrincham Market place—Executions for burglaries at Bowdon—A man hanged for poaching near Altrincham—The ancient custom of souling—The entertaining play of St. George and the dragon—Wassailing and Christmas carols—The barley hump and Dunham Ale—The lions of Dunham—Altrincham races—Dunham Parks and the Hall—De Quincy's description of Altrincham 139

CHAPTER XII.

Ecclesiastical Altrincham: The Wesleyan Methodist Churches—Wesley's visits to Altrincham—St. George's Church; its Schools, etc.—An Altrincham Centenarian—The Unitarians; their early history; description of the New Chapel in Dunham Road—The Methodist New Connexion—The Independents or Congregationalists, with some notices of their Pastors and work—St. Margaret's, Dunham Massey—St. John's—St. Peter's, Peel Causeway—The Old Downs Chapel—The Primitive Methodists—Baptists, etc. 147

CHAPTER XIII.

More looks into old books—Visit of strolling players—Disappearance of town documents—Appointment of town's attorney—Wages a century ago—Disturbances in Altrincham—Another Altrincham industry—The fire engine—The old handcuffs—A jury list—The expenses of the great well—Altrincham highways indicted—Hard times; a display of public spirit—The select vestry—Extracts from the books; a stray parcel of gloves—How the town got a sun-dial—Substitutes for the Militia—Disrespect for proclamations—A worthy overseer—Dread of Hydrophobia, etc. 175

CHAPTER XIV.

Description of Altrincham and Bowdon 60 years ago—The Old Market Place; its ancient cross, lockups, and Star chamber—Higher Town boys v. those of Lower Town—The town field - An Altrincham Carnival - The loyalty of the town—The first Altrincham undertaker—Altrincham woolcombers and their Bishop Blaize festival—Bowdon bull baiters and Altrincham cockfighters—Salt works at Dunham—The destruction of small birds—The churchwardens and their duties—Formation of the Altrincham Poor Law Union; the old workhouse and its management—Cutting of the Bowdon line—Lloyd's Hospital—Introduction of coal gas into Altrincham—Formation of the Gas Company; negotiations for the purchase of the works and their results—Altrincham and Bowdon Literary Institution; Free Library and Technical Schools—Royal Visit—Formation of the Altrincham Parliamentary Division; its members, past and present—The electric light, etc. 188

CHAPTER XV.

What Sale was; a glance at the past; the Masseys of Sale—a gracious permission to marry from the Pope—A reminiscence of the civil war; Lord Strange at Ashton-on-Mersey—Some looks into old township books—The official mole catcher—Sale "Vineyards"—Constables' staves—The poor law and its administration—troublous times—A lady's interest in township matters—A local Hampden, Sale township schools—Sale Volunteers, past and present—Sale Burial Board, etc. 223

CHAPTER XVI.

Ashton-on-Mersey and its parish—The beginnings of modern non-conformity—Old Cross Street Chapel—Some notices of old Vicars—Restoration of St. Martin's—St. Anne's; St. John's, Brooklands; St. Paul's; St. Mary's; Wesleyanism; Congregationalism—Sale Local Board—Progress of Sale—Sanitary arrangements, etc. ... 241

CHAPTER XVII.

Wythenshawe Hall—Carrington Moss, with an account of Carrington fight, a memorable local event—Manchester Ship Canal—A Bishop from Partington—Baguley Hall and the Leighs—Riddings Hall—The Gerrards and the Vaudreys—Edleston's Lepidoptera of the Bollin Valley; ornithology etc.—Ashley Hall, a notable meeting; a little known tragedy—The murder at the Bleeding Wolf, etc. ... 257

APPENDIX.

Cheshire County Council—Bucklow Union and Rural District Council—Magistrates for Altrincham Division—Altrincham Local Board; list of members and contested elections, etc.—List of towns and villages in the neighbourhood, with population, acreage, rateable value, distances from Chester, Altrincham, etc.—Sale Local Board; list of members—Altrincham, Bowdon, and Sale Urban District Councils, etc.—Debts of local authorities. 293

ILLUSTRATIONS.

	PAGE
Bowdon Church, 1858	Frontispiece
Burying Lane (now The Firs), Bowdon	25
Bowdon Parish Church—restored	38
St. Margaret's Church, Dunham	46
Scolds' Bridles	75
Earl and Countess of Stamford	91
Dunham Hall, 1697	62
The Hall, Dunham Park	86
Oldfield Hall, Altrincham	102
Market Place, Altrincham, 1745	131
Market Place, Altrincham, 1858	198
Ashley Mill (now dismantled)	214
Bowdon Wesleyan Chapel	149
The Old Church, Ringway	156
Rev. George London	151
Bowdon Downs Congregational Church; interior lighted by electricity	161
St. Peter's Church, Peel Causeway	174
The Old Church, Ashton-on-Mersey	179
Altrincham in the Jubilee year; visit of the Prince of Wales	195
Altrincham Free Library and Technical School	211
Past and Present Members for the Altrincham Parliamentary Division:—Sir William C. Brooks; the late Mr. John Brooks; Mr. Coningsby Disraeli	217
Lord Strange's Forces Crossing to Besiege Manchester	225
Review of the Manchester and Salford Volunteers on Sale Moor, April 12th, 1804, by Prince William of Gloucester	237
Lych Gate, Ashton-on-Mersey	242
St. Anne's Church, Sale	247
St. Mary's Church, Ashton-on-Mersey	253
Wythenshawe Hall	261
Altrincham Electrical Works, Broadheath	271
Rostherne Church	284
Altrincham Cemetery Chapel, Hale	286
Plan of Stamford Park, Altrincham	291

INDEX.

	PAGE
A hard winter	182, 183
Advowson, Bowdon	12
Altrincham, Free traffic granted	13
,, Charter	60 to 82
,, Landlord and landlady of olden time	134
,, Sir Walter Scott's description of	134
,, Sir Peter Leycester's description of	135
,, Indications of progress	139
,, Manufactures at	129, 139
,, Races at	144
,, Riots at	176
,, De Quincy's description of	143
,, Footpaths indicted	182
,, Fire Brigade	177
,, Sixty years ago	188
,, Union	198
,, Provident Dispensary	204, 205
,, Introduction of coal gas	208
,, Gas Company	209, 210
,, and Bowdon Literary Institute	210
,, and Free Libraries Act	213
,, Local Board, formation of	214
,, List of members (see Appendix)	
,, Contested elections (see Appendix)	
,, Statement of debts, &c. (see Appendix)	
,, Urban District Council (see Appendix)	
,, Cemetery	221
,, Introduction of electricity	219, 220
,, Parliamentary Division	216, 219
Appendix	293 to 326
Ashley	288
,, Hall	289
,, Church	290
Ashton-on-Mersey, Parish of	241 to 254
,, Vicars	242
,, Cross Street	245
Ashton Wakes, incident of	228, 229
Baguley	270
Bank Hall, Hale	275
Baptist Chapel, Bowdon	173
Banns, Curious mode of publication	44
Barleyhump, The	143
Beeston Castle	100
Benefactions, Bowdon	59
Bishop Blaize Festival	193
Bloody Field, Story of	133
Booth, Derivation of	86
,, John	86

INDEX.

	PAGE
Booth, William	86, 87, 88
,, George	89, 93
,, William	89
,, Henry	24 to 28
,, Langham	28
,, Sir George	19, 98, 99
,, Robert	86, 87
,, Sir George, defeat and capture of	103
,, ,, grant by Parliament for distinguished services	104
,, ,, death of	105
,, Nathaniel	120
Botany, of Cotterill, &c.	276
Bowdon, Derivation of	1
,, Doomsday Entry	2
,, Family of	128
,, Free School at	129
,, Church	16
,, Restoration of	39 to 42
,, Registers	43, 44, 46
,, Wakes	194
,, List of Vicars	58
,, Notices of	55 to 58
,, Local Board	215
,, Urban District Council (see Appendix)	
Brereton	21, 23, 269, 270
,, Traditions	21
,, Sir William	21, 99
,, Jane	21
,, William	21
Briefs Collected	54
British Road	1, 2, 3
Broadheath	3
Bull Baiting at Bowdon	194
Burgesses Election of	73
Burying in Linen	51
Carrington Chapel	20
,, Moss	264, 265
,, Fight or Feight	265, 266, 267
Charities	206, 207, 208
Chartists at Altrincham	202
Charter, Altrincham (translation)	79, 80
Civil War	100
Congregational Churches	159, 161, 163, 164, 246, 247
Cross Street Chapel	245, 246
Curious Customs	143
Court Leet, Altrincham	60 to 82
,, ,, Mayoral Oath	62
,, ,, Proclamation	63
,, ,, Uses of	63, 64

INDEX

	PAGE
Court Leet, Duties of Members	70 to 74
,, ,, Mayor's Land Charity	78, 79
Cock Fighting at Altrincham	194
Delamer, Lord	117
,, Trial of	108 to 116
,, Created Earl of Warrington	117
,, His views on Monarchy	118
,, Prayers, &c.	117, 118
Destruction of small Birds	198
Dick Turpin at Hoo Green	137
Dunham Castle	8 to 13
,, Doomsday Entry	7
,, Hall, Ancient Mansions	105
,, Ale	143
Executions for Burglaries at Bowdon	142
Extracts from old Minute Books	184 to 187
Gerrard of Riddings	21
Grey, Hon. Booth	69, 121
,, Family, Antiquity of	121
,, Lady Jane	121
,, Rev. Harry, Eight Earl, a Romance of the Peerage	123
,, Pedigree, to face page	127
Guy Fawkes at Altrincham	130, 134
Hale Barns	285, 286
Linen Manufacture	129
Lloyd's Hospital	204
Masey or Massey of Dunham	6
,, Reference to	11 to 15
Massey of Sale	222 to 227
Manchester Ship Canal	267, 268, 269
Minute Books, Disappearance of	175
Mayor's Land Charity (see Court Leet)	
Manor of Dunham	85
Manchester South Junction & Altrincham Railway	202, 203
Martindale, Adam, at Dunham	135, 136
Methodist New Connexion	139
Members of Parliament	216, 219
Mize, or old rate	59
Oldest Tombstone	33
Old Tombstones, Inscriptions on	33 to 37
Old Jury List	177
Obsolete Punishments	140, 141
Presbyterianism	173, 249
Primitive Methodism	174, 249
Prince Charles at Altrincham	138
Queen's Jubilee Festivities	215
Rateable Value (see Appendix)	
Rider, Bishop of Killaloe	269

B

	PAGE
Roman Road	9
,, Remains, Hale	283
Roman Catholic Church	173
Salt Works at Dunham	197
Sale, Description of	222
,, Family	224
,, Overseers in	224
,, Vineyards	228
,, and Luddites	230
,, Lady Overseer	231
,, A village Hampden	233
,, New township schools	234, 235, 236
,, Moor	236
,, Burial Board	240
,, Local Board	255, 256
,, Urban District Council (see Appendix)	
St. Anne's, Sale	249, 250, 251
St. Elizabeth's, Altrincham	172
St. George's, Altrincham	150, 153, 154, 155
,, ,, Schools	154
,, ,, List of Ministers	155
St. John's, Altrincham	171
St. John's, Brooklands	251
St. Margaret's, Dunham Massey	165, 166, 167, 168, 169
,, Vicars of	169, 170
St. Mary's, Ashton-on-Mersey	252, 253
St. Martin's ,, (see Ashton Parish)	
St. Paul's, Sale	252
St. Peter's, Peel Causeway	174
Select Vestry, Altrincham	199, 200, 201
Sparrows, Destruction of	229
Strange, Lord at Ashton	129, 130
Tattons of Wythenshawe	22, 257, 258, 259, 260, 262
Timperley	273
Tumuli and Urns, Dunham Park	3, 4
Unitarian Chapels, Altrincham	155, 156, 157, 158
,, ,, Sale	245, 246
Vandrey, Will of	273, 274
Volunteer Movement, Sale	236, 239
Vertebrate Fauna	276 to 283
Watling Street	2, 3
Warburton	23
Warrington, Mary, Countess of	27
Warrington, Purchase of	96
,, Earldom extinct	120
,, Earldom revived	123
Wesley's visits to Altrincham	147, 148
Wesleyan Methodism	147, 148, 149, 249
Wythenshawe Hall, &c.	259 to 263

HISTORY OF

ALTRINCHAM & BOWDON.

CHAPTER I.

Bowdon:—A peep at the past, geological, historical, and romantic.—Boaden Downs—Watling Street, signs of Roman occupation—The tumulus in the Park—An old Saxon coin—The Barons of Dunham, their position and power—The Crusader's Cedar—The legend of the Seven Sisters—" The last of the Barons."

BOWDON, eight centuries ago, was spelled Bogedon, or the *hill* or *down* by a bog. It was so written in the Domesday Book, and was comprised in the ancient Cheshire hundred of Bochelau, whence our modern Bucklow, in the eastern division of which it is still included. It has also been written Bodon, Bodeon, Bawdon, Boaden, Bauden, Boden, and Bowden; but the modernized spelling of Bowdon now prevails. This is derived from two Anglo-Saxon words signifying Bode, a dwelling, and don or dun, a plain upon a rising hill or down.

Geologists tell us, with the charming uncertainty they always attach to their "periods," that Bowdon has little interest for them,—that it was once an enormous sandbank, left by the receding waves of a restless ocean, to be at a subsequent time transformed by the God of Nature into a lovely garden, the loveliness of which was to be heightened and enhanced by the ingenuity and art of man.

It may be very safely assumed that it was not then the pleasant place of residence it has since become. It had not the same delightful prospects of pastoral scenery, of grassy plain and lovely woodland, hemmed in by masses of billowy vegetation. The pre-historic Bogedonian—if there was such a creature—looking southwards from the hill side, would have seen the waves beating at the foot of the vale, where the shingle of the sea beach was quite recently uncovered; later still, he might have viewed what is now called Alderley Edge, and the more distant Mow Cop, looking out on a vast expanse of moor and morass, studded here and there with a consumptive dwarf oak ; but he could have formed no conception of the changes to be wrought, as if by fairy wand, in future ages. The "proud hill's crest" had not become dotted with those stately homes which in so marked a degree contribute to set off Nature's beauties. It had not even those prim ivy-covered quaint old houses which peep out at the passer-by from their nests of umbrageous foliage and over-hanging trees, as if very modesty prevented their coming to the front in all the boldness of modern paint and stucco. "Sleepy hollow," as Altrincham has been termed, was unknown, and that almost universal edible the potato did not flourish in unchecked luxuriance on the Downs, and form a special cry in the adjacent market of Cottonopolis. All that can, with any degree of confidence, be relied upon as giving Bowdon a place in early English history is the mention of it which occurs in the Domesday Book, of which more hereafter, and when among other things, there was a Church and a Priest, with his half-a-hide of land, a hide being as much as one plough would cultivate in a year, 60 to 120 acres according to the peculiar reckoning of the times, and which said Priest lived contentedly amongst his meagre and widely-scattered flock, and was passing rich on the forty pounds a year of the period.

There are, however, evidences of this portion of the district having been inhabited long before the Conquest. The British road, well known by the name of Watling Street, runs through it, and was adapted by the Romans to suit their own purposes. The ancient Roman Road, as traced by that eminent authority, Whitaker, commences at the ford of the Mersey called Stretford, continues to Broadheath, where the Roman Road keeps the middle of the heath, and was discovered on the cutting of the Bridgewater Canal which crosses its line. It is then seen in the enclosures about Oldfield Hall, and in crossing the Moss is known by the name of Upcast. It afterwards ascends the hill, enters (skirts) Dunham Park, passes on to Street head, and crossing the Bollin falls into the modern road at Newbridge Watkins, in his work on Roman Cheshire, published in 1886, has with painstaking ability made this particular subject his own. The main road remains, so far as this district is concerned, pretty much as given above, but he adds, " There appear to have been two small roads branching off to east from that between Manchester and Northwich at Dunham Park, one which for part of its length is now the modernised Long Lane, and seems to have led to a village at Hale, and may thence have been continued towards Wilmslow, where there is a Pepper Street. It would, before arriving at this point, cross the road from Stockport to Kinderton. The other, known as Peel Causeway, is only traceable as a fragment, and I am doubtful of its Roman origin." This part was comprised in the Roman province of Flavia Cæsariensis; and subsequently, in the sixth century, by a course of events in which Britain had passed through the fiery ordeal of Saxon subjugation and civil war, it became included in the Kingdom of Mercia. No doubt, the army of Danes, who are said to have taken possession of Chester in the latter end of the year 894 (according to the Saxon chronicle), marched through it from Northumberland. There are still most conclusive evidence of Saxon and Danish occupation in the tumuli or barrows which are to be seen in Dunham New Park. One of them is marked on the Ordnance Survey Map, and there are also others near Bollington and at Baguley, but both these are either more level, or considerably reduced in size. These tumuli are the most ancient form of burial places known, and were in extensive use amongst the Romans and Danes, who probably derived it in their turn from the Greeks, for the custom is mentioned by Homer. Some of these tumuli, as at Marathon, are very large, and it is said that the higher they are the greater must the deceased have been held in esteem by their fellows. The tumulus marked on the Ordnance Survey Map exists on the north side of the New Park, and is known more generally by the name of Beech Mount, being marked by a clump of these noble trees, some of which are beginning to exhibit signs of decrepitude and old age. In his work, "Britannia Romana," published by Horsley in 1732, he refers to this, when discussing the place where the Roman station, Condate,—the exact site of which has been the subject of much controversy amongst antiquarians—shall be placed. He says:—"The urns which have been found, and the barrows that are in Dunham Park, belonging to the Earl of Warrington, and the military way near it, render it highly probable that the Roman Road has gone directly from Manchester to Chester through or near to Northwich, the piece of Roman Road by Altrincham pointing directly towards Chester and Manchester, and not at all towards Congleton. It is in the middle of a field near the road which now leads from Manchester to Chester and is called the Street. This leaves little room to doubt that the military road, and consequently, the iter (way) has proceeded this way to Chester, which is also further confirmed by the name of Stretford on the Mersey."

Thus, in a somewhat interesting manner, is related an important fact. It is in this road that the Romans have left a mark of their enduring greatness, when all appearances of ancient Saxon power have been completely effaced. These urns speak to us of Rome in her palmy days; but the mounds tell a story which extends beyond. Imagination pictures a somewhat rugged country, studded with the kraals or mud dwellings of the aboriginal inhabitants,—a time when, according to Lucian, the monk, the County of Chester exported *slaves and horses*. Near the great highroad would be the dwelling of the hardy chieftain. At his death, guided by those æsthetic tastes instinct even in savage nations, the nearest spot on which nature had greatly lavished her beauties would be selected for his burial place, and at what would then be the head of a mossy dell would his remains be laid. There would be the long procession of bearded warriors and slaves, headed by weirdly robed priests, who, amidst moanings and lamentations, would perform, with mysterious and perhaps ghastly rites, the last offices for the dead. The huge tumulus would be raised, with nothing but its height to remind the people that buried greatness there reposed in its last long sleep; with no image or legendary scroll to record, for the information of succeeding generations, the names and deeds of the mighty dead; his very remembrance would in time be blotted out. But he would have a grand burial place, not perhaps graced with the virtues of consecration, except in the sense in which Nature reflects Nature's Deity. There, we may leave him in Nature's presence-chamber itself,—and if we could have seen it then, standing out like the refreshing greenery of the desert oasis, in "the forest primeval," where

> The murmuring pines and the hemlocks
> Bearded with moss, and in garments green, indistinct in the twilight,
> Stand like Druids of old, with voices sad and prophetic;
> Stand like harpers hoar, with beards that rest on their bosoms.

Another interesting memento of the ancient associations of Bowdon may here be mentioned. Several years ago, a bystander, who was watching the sexton of the Parish Church open out a grave, observed in one of the shovels full of earth thrown out, something black and round. This, on rubbing, gave out a bright appearance, and, on being placed in the hands of an antiquary, proved to be a silver penny of Eadmund, one of the early Saxon Kings, and grandson of Alfred the Great. On the obverse was *Eadmund Rex*, in the centre being a small cross. On the reverse, amongst other things, was the word *Ingel || Gar*, M T., or really Ingelgar Moneyer. Probably the sandy soil into which the coin had been dropped prevented corrosion, as it was in an admirable state of preservation. The capital letters were well formed, and differed very little from our modern ones, except the G, which was very square in form, and the M, which consisted of two outer stems like capital I's connected not by an inner acute angle like a V, but by a slight curve or festoon at the top. This Ingelgar was, during the years 941-945, a moneyer to Anlaf, at that period King of Northumbria, who, in the latter year, was expelled by Eadmund. Ingelgar, in addition to Anlaf, was moneyer to three other Kings; Eric, also a King of Northumbria, and to Eadmund, and his brother and successor Eadred. The coin was thought to have been struck at Manchester, on account of its proximity to Bowdon; but as there was also a Mint at Chester, there is no conclusive evidence on this point.

We now leave for the present speculation behind, and proceed to the consideration of authentic records. With the advent of William the Conqueror, and the consolidation of his power in England, we see the establishment of a feudalism which was to leave its mark and impress on the people to our own time. The County of Chester, which was then looked upon in the light of a little kingdom, was amongst the last in England to yield to his army, and the city did not fall into his hands until 1070. Shortly afterwards the Earldom of Chester was given by the King to his nephew, Hugh D'Avaranches, son of Richard Gosse, and surnamed Hugh la Loup, or Hugh Lupus, on account of his bearing a wolf's head on his shield. The Earl had his Council of Barons spiritual and temporal, with all the usual officers of the Court and a reigning Sovereign. The County was parted amongst the Normans, and the old Saxon possessors turned out. Amongst the Normans in the Roll of Battle Abbey, quoted by Hollinshed, appears the name of Hamound. This again is given in ancient charters as Hamund; and as he was a most important personage, it is beyond doubt that he is the same Hamunde or Hamo who held the Barony of Doneham or Dunham, at the time of Domesday Survey, in 1086, and who dwelt at the Castle, which in all probability was founded by a Saxon predecessor. These Barons held their Lordships from the Earl of Chester, and the tenants of the farms from the barons. In an old poem written about 300 years ago, it is said of the first Earl of Chester, that

> On Hamon Massey he did bestow
> The Dunham Massey barony;
> To whom there did succeed in rowe
> Five heires of his successively.
> From henceforth 'mongst the female heires
> It scattered was for many years;
> Yet most part, after ages passed,
> To Fitton of Bollin came at last.

Another version gives it :—

> Vpon Hughe Massey he did bestow
> the Dunham Massey barronye,
> to whom their did succeed in row
> 8 (5) heyres of his successivelye;
> from thenceforth mongst the femall heyres
> it scattered was for many yceres,
> yet most part after ages past
> a Boothe of Du[n]ham came at last.

The entry in Domesday Book says that Hamon holds Doneham; Eluard held it, and was a freeman; there is one hide of land rateable to the gelt; the land is three carucates; one is demesne; and there are two neatherds, two villeins, and one bordar; and one acre of wood, and one house in the city (of Chester); in the time of King Edward it was worth 12s.; now 10s. It was waste.

It also states that the same Hamo "holds Bogedone; Eluard held it and was a free man; there is one hide rateable to the gelt; the land is two carucates; there are two foreigners having one carucate; there is a priest and a church to which half this hide belongs; also a grinding mill rendering 16 pence; it was waste, and so [the Earl] found it."

It may be well to explain the meaning of one or two of these terms. The quantity of a hide, as has been already mentioned, appears to have varied considerably. The land rateable to the gelt was that which was taxed for the purpose of subsidizing the invading Danes, and a carucate, or caroc, or ploughland, was generally eight oxgangs, or bovates—224 acres. There do not seem to have been any radmen or roadmen in either township, although there was one in Hale; but those of a lower order, viz., neatherds, &c., are noted. Radmen were those who served their superior lords on horseback, and were freemen in a certain sense. Villeins were those whose estate of vassallage almost amounted to slavery; neatherds or bovarii were employed in attending to the cattle, and in other servile work; and bordars, or boors, held small portions of land, and were probably bound to supply the table of the Lord of the Manor with eggs, poultry, &c.

That historian and antiquarian *par excellence*, Sir Peter Leycester, shrewdly guesses that Hamon the Norman dispossessed Eluard the Saxon of his lands in this neighbourhood, after having had them "given" to him by the Earl; but in addition to these he held Hale, Ashley, half of Owlerton—now Ollerbarrow—Bromhale, Puddington in Wirrall, and other lands, by military service; he being bound to attend the King in time of war with a certain number of horse and foot, and immediately repair to the King's summons with his whole posse should an enemy's army come into Cheshire, or should Chester Castle be besieged. An engraving in King's "Vale Royal" represents the Earl of Chester in Parliament assembled, his eight barons seated on each side of him, and amongst them, the first on his left-hand side, distinguished by his arms—quarterly, gules and or, in the first quarter a lion passant, argent,—is to be seen Hamo of Dunham. At the barrier which divides the room into two portions, are a number of adherents, who appear to be pressing their claims to lands, which having been won by the sword, will be so held and esteemed good title to them in the future.

The Castle of Dunham was greatly strengthened by Hamon, so as to resist successfully the marauding propensities of avaricious neighbours. He was one of the most influential of the barons, from the fact of his Castle being situated near the great Roman road, it formed a powerful position of defence in case of invasion. The counties palatine, says one writer, were judged to be in greater danger than the others, and greater attention therefore was paid to their defences. The adjoining County Palatine of Lancaster was surrounded by a chain of forts, one of which was at Widnes, where a baron was stationed to protect that side from the incursions of the Cheshire people; and the jealousy being mutual, opposite to this on the Cheshire side was Halton Castle, placed in such a manner as to guard the county from any surprise either from Warrington, another Lancashire barony, or Runcorn Ferry. The next barony was Newton, erected as well to strengthen Warrington as to oppose any passage out of Cheshire, and opposite to this was placed Hamon at Dunham. Hamon in his lifetime gave to St. Werburgh's at Chester, the village of Northerden (Northenden), in the Maxfield or Macclesfield Hundred. He had a son and heir, named after him, Hamon, and also Robert Massey, who was a witness to the first Randle's charter of confirmation to the Abbey of St. Werburgh in Chester, about A.D. 1124.

The second Hamon had issue, Hamon, a son and heir, and Robert Massey, from whom sprang the Masseys of Sale. This is probably the Hamon Massey who is noticed in one of the ancient chronicles as having held the Castle of Dunham against Henry II. in 1173, during the rebellion of which Hugh, Earl of Chester, was principal leader. He gave the lands of Bramhall, or Bromale, to Matthew de Bromale by charter, of which the following is a translation:—

Hamo de Masci to all his friends, both clerical and lay, as well present as to come, sends greeting. Know ye all that I have granted, &c., to Matthew de Bromale, Bromale and Dokenfeld and two parts of Baguley, which his father held of me and my heirs in fee [by the service] of a breastplate [meaning that he should render or pay for his lands a man armed with a breastplate for military defence, or its equivalent in money, at a later period, every year] to him and his heirs, to hold of me and my heirs freely and quietly, &c., making to me and my heirs the free service in fee of one breastplate; and know ye that I have quit claimed the said Matthew and his heirs and the aforesaid lands, to me and my heirs, of the service and custom which I, the said Hamo, used to demand from them, namely, of ploughing, mucking, and sowing corn, and of making hay, and doing homage of estovers [providing food], pannage, and of all other services except the service of the fee of one breastplate. These being witnesses: Roger de Massie, William de Carington, Robert de Massie, and Richard de Fitton, and very many others, both seeing and hearing the same.

The third Hamon married Agatha de Theray, and had several children, the eldest of whom was a son named after his father. He died about the end of the reign of King John, or the beginning of that of Henry III., and his wife Agatha survived him. He is said to have given to his brother John Massey all the land of Moreton. He also confirmed to Robert, son of Waltheof or Fitz Waltheof, all his father's lands in Bredbury, Brinnington, and Etchells, by a very interesting charter, which has been translated as follows:—

Hamo de Masci to all his men, whether French or English, clerical or lay, as well in the future as now living, sendeth greeting. Be it known to you all that I have regranted to Robert, the son of Waltheof, all the land which Waltheof, his father, held of me and my ancestors for his inheritence, that is to say Hecheles (Etchells) with all that appertains to it, to him and his heirs, holding of me and my heirs freely, quietly, and peaceably, by the service of half a knight's fee. And I [the said] Hamo reserve to my own use, stag, hind and boar in Hulreswood, and the other liberties shall remain to Robert, the son of Waltheof, and his heirs. And I [the said] Hamo, regrant to Robert, the son of Waltheof, Bredburie and Brinintone, with their appurtenances, as his inheritence to him and his heirs, to hold of me and my heirs, by the service of carrying my bed, my arms or my clothing, whenever the Earl [of Chester] in his own proper person shall go into Wales. And I [the said] Hamo will fully furnish [the said] Robert, the son of Waltheof, and his heirs, with a sumpter beast, and a man and a sack, and we will find estovers [sufficient food] for the man and the sumpter beast aforesaid whilst he is with us in the field, until he shall be returned to the said Robert or his heirs. And Robert, the son of Waltheof, shall pay aid to ransom my body from captivity and detention, and to make my eldest son a knight, and to give my eldest daughter a marriage portion, in consideration of which [the said] Robert has given me a gold ring.

The conditions named in this charter were usual under the feudal system, when the kingdom was really the encampment of a great army and military ideas predominated. While the vassal was thus bound to render service to his lord, and to attend as assessor in his court of justice, the lord in his turn was bound to afford him protection in case of his fief being attacked; but the defence of each other's person was reciprocal.

As freedom broadens down, we frequently find in subsequent writings the Barons of Dunham conceding to their squires the right that neither they nor their heirs or tenants shall be impleaded or brought to trial for any offence in the Court at Dunham, which was a most valuable right, as the barons had most extraordinary privileges, on their own estates, and in their hands was reposed the power of life and death. So late as the year 1597 this right was exercised in the Baronial Court of Kinderton, where Hugh Stringer was tried for murder, convicted and executed.

It was probably about this period that Roger de Masci, of Hale, son of Geffrey Masci (being possessed of one half the lands in "Bodeon"), sold them unto Agatha de Massey for the sum of £4 7s. in money, and two robes, one for himself and the other for his wife, "rending therefor yearly one pound of cumming seed at the feast of Saint Martin." These lands, Agatha, by another deed, in which she styles herself de Theray, gave to Robert her younger son, whom she made heir thereof by the consent of Hamon, her eldest son.

supposed to be the last relic; and tradition affirms that a fine old cedar, long, long ago killed by the ivy, was brought a sapling from the Holy Land by one of the old crusading Barons of Dunham, and that it died out with the last of the race! Probably, too, the fact of the last of these barons dying without leaving a lawful son to succeed him, gave rise to the romantic legend of the "Seven Sisters," in connection with the park at Dunham, where there is a clump of trees which is known by this name. Many people are acquainted with it, and, no doubt, lament the tragic end of the youthful heir, who was struck dead by lightning just as he was passing the "Seven Sisters."

> And each fatal tree was stained with gore;
> And so was the bloody earth;
> And the same night saw his dreadful death
> That first beheld his birth.

And the legend closes:—

> The seven sister trees may still be seen,
> Though the mortal ones are fled;—
> And none of that fated house were left,
> When the squire himself was dead.

Hamon also reminds us in a most striking manner of Longfellow's melodious poem, "The Norman Baron." We can well picture to ourselves the stately Castle of Dunham. In his chamber on Christmas Eve, lies the dying baron. The King of Terrors has already laid his relentless hand upon him; and the humble monk, seated by the bed side, mutters the "prayer and pater noster" which shall usher the fast fleeting soul into Eternity. Outside, the tempest thunders, and shakes the Castle turret, but the sufferer is unmindful of it. Within its precincts serf and vassal are holding their Christmas festival. As their lays they chaunt, the sound rises above that of the tempest, and the dying baron turns his weary head to listen to the carol, in

ROBERT DEL BOOTH or BOTH, yr Son of John Booth of Barton, Lancashire, d. 1400, m. Dowe, yr dau. and cohetress of Sir. Wm. Venables, d. 1453.

| 1 WILLIAM BOOTH, Son and Heir, | 2 Raufe, m. Margaret, dau. | 3 Geffrey. | 5 Lucy, m. to John Chantler, of Barbe. | 10 John Bishop, of Exeter, warden of

supposed to be the last relic; and tradition affirms that a fine old cedar, long, long ago killed by the ivy, was brought a sapling from the Holy Land by one of the old crusading Barons of Dunham, and that it died out with the last of the race! Probably, too, the fact of the last of these barons dying without leaving a lawful son to succeed him, gave rise to the romantic legend of the "Seven Sisters," in connection with the park at Dunham, where there is a clump of trees which is known by this name. Many people are acquainted with it, and, no doubt, lament the tragic end of the youthful heir, who was struck dead by lightning just as he was passing the "Seven Sisters."

> And each fatal tree was stained with gore;
> And so was the bloody earth;
> And the same night saw his dreadful death
> That first beheld his birth.

And the legend closes:—

> The seven sister trees may still be seen,
> Though the mortal ones are fled;—
> And none of that fated house were left,
> When the squire himself was dead.

Hamon also reminds us in a most striking manner of Longfellow's melodious poem, "The Norman Baron." We can well picture to ourselves the stately Castle of Dunham. In his chamber on Christmas Eve, lies the dying baron. The King of Terrors has already laid his relentless hand upon him; and the humble monk, seated by the bed side, mutters the "prayer and pater noster" which shall usher the fast fleeting soul into Eternity. Outside, the tempest thunders, and shakes the Castle turret, but the sufferer is unmindful of it. Within its precincts serf and vassal are holding their Christmas festival. As their lays they chaunt, the sound rises above that of the tempest, and the dying baron turns his weary head to listen to the carol, in

Genealogical Table of the House of Dunham.

which is heralded the birth of the manger-cradled stranger, Christ, who was born to set us free. In an instant, the spirit of repentance appears. He thinks of the justice, long withheld, due to those under his iron rule, and they are by him freed again. As on the sacred missal he inscribes their freedom, death relaxes his iron features, and the monk repeats a deep Amen.

Many centuries have been numbered
Since in death the baron slumbered,
By the convent's sculptured portal,
  Mingling with the common dust:

But the good deed, through the ages
Living in historic pages,
Brighter grows and gleams immortal,
  Unconsumed by moth or rust.

CHAPTER II.

The Parish Church :—Its claims to antiquity—The yew trees, a relic of Saxon Christianity—The wakes, their origin and use—An old bead roll and its record—Description of the old church—Value of the living six centuries ago—The ringers' orders—A law suit—Another bead roll and its record—Memorials of old families—The Brereton monuments—The Dunham Chapel, &c.

IT is not stated precisely when the Church of Bowdon was originally founded. It cannot boast a date like that at Rostherne, of 1188, although, there is no doubt, Bowdon is much older; neither is it recorded that it had "a priory of regular canons of the Order of St. Augustine," like its relation at Mobberley, or any of the Præmonstatensians, such as dwelt at Warburton, anciently spelled Wurburgetone ; but it is certain that at the Domesday Survey, as already noticed, there was a priest attached to the church, munificently endowed, probably with many "fat fallows." It is also certain that the church existed a long time prior to the Conquest. The planting of yew trees in churchyards, on account of their sombre and funereal aspect, is a relic of the Saxon Christianity which had spread over the land, and the custom prevailed at Bowdon. There are two or three in the churchyard, and one in particular is, judging from calculations made of the growth of such trees, upwards of 800 years old. According to one authority, it is even said to have been planted in the seventh century. It is a gnarled sturdy-looking veteran, but much the worse for its thousand years' (supposed) exposure on the hilltop.

The view from the churchyard is the finest in the district. It embraces a vast expanse of lovely scenery, including the beautiful valley of the Bollin, backed in the distance by Alderley Edge, the hills of Derbyshire and Staffordshire, and many other features of interest. The church is dedicated to St. Mary, whose "feast" is kept annually by wakes held in the month of September. This feast was formerly celebrated on the 8th September, being the nativity of the Virgin, but it is now held on the 1st Sunday after the full moon succeeding the 14th September. The event, however, now evokes little or no interest. Leycester says that the word Wakes or fast day is derived from the Latin Vigilæ à Vigilando, because at such times people prayed most on the night before such fast day in the churches: "yet we find this primitive custom abused in the reign of King Edgar, A.D. 967, and at last it turned into a feasting and merriment of neighbours." Who will say after this that history does not repeat itself?

From extracts taken from the Bead Roll, A.D. 1298, it is shown that "Robertus de Masci, by ye consent of his wife and heirs male of his body, gave and devised unto Adam de Bodon, two oxganges (56 acres) of land in Bodon, rending yearly one penny upon the Altar of St. Mary the Virgin at Bodon on the nativity of St. Mary the Virgin, which is the eighth day of September in perpetual alms for the Salvation of the Souls of Robertus de Masci, his wife, ancestors and heirs, and for the souls of Mathew de Bodon and Hale." Baron Masci, son and heir to the fourth Hamon de Masci, gave to God, the blessed Virgin Mary, and St. James, and to the Prior and Convent of Birkenhead half-an acre of land in Doneham Masci, together with the advowson of the church of our good lady Saint Mary in Bowdon, A.D. 1278; "for in that year was Richard Masci, one of the witnesses, Sheriff of Chester." After the dissolution of the Abbeys in the reign of Henry VIII, a new Bishopric was created at Chester, whereunto was given amongst other things the church of Bowdon.

The advowson of the Vicarage continues attached to the See of Chester. The latter is held by lease of lives by the Earl of Stamford and Warrington. The church was valued in the tax roll of Pope Nicholas in the thirteenth century at £11 6s. 8d., and at £24 per annum in the King's book. In 1666, according to Sir Peter Leycester, it was £120 per annum; two hundred years or so later it is given at £900 in the Clergy List.

A description of the church as it anciently stood will not be found uninteresting. The exterior was chiefly in the Norman style of architecture, introducing at the eastern termination, or at the Carrington and Dunham Chancels, the pointed and more fanciful Gothic. The tower was also in the Norman style embattled and quadrangular, and contained a peal of sonorous bells. In the belfry is the following :—

THE RINGERS' ORDERS.

You ringers all, observe these orders well—
He pays his sixpence that o'erturns a bell,
And he that rings with either spur or hat
Must pay his sixpence certainly for that ;
And he that rings and does disturb the peal
Must pay his sixpence or a gun of ale.
These laws elsewhere in every church are used,
That bells and ringers may not be abused.

James Millatt, Ferdinand Laughton, George Wright, and James Fletcher, *Churchwardens ;* Joseph Drinkwater, John Pickering, Aaron Eccles, Peter Pickering, John Dean, John Hobbert, *Parish Ringers*.

Formerly, the sixth bell was tolled for a funeral, and after being tolled (if for a male) the whole six bells were tolled thrice each ; (if for a female) only twice each. The curfew was rung on the fifth bell, and the practice is still continued, although the day of the month is not tolled as it was up to 1864 or 1865.

The interior of the church consisted of a nave, chancel, and side aisles with spacious galleries ending in two private chancels appropriated and belonging to the Lords of Dunham Massey. Regarding these chancels, it appears that a dispute arose at the death of John Carrington, between his executors and the Brereton family, as to the right of legal possession of Carrington chapel, dedicated to St. Nicholas. The Breretons claimed it by reason of being possessed of one-fourth of the lands in Bowdon, and the Booth family by heirship. The enquiry in 1557 by the Court of Chancery, resulted in the claim of the latter family being confirmed. These chapels were divided from the rest of the church the Dunham one by two pointed arches and the Carrington one by three, resting on short octagonal pillars. Connected with them were originally two chantry priests, John Percivall and Henry Tipping.

There was also a head roll belonging to the chantry to the following effect :—

Pray for ye good estate of me, Sr. Wm. Booth, Maude my wife, Lawrence Bishope, George sonne and heir apparent of me, ye said Wm., Katherine his wife, Wm. sonne of the said George Bouthe, Richard Bouthe, John Bouthe, and Wm. Bouthe, sonnes of me yt said Wm. Geffrey Bouthe and Hamnett Bouthe, Clerkes, brethren of yt sd Sr. Wm. Bouthe, Lucy late wife of John Chantrill, Ellen wife of Robert Leigh, and Allison wife of Robert Hesketh, sisters of me yt said Wm. Thomas Duncalfe and James Hall, p'eones of Northen, for ye souls late of my father and mother, that is to say, Robert Bouthe, Knt, Jane his wife, Wm. Bouthe late Archbishop of York, Rafe Bouthe my sonne, Jonet, late wife of Will Holte, my daughter Kate Bouthe, Mr. Edmond Bouthe Clarke, Piers Bouthe Clerk, and Robert Bouthe brethren of me, ye said Wm., Jonet late wife of Will., Mainwaringe, and Margaret late wife of James Scaresbrooke, my susters, and especially for all the . . . .

There was formerly an inscription over this chapel :—

This is Dunham Chapel, repaired by and belonging to the Lords of Dunham Massey.

The arms of the Booths, surmounting with the motto, " Quod ero spero " ; and on the other :—

This is Carrington Chapel, repaired by and belonging to the Lords of Dunham and Carrington.

In the chapel belonging to Sir George Bouthe, " on a faire stone of marble with beasts about it," was "the picture of a man and woman engraven in brass." The "two recumbent figures had clasped hands : the male figure in plate armour, under his feet six kneeling figures (infants), and seven under those of his wife ; in three angles of the tomb, the arms of Massey of Doneham, quartering those of the Bouthes, and the fourth, those of Butler, Baron of Warrington." The inscription translated read :—

Of your charity pray for the souls of George Bouthe, Esquire, and Elizabeth his wife, and of the said Thomas Butler of Bewsey, Knt, which George and Elizabeth, had together at the time of the death of the said George Bouthe, three sons, George, Jo, and Robert.

The Booths, at this time, appear to have used the arms of the Norman founder of the Barony.

In the east window were the words :—

W'ch chapelle and chamber was erected by Sr Wm. Booth, about Edward IV. raigne.

And in Latin the following :—

Pray for the souls of Will Booth Knt, and Matilda his wife, daughter of John Dutton Esqr., and for the soul of George Booth, son and heir, who it is said built this chapel.

There were other memorials existing in the same chapel in the 16th and 17th centuries. Upon an "alabaster stone" this monument, engraven with an inscription, about the stone : A knight in plate armour, recumbent, his head resting on a helmet, the crest of which is a lion passant, on each side a recumbent female ; over his head the coat of Mascy of Dunham ; over the dexter lady, argent, an eagle, displayed azure ; at her feet four children. Over the sinister lady the coat of Fitton, and at her feet four children. In Latin were the words :—

Here lies the body of Sir William Booth, knight, who died on 9th Nov., 1519, and Margarete and Helena, wives of the said William : upon whose souls God be merciful. Amen.

There was a little monument to two of the children of Sir George Bouthe, Francis and George, who died in infancy. There were no arms upon it, but two little children with two torches turned downwards.

In the Carrington chapel were many similar inscriptions and arms of the Vawdreys, Baguleys, Leghs of Baguley, the Lords of Carrington, &c. On the Carrington side of the chancel there is an ancient monument of the Brereton family erected in the years 1627 to 1637. Although bearing marks of great exposure, sufficient of it is still to be seen to show that it is a real work of art. The husband and wife are recumbent, arrayed in robes and ruffles, peculiar to the time ; and underneath, in bas-relief, are their eight children in surcoats. The third holds a skull in his hands ; and between the sixth and seventh is an infant in swaddling clothes. There is impaled beneath a canopy of frieze in the arabesque, two escutcheons, Brereton and Warburton arms conjoined. The family arms are charged with 27 quarterings (18 Breretons and 9 Warburtons) impaling Hugh Lupus, Cholmondeley, Booth, Warburton, Egerton, and others : and there is a beautiful Latin inscription, of which the following is a translation :—

Under this monument lie interred the bodies of Wm. Brereton, of Ashley, in the county of Chester, Esq., and Jane his wife ; the former of whom derived origin and descent from the ancient and illustrious family of Lord William Brereton, of Brereton, in the aforesaid county ; the latter was one of the daughters and co heiresses of Peter Warburton, of Arley, in the said county, Esquire, lately deceased. They bore male children, Richard, Thomas, William (peacefully sleeping in the Lord) and Peter ; females, Frances, Maria, (also overcome by the bonds of death), Ann and Catherine. They enjoyed themselves in conjugal and chaste love ; they adhered strictly to and exercised the principles of the true and orthodox religion (as Christians ought to do) ; and having walked this life righteously and holy, are now awaiting the joyful and glorious resurrection by the body of Christ to be conveyed to the heavenly abode of rest, unto which they were called. Jane, his wife, died March 2nd, 1627, aged 63 years ; William died August 29th, 1630, also aged 63.

There is a tradition concerning this couple that the wife, Jane Brereton, was murdered, and that her hands were cut off. There are no hands on the female effigy ; but it is just possible that it may have been an act of vandalism on the part of some evil-disposed persons in former times.

While on the subject of the chancel, it may be mentioned that in the window in or about the year 1600, were five coats of arms. In the first, Tatton impaling Davenport ; second, Tatton impaling Booth ; third, the Bishopric of Chester ; fourth, Tatton impaling Fitton ; fifth, Tatton, with a label, impaling Warren.

In the floor of the chancel, within the rails of the altar, was a somewhat curious inscription, in Latin :—

In this place is interred the remains of—Gerrard, of Riddings the first and last of that name—on the day in the year of our Lord 1672.

In the body of the church, on the south side, there was a monument of Sir William Baguley, Knight. It was a full-length effigy, cut in free stone, and represented a warrior in mail. The surcoat and shield were emblazoned with the arms of Baguley, or Bagleigh. As it appeared to be in the way, it was taken out of the church, and for several years graced the grotto of a gentleman's garden at Partington. It attracted some attention at a later period, and through the instrumentality of the late T. W. Tatton, Esq., of Wythenshawe, it ultimately found a more appropriate resting place at Baguley Old Hall, from whence the original had sprung.

There must have been many representations on painted glass, for which Cheshire churches are famous, at Bowdon. In the head of the south aisle was a very ancient coat of arms of the Baguleys; under which was a memorial of the Leghs of Baguley; underneath was a kneeling male figure with one son and four daughters kneeling behind him. In the second window on the south side, Sir Thomas Butler, in coat armour, with two sons and eight daughters kneeling behind him. In the west window were the arms of the Barony of Dunham Massey. In a higher window on the south side were certain coats of arms, and an inscription in Latin, desiring prayers for James Hall, Rector of Northen, who bequeathed the window. On the north side, in the second window from the "bell-house," as it is quaintly termed, were two kneeling figures, the man habited in a surcoat emblazoned with the arms of Ashley, with five sons and four daughters, ranged severally behind them. Over them were the arms of Ashley, an ashbranch with ash keys dependant. In Latin there was a request to pray for the souls of John Ashley and Alice, his wife, who caused the window to be erected A.D. 1530. In the next window on the north side, were the arms of the Carringtons, quartering the same coat with a helmet and crest over. In the compartment on the dexter side of the shield was a man in armour, kneeling, his surcoat emblazoned with the arms of Carrington, one son behind him in this compartment and another in the next.

In the compartment on the other side were two kneeling females, their arms severally emblazoned with those of Brereton and Warburton. Behind the first was one daughter, and four behind the other. This was erected in 1530 by the Carringtons. In another window on the north side were two figures kneeling on cushions. The male figure's surcoat was emblazoned with the arms of Ashton, and the dress of the female with that of Butler. Over them were the arms of Mascy of Dunham, quartering Ashton, Stayley, Fitton, and Thornton. Four sons and nine daughters knelt severally behind them; and an inscription requested prayers for the good estate of George Bouthe and Elizabeth his wife, who erected the window in 1530.

In another light of the same window were the arms of Mascy of Dunham, surmounted with a crosier; this window being presented by John Sharpe, Prior of Birkenhead, in the same year. The same coat of arms was repeated in the roof of the north aisle, but it has been obliterated, and the marks of the chisel which has been used may still be seen.

In the lowermost window on the north side was another memorial to a Prior of Birkenhead, Robert Millington, or Millenton. There were the arms of Millington and an ecclesiastic kneeling, holding a cup in his left hand.

In the east window of the north aisle, over against the chancel, was a window bequeathed by Hamonis Carrington, and surmounted by the Carrington arms.

On a flag in the middle aisle was a memorial to the Rev. P. Lancaster, A.M., who died March 7th, 1763; but prior to the restoration of the church, there was a large number of inscriptions on stones in the interior to the servants of the Dunham family.

In the Dunham Chapel are two large mural monuments. One has a shield of 60 quarterings of the Booth family placed against a pyramid, and resting on a sarcophagus. At the sides of the pyramids are two medallions to the memory of Langham and Henry Booth, younger sons of the then Earl of Warrington, who

E

died in 1724, and in 1727. The other is divided into two tablets; the first to the memory of Henry Booth, Earl of Warrington and Baron Delamer, who died in 1693-4; the second to the memory of his Countess, sole daughter and heiress of Sir James Langham. In the charging of the surcoat, Booth has nine quarterings impaling six of Langhams. The inscription regarding the Earl is as follows:—

<pre>
                Beneath
              lieth the body of
         the Right Honourable Henry Booth,
         Earl of Warrington and Baron Delamer,
                of Dunham Massey;
                  a person of
               unblemished honor,
                impartial justice,
                 strict integrity,
              an illustrious example of
           steady and unalterable adherence to
          the liberties and properties of his country,
                in the worst of times
              rejecting all offers to allure
                      and
            despising all danger to deter
                  him therefrom,
               for which he was
        thrice committed close prisoner to the tower of
                    London,
                and at length
                tried for his life
      upon a false accusation of high treason, from which he was
               unanimously acquitted
        by his peers, on the 14th January, MDCLXXXV-VI. (1685-6),
                  which day
          he afterwards annually commemorated
         by acts of devotion and charity.
                 In the year
               MDCLXXXVIII (1688)
         he greatly signalised himself at the
                  REVOLUTION
                 on behalf of
       the Protestant religion and the rights of the Nation,
             without mixture of self interest,
           preferring the good of his country
              to the favor of the prince
            who then ascended the throne,
</pre>

BURYING LANE (NOW THE FIRS), BOWDON.

and
having served his generation according to the will of God,
was gathered to his fathers in peace,
on the second day of January, 169¾ (1693-4),
in the XLII. (forty-second) year of his age,
whose mortal remains were here entombed
on the same memorable day on which, eight years before,
his trial had been.

The companion inscription sets forth the many virtues and good qualities of Mary, Countess of Warrington, his wife, as follows :—

Also rest by him the earthly remains of the Rt. Honble. Mary, Countess of Warrington, his wife, sole daughter and heir of Sir James Langham, of Cottersbrooke, in the county of Northampton, Knt. and Bart. ; a Lady of ingenuous parts, singular discretion, consummate judgement, great humility, meek and compassionate temper, extensive charity, exemplary and unaffected piety, perfect resignation to God's will ; lowly in prosperity and patient in adversity, prudent in her affairs, and endowed with all other virtuous qualities ; a conscientious discharger of her duty in all relations, being a faithful, affectionate, obliging, and observant Wife, alleviating the cares and afflictions of her husband, by willingly sharing with him therein ; a tender, indulgent, and careful Mother, a dutiful and respectful Daughter, gentle and kind to her servants ; courteous and beneficent to her neighbours, a sincere friend, a lover and valuer of all good people, justly beloved and admired by all who knew her, who having perfected holiness in the fear of God was by Him received to an early and eternal Rest from her labours on the 23rd of March, 169¡, in the XXXVII. year of her age, calmly, composedly meeting and desiring death, with joyful hope and steadfastness of faith, a lively draught of real worth and goodness.

A pattern deserving an imitation,
Of whom the world was not worthy.

Heb. xi., 38.

Underneath are the words :—

To perpetuate the remembrance of so much virtue till that great day come, wherein it shall be openly rewarded, this monument is erected as a mark of dutiful respect and affection by the care of their son George, Earl of Warrington, who reveres their memory.

Mottoes : *Ero quod spero* (Let me be what I wish or profess to be) ; and *A ma puissance* (According to my power).

On the second monument is the following :—

This monument is
erected
to the ever valuable memory of the Honorable
Langham and Henry Booth,

younger sons of the
Right Honorable Henry late Earl of
Warrington.
Both of them began their earthly pilgrimage on the
Lord's Day
and,
after having fought a good fight
cheerfully resigned their souls into the mercifull
hands of their God and Saviour
JESUS CHRIST,
finishing their course in ye xi.. year of their respective ages,
the former on the xii. of May, mdccxiv. (1714)
the latter on the 11 Febr. mdccxxvii., do now rest in hope to receive
their bodies
immortal and glorious
in the great day of the Lord.

In the sight of the unwise they seemed to die, but they are in peace and their hope full of Immortality, for God proved them and found them Worthy of Himself; for Hnble. age is not measured by Number of years, but they being made perfect in a short time, fulfilled a long time, and pleasing God were beloved of Him, so that living among sinners they were TRANSLATED.— *Wis.* iii. *and* iv.

On a brass which was formerly fixed in a stone at the descent to the family vault of the Earls of Stamford and Warrington, &c., was an inscription of which the following is a translation. It was not replaced at the restoration of the church :—

Under this monument are interred the remains of George, Lord Delamer, Baron of the ancient and noble house of Dunham Massey, who was distinguished by his piety, fidelity, and affection to God, King, and Country, and who in the sixty-second year of his age exchanged an earthly coronet for a celestial crown, and died on the 10th day of August, in the year of our Salvation 1684. William Andrews, deploring the death of his most honourable Lord (in whose service he had continued for upwards of 30 years, faithfully emulating and partaking in the loyalty which his master showed to his King), this monument to his ever-blessed and happy memory has been erected, consecrated, and preserved, and a hope added that when his life at the same time with his official duty to that noble family came to an end, at the entrance to this tomb his ashes might rest, until the day when they might rise, together with those of his master, into the new and eternal life. Died 25th day of July, 1685.

In the south-east angle of this chapel is a portion of a piscina, much defaced, formerly used for holy water.

CHAPTER III.

Description of the old church, continued—The tales told by the tombstones and the tablets—A curious old stone.

THERE still remains something to be said about the old structure, and having described the Dunham and Carrington Chapels, we pass on to the other parts of the church. The vestry was situated under the belfry, and occupied the ancient western entrance, and at the north entrance were the font and the gallery stairs and near the south porch the organ gallery stairs. The galleries were of fair dimensions. The organ gallery was built under a faculty from the Bishop of Chester, and the organ was presented by the Earl of Stamford and Warrington in 1822. This was afterwards pulled down, and a new one built in the Carrington Chapel, which in its turn gave place in 1876 to a noble instrument built by Messrs. Jardine and Co., of Manchester. The galleries on the north side were enlarged and re-built in the year 1841, at the sole expense of the vicar, the Rev. W. H. G. Mann, M.A. The side aisles of the church had handsome carved oak roofs. On the south side the roof had remained unfinished for centuries, and had become so dilapidated as to render its restoration necessary. This was undertaken by Mr. Kay, of Manchester, and was executed by him with such exactness as to preserve its pristine effect. There was some exquisite carving, and the cluster points all varied in pattern. The ceilings were divided from the nave by five pointed arches on each side, resting on short octagonal pillars with capitals. The roof appears to have been taken down about 1778, and the walls raised; at which time John Coe, Richard Leather, Thomas Ashley, and John Slater were churchwardens.

There are several monuments in various parts of the church which have not been hitherto mentioned. Prominent amongst them is a fine mural one to the memory of Thomas and Harriet Assheton, of Ashley, and their son, Thomas Assheton Smith, descendants of the ancient family of the Breretons of Bowdon :—

> In a vault near this place were interred
> the remains of Thomas Assheton, of Assheley, Esq.,
> on the 9th day of July, 1759, aged 64.
> Also in the same vault, Harriet Assheton,
> who died at Manchester, Jan., 1773, aged 74 ;
> also, the remains
> of Thomas Assheton Smith, of Assheley, Esq.,
> son of the above Thomas and Harriet,
> who died April 16th, 1774, aged 49 years,
> to whose memory Wm. Henry Assheton Smith, Esq.,
> erects this monument.
> Quis desiderio sit pudor aut modus
> Tam cari capitis.
> Also the remains of
> William Henry Assheton Smith, Esq.,
> younger son of the above,
> Thomas Assheton Smith, Esq.,
> who died at Hailey, in the county of Oxford,
> March 4th, 1839, aged 82 years.

> Sacred
> to the memory of
> Hugh Fitz-Patrick Hall, Esq.,
> of Jamaica, and late of Ashley, in this county,
> who died on the 27th day of June, 1788,
> in the 38th year of his age ;
> also, Martha his wife,
> the second daughter of
> Marsden Kenyon, Esq.,
> of Manchester,
> who died on the 14th day of Jan., 1780,
> in the 26th year of her age.

In a recess at the south entrance to the organ gallery was a tablet to the memory of a most unostentatious man, the Rev. Thomas Whittaker, sometime perpetual curate of Ringway :—

> What he was as a scholar he desired not to have recorded,
> What he was as a minister of Christ
> ought ever to be had in remembrance ;

and when those who revered him as a guide,
a counsellor, and a friend are seen no more,
let this humble memorial testify
how diligently he instructed the young,
warned the careless, sought out the neglected,
comforted the afflicted, and preached to all
the doctrine of his God and Saviour,
which he cordially embraced,
which his life adorned, and whose consolations
he enjoyed in his last hours.
he died May VII, MDCCCXVIII. (1818),
aged LXIII (63) years.
God forbid that I should glory save in
the Cross of Christ my Lord.—*Gal.* vi. 5.

In the middle aisle was a tablet with a Latin inscription to the memory of John Baldwin, LL.B. :—

Who was placed over the parish of Bowdon as Vicar more than forty-three years. To him was entrusted the joyful gift of the ministry, which he diligently performed ; and at length, having concluded his labours, peacefully returned his soul to God in the year of safety, on the 3rd day of July, 1815, aged 69.

On the same stone is also an inscription to—

John Baldwin, junior, his only and much beloved son, who had scarcely entered into the sacred office, in which he dutifully pointed out the way of the blessed, when he expired, having fulfilled the task imposed, on the 16th January, in the year of safety, 1817, aged 25 years. Wife, husband, mother, son, bewailing.

There are the following inscriptions in other parts of the church :—

This humble tablet
in conformity with the unassuming tenor of his mind
records the death of
William Harle Nicholls, M.D.,
a native of the city of Durham,
whose character as a man
reflects honour upon human nature ;
visiting at Altrincham upon a tour of observation,
he was arrested by a call from his Creator
May 28th, 1830, in the 69th year of his age,
and was interred in the cemetery
of this church.

Sacred
to the memory of
the Reverend Daniel Whittle, A.M.,
late of Hollingworth Hall, in this county,
who after a ministry, short but faithful and approved,
at Saint George's Chapel, in Altrincham,
in the prime of life, in the midst of usefulness
was by his Master summoned away from his work,
with him to rest, with him to reign,
on 22nd April, A.D. 1834;
born 26th Jan., A.D. 1800.
Looking for that * * * Titus ii. 13.

To the memory of
Edward Jeremiah Lloyd,
of Oldfield Hall,
a magistrate for the counties of
Chester and Lancaster,
and a Captain in the Earl of Chester's Yeomanry Cavalry,
who closed an exemplary and useful life
on the 3rd day of July, 1830,
in the 61st year of his age.
Distinguished by the urbanity of his manners
and the kindness of his disposition
no less than by his undeviating honour
and exact sense of justice:
accessible and benevolent to the poor,
considerate and attentive to all,
he engaged in a remarkable degree the affections,
while he commanded the respect
of every class of society.
to testify their appreciation of his worth
and to record so eminent an example of excellence;
the inhabitants of this neighbourhood
and the members of the corps to which he belonged,
have caused this tablet
to be erected.

---

†

I.H.S.

Sacred to the Memory of Thomas Bagshaw, of Altrincham, late of Manchester, who died October 15th, 1843, in the 70th year of his age. His loss was deeply lamented by all who knew him, for through a long and peaceful life he worthily sustained the character of a faithful and sincere friend, a truly honorable man, and a benefactor of mankind. As a grateful tribute to his departed worth, and as a mark of the deep esteem with which his memory is cherished, this tablet is erected by his sole surviving Niece, S.B.

"The praise of Man is fluctuating and perisheth,
The testimony of a good conscience endureth for ever."

Passing from the interior to the exterior, we enter the church-yard to note many points of interest to be discerned there. Some of the old inscriptions are rather curious.

On a stone, on the north side, is the following:—

The body that this stone doth here embrace,
So like to Leah, with a Rachael's face,
Sarah's obedience, likewise Lydia's heart,
With Martha's care, and Mary's better part.

This was formerly to be seen under the chancel window:—
Here lie the bodies of a daughter of John Cooke, of Altrincham, an attorney at law, and Sarah his wife, who, though full grown (and a while before alive), was born dead the 16th and buried 17th March, 1749.

Near the old yew tree is:—
Here lieth the body of John Pixton, of Altrincham, who died 27th Sepr., 1843, in the 96th year of his age; Mary, wife of John Pixton, of Altrincham, who died 21st February, 1841, in the 93rd year of her age.

Twenty years they lived a single life,
Seventy-two they lived a married life,
Three years he lived a widower chaste,
And now hath left the world and gone to rest.

On one of the stones is an old heading in Roman letters I.B. 1633, enclosed in a square; but the oldest inscription to be found in the yard is on a long narrow stone, also not far from the old yew tree. Owing to the way in which the words are divided, it is somewhat difficult to decipher at first sight, but it reads as follows:—

Here lyeth the bodie of William Artinstall, de Ringey, deceased November xxvii, Ao. Do. 1617; also the bodie of Laurence Artinstall, of Ringey, who departed this life August 4th, Anno. Dom. 1684.

On the grave of Francis Booth, who was Clerk of the church 40 years (it is a remarkable fact that there have only been three clerks during 120 years, Mr. H. Service being the last, who served forty), is an inscription at once unique and suggestive. It reads :—

> I oft have viewed the gloomy place
> Which claims the relicks of the human race,
> And read on the insculptured stone
> Here lies the body of . . .
> . . but now my own
> Dissolves to native dust, and as you see
> Another hero has done the same for me.
>
> Our life is but a winter's day,
> Some only breakfast and away,
> Others to dinner stay and are full fed,
> The oldest man but sups and goes to bed ;
> Large is his debt who lingers out the day.
> Who goes the soonest has the least to pay.

On the tombstone of John Bray, of Dunham, who was 81 at the time of his death, and his wife Martha, aged 91, are the following lines :—

> Our term of life is 70 years—an age that few survive,
> But if we've more than common strength, to 80 we arrive ;
> And then our boasted strength decays, to sorrow turned and pain ;
> And soon the slender thread is cut, and we no longer reign.

Near the tower is another stone, inscribed to the memory of Peter Shaw, of Bowdon, who died in 1825, aged 74 years. He was the faithful servant of Mr. Thomas Davenport, of Oldfield, "for 24 years and upwards" :—

> Farewell, vain world, I've seen enough of thee,
> And now am careless what thou sayest of me,
> Thy smiles I court not, nor thy frowns I fear,
> My cares are past, my head lies quiet here.
> What faults you saw in me take care to shun,
> And look at home—enough there's to be done.—
> Where'er I lived or died, it matters not,
> To whom related or by whom begot.
> I was, now am not, ask no more of me,
> 'Tis all I am, and all that you shall be.

There are references on some of the stones to the ancient family of Vawdrey, frequently alluded to in the annals of the parish. There are two such references which may be quoted as possessing great interest :—

William Vawdrey, of Owlerbarrow, gent., sonne to John Vawdrey of Banke, gent, was borne the 20th day of Nov. Anno Dom. 1606. He married Mary, the daughter and hærotrix of John Massey, gent, and after, Alice, sister to Sir Edward Moore of Thelewell, baronet, and had by them sixteen sonnes and daughters. Departed this life and was buried the 12th day of May, Anno Dom. 1665.

On the stone are the arms of the Vawdreys. Also :—

The mortalitie and death of the sonnes and daughters of William Vawdrey of Owlerbarrow, gent., by Alice his wife:
    Alice, second November, 1650.
    Richard, 17th December, 1650.
    John, 23rd January, 1651.
    Thomas, 16th July, 1654.
    Henry, 3rd December, 1654.
and William, seventh sonne, likewise departed this life 22nd day of January, 1664.

On a raised tombstone, surrounded by iron railings, within a few yards of the tower on the south-west side, is an inscription to the memory of Robert Rothwell, of Agden, who, with his wife and children, who apparently all died young, is interred here, having died at the age of 45.

    Beneath this rustic monument there lies
    One whose pure soul beat high in virtue's cause ;
    Religion's favorite child, he was the boast—
    And champion of the poor, blessing and blest !
    Within the narrow circle of his friends he lived
        Unknown to fame :
    Unknown he died.
    Alas ! too soon in manhood's prime he fell.
    Say ye who knew him best was not his life
    A perfect model of a Christian's course?
    And stranger whosee'er thou art whose steps,
       or chance or melancholy this way leads
    If thou dost honour merit, pause ! 'tis hallowd ground,
    Here in the arms of death a village Hambden (?) sleeps.

On the gravestone of a young girl who died suddenly, is the following :—

> Warned by my fate be ever on your guard
> Lest sudden death should meet you unprepared
> Innocent and young I saw no danger near
> Stranger both to sickness, pain and fear.

Inscriptions are to be found to the memory of two infant sons of a former Vicar, the Rev. W. H. G. Mann :—

> Bold Infidelity turn pale and die !
> Beneath this stone an infant's ashes lie.
> Say, is it lost or saved ?
> If death's by sin, it sinned, for it lies here ;
> If heaven's by works, in heaven it can't appear.
> Ah Reason ! how depraved !
> Revere the Bible's sacred page—the knot's untied
> It died through Adam's sin—it lives for Jesu's shed.

On the second boy, which died aged one year, is the following :—

> To us for just 12 anxious months his infant smiles were given,
> And then he bade farewell to earth and went to live in heaven ;
> We cannot tell what form is his, what looks he weareth now,
> Nor guess how bright a glory crowns his shining seraph brow ;
> But we know, for God has told us this, that he is now at rest
> Where other blessed infants lie on their Saviour's loving breast ;
> We know too we shall meet our babe through the same Saviour's grace,
> Where God for aye shall wipe away all tears from every face.

On a raised tombstone on the westerly side is an inscription to the memory of an aged lady :—

> The storms of life are now o'er blown,
> Fear, trouble, care, grief, pain are gone,
> And God in Christ will hence display
> The sunshine of eternal day.

Perhaps the very last of these rhyming inscriptions is the one which perpetuates the memory of one who in life was one of our worthiest citizens :—

In affectionate remembrance of Joseph Owen, who died April 4th, 1866, in his 51st year,

> Yes, he is gone, of parents best :
> A master, kindly, just ;
> His sleep will be the Christian's rest
> Who lived a life of trust.
> Yes, gone ! in life's fair noon removed,
> When all was doubly dear,
> But those he cherished—her he loved
> Will commune with him here.

A notable monument near the centre of the churchyard, which bears by its freshness the mark of loving and tender care, is that to the memory of David Stott, founder of St. Paul's Sunday School, Bennett Street, Manchester, who died February 26th, 1848, aged 68 years. The inscription runs :—

He founded this institution in the year 1801, and was permitted in the goodness of God to labour in the management of it until the last week of his life. His gentleness and devotion amply fitted him for a Sunday School Instructor; his benevolence and discretion enabled him to foster this Institution, equally eminent for its usefulness, with success. He was also the originator of sick and burial societies in connection with Sunday Schools, and was a noble example of what may be effected by the influence of christian principles, affection and perseverance, when devoted to the service of the Saviour. This tribute of affection is erected in veneration of his efforts and example, by the visitors, teachers and friends of the said school.

In the same grave rest the remains of his wife, Jane, who died May 11th, 1851, aged 70 years.

CHAPTER IV.

The Parish Church, its restoration—Reminders and relics of antiquity—Description of restored edifice—Tablets to the Ven. Archdeacon Pollock, and to the first Vicar of St. Margaret's—The stained glass windows and their donors—A run through the registers—Curious and interesting extracts—the Bowdon Proverb—Notices of Vicars, with list—The ancient rating valuation, or mize—-List of benefactions, &c.

THE hoary pile which had served the spiritual wants of the parish for so many centuries at length fell into irreparable decay, and the substitution of an edifice more calculated to meet the increased requirements of the age was rendered necessary. It is a matter for thankfulness that Bowdon has escaped that spirit of vandalism which demolishes while it does not reproduce, and that the restoration of its parish church is essentially so both in spirit and in fact. As nearly as possible the old type has been adhered to.

In 1854 attention was drawn to the state of the church, and two years afterwards plans were prepared; but these were objected to for many reasons, and ultimately, after some competition, Mr. W. H. Brakspear was entrusted with the important work. In the demolition of the ancient structure the remains of two churches formerly existing on the site were discovered. These were unmistakably portions of the ancient Norman church, probably of the twelfth century, and a decorated church of the fourteenth century. The traces of Norman work were, indeed, very numerous. A piscina, cusped-headed, having marks of four crockets and a finial, was also found; but whether this was from the high altar or not is uncertain. Another feature of interest was the stone figure of a recumbent Knight, in armour, greatly worn, found in the foundations of the nave pier.

The first, or foundation, stone was laid on Wednesday, 18th August, 1858, in the presence of a large concourse of spectators, by the Bishop of Chester. The Vicar (Rev. W. Pollock) on that occasion announced that there had been received from various sources the sum of £6,000. The Nonconformists had responded to his appeal in a way which called forth his warmest gratitude. The silver trowel which he presented to the Bishop bore the following inscription :—

To John, Lord Bishop of the diocese, and patron of the living, on his laying the first stone, in the restoration of their ancient Parish Church, by the Vicar and Building Committee, on behalf of the parishioners of Bowdon, 18th August, 1858. Reverend William Pollock, M.A., Vicar, John Mort, A. W. Mills, John Reid, and John Warburton, Churchwardens.

It has been erected on a more extended scale, but occupies the same site, and to some extent rests on the old foundation. By the introduction of north and south transepts, the increase in size has been made principally towards the east, which consequently required a greater height than before existed. Thus the aisles, walls, clerestory, and tower have been considerably increased in size. All the architectural features of any value have been reproduced, and the north and south aisle ceilings of carved oak remain entire, and have been carefully restored. Those portions of the old church that had been preserved from an earlier building have also been utilized, which will explain why the architecture of the middle and third pointed periods are found side by side. The general character of the architecture, however, is that of the perpendicular, or third pointed period.

The arcades of the nave have been somewhat extended in their span, and transept arches introduced, otherwise they may be considered a restoration. The aisles and chapels being of unusual width, they have been spanned by two arches of similar design to those of the nave. There are also two arches on either side of the chancel, opening out of the chapel. The chancel has a massive arch of separation from the nave, in the deep hollow moulding of which is arranged, at certain distances, carved flowers and foliage, which also with the mouldings to some extent return down the pier. There is a lofty arch and stone carved screen opening out of the tower and inner porch, which has a rich continuous carved hollow mould in the arch and piers. Over this arch is a circular traceried opening for ventilation, connected with an exhauster in the tower above. The whole of the interior is lined with finely worked ashlar, with the exception of the Vestry, which has since been extended so as to give accommodation to the choir and clergy.

The two chapels, as is well known, were formerly the mortuary chapels of the ancestors of the Earls of Stamford and Warrington, and under the South or Dunham Chapel is the present family vault. To give the true character to these chapels, monumental arches and copestones have been introduced externally immediately above the base mould, and above each is a circular window with tracery arranged as a cross.

The tower, which was only intended to be taken partly down, was found too dilapidated, and had to be wholly rebuilt. The restored one is certainly a striking conception. Its height from the ground to the top of the parapet is 91 feet 6 inches, being 31 feet 6 inches higher than the old one. It is surmounted by eight richly crocketed pinnacles, the four corner ones being terminated with gilt copper vanes.

The interior is lighted with gas. Four polished brass coronæ, of eight lights each, are in the nave ; one in each of the transepts ; one in the chancel ; three in each aisle, and one in the Dunham Chapel, of six lights each.

Most of the tablets formerly in the old church are to be found in the restored edifice. There are also additional ones, of which it becomes necessary to speak. First and foremost is the following :

This tablet and the monument over his grave were erected by the parishioners in loving memory of William Pollock, D.D., who, after much and varied pastoral work, diligently and faithfully done, in the diocese at Stockport, Macclesfield, St. Helens, and Liverpool, was appointed Vicar of this parish in 1856, and subsequently Rural Dean of Frodsham East, honorary Canon of Chester Cathedral and Archdeacon of Chester. The complete reconstruction of this church, the building of St. Mark's Church at Dunham, and the Bowdon and Ashley Parochial Schools, are among the memorials of the great influence which the love and respect he inspired enabled him to exercise. Born 12th April, 1812; died 11th October, 1873. "Blessed are the dead which die in the Lord."

Also :—

This tablet is placed by grateful friends of the Rev. John Kingsley, M.A., Vicar of St. Margaret's, Dunham Massey, to record his faithful services while curate of the parish church during a period of twenty years. He died in the sixty-first year of his age, and was buried in this churchyard on the 18th day of November, 1869. "Verily, I say unto you, Inasmuch as ye have done it unto one of the least of these my brethren, ye have done it unto me."—*St. Matthew* xxv. 40.

The following is the inscription on a brass at the west end of the south aisle wall :—

This church of St. Mary, at first erected in Saxon times, and afterwards thrice restored, viz., about the years of grace 1100, 1320, and 1510, was rebuilt and enlarged by voluntary subscriptions, the good work being completed according to the good hand of our God upon us, A.D. 1860. William Pollock, M.A., Vicar; John Mort, Alexander W. Mills, D. A. Clarke, John Reid, M. E. Lycett, Churchwardens; W. H. Brakspear, Architect. "'The place whereon thou standest is holy ground.'"

There are several stained glass windows of great beauty. The large east window has for its subject the crucifixion, the centre light containing the figure of Our Saviour, and on each side are the malefactors, which, however, are not made too prominent. The other lights and tracery are filled with pictures of the Ascension, the scene on the morning of the resurrection, the Marys going to the sepulchre with angels, Abraham offering up his son Isaac, and Moses lifting up the brazen serpent, both events being typical of the Crucifixion. Underneath are the words :—

In memory of Mary, the Wife of William Neild, Esquire, of High Lawn, who died March 16th, 1859.

The north and south transept windows are the gifts of Lady Murray, a descendant of the ancient family of Rigby, of Oldfield Hall, and of E. Joynson, Esq., J.P., of Bowdon. One represents the Miracles; the other the Parables of Our Lord. The window of the west end is the gift of John Clegg, Esq., J.P., of Altrincham. There is a small chancel window erected by W. D. Nicholls, Esq., and his sisters, to the memory of their father.

Other windows are to the memory of Peter Hartley, late of Altrincham, by his children, " in token of their love and esteem for their father, A.D., mdccclxxix. ; " " to the glory of God and in loving memory of Edward Dowling, of this parish, who, on the 30th August, 1889, on a mountain in Calvary was called to behold the things unseen ; " one erected by Mrs. Sarah France in loving memory of her father and mother, Mr. and Mrs. W. Goulden, who died in 1857 and 1863 respectively ; and a chancel window " in loving remembrance of Robert Alsop Warburton, of Bowdon, born March 5th, 1820, died December 31st, 1879," presented by his wife and children.

The font is a massive octagonal one, richly cut, of Painswick stone, and the basin rests on a shaft of Devonshire marble. It was the gift of Miss Joynson. The oak lectern was the gift of Miss Pollock.

The restored church contains 1,164 sittings, exclusive of those for the private accommodation of the Earl of Stamford and Warrington, being an increase of 359 sittings on the former number. The entire cost of the building and works in connection therewith was £12,371 16s 7d., exclusive of the sum of £1,748 10s. which was allowed by the contractor on account of old materials Of this amount £11,447 was contributed by resident parishes, or persons owning property in the parish ; £521 by strangers ; £210 by the Incorporated Society for the building and enlarging of Churches ; and £150 by the Diocesan Church Building Society.

The Registers of the baptisms, marriages, and burials date from the year 1628 ; but there are incomplete copies preserved at Chester from the beginning of 1600. Not the least interesting feature connected with those at Bowdon is an index which was compiled several years ago by Mr. Rushton, a son of the Ven.

Archdeacon Rushton, formerly of Manchester. The work of reference is thus rendered remarkably easy, and ample testimony to his painstaking endeavours is borne by the fact that not a single error has yet been discovered. The first volume contains records under all three divisions, from 1628 to 1653. It is headed :—

"A Register Book of all Weddings, Christenings, and Burials, in the Parish Church of Bowdon, in the year of our Lord, 1628."

The first entry states that :—

Robert Tatton, of Withenshaw, Esquire, and Anne Brereton, daughter of the Right Worshipful William Brereton, of Ashley, Esquire, were marryed the eight day of January, Anno Dom. 1628.

This is an important event, and is more elaborately set forth than the rest. The parchment on which the entries are made is very stout but it is obvious that little care has been bestowed on its preservation in former years, as damp, the arch-enemy of ancient documents, has been at work and succeeded in effectually obliterating some of the written characters In 1646, the marriages are entered at greater length, as are also the baptisms. One of the clerks, Thomas Sanderson, was most particular. We find that—

Alexander Sanderson, sonne to Thomas Sanderson, clarke of Bowdon, was born upon Saint Michael and All Angels dayo, between the hours of five and six of the clock in the morninge, being the 28th day of September, in anno 1636.

At the foot of the volume it is announced that—

George Booth, Knit and Barronett, is one of his Matie's justices of peace within the County of Chester, as attested by Peter Drinkwater, clerk.

The first name amongst the burials is that of " Henry Arstall de Ringey, January 19th, 1628."

A stranger yt (that) plaid on a tabret and whistle.

There is nothing to indicate where this wandering minstrel of some accomplishment died ; but that he found a stranger's grave at Bowdon, and went down to it apparently " unwept, unhonoured, and unsung," is clear.

Alexander Owen, clerk of Bowdon, was buryed ye third day of February, Anno Domini 1628.

"Margaret Pagett, wife of Mr. Thomas Pagett, minister and preacher at Bowdon, Aug. ultimo, 1628."

Robert Janny, Vicar of Bowdon, departed this life the 8th day of January, and was buryed the 9th in anno, 1636.

A poore boy out of the Woodhouses was buryed 8th day of November, 1640.

Dorrity Smith, daughter to George Smith, being a stranger, and another a child that was not baptised of his, March 18th, 1640.

"Two infants of one Sarah May.

A poor child of a stranger, 1647.

Amongst the concluding entries in the first volume is the following :—

Sir George Booth, of Dunham Massey, Knight and Baronett, departed this lyfe the 24th day of October, and was buryed the 28th day of November, in the year of our Lord God, one thousand six hundred and fiftie two, 1652.

The second volume contains baptisms and burials from 1653 to 1681, and marriages from 1653 to 1664, and from 1673 to 1681, nine years being missing. The latter are, however, to be found at Chester for the years 1666, 1668 to 1673, but for 1665 and 1667 there are no records. On a kind of rider attached to the ordinary register is a list of still-born children ; thus :—

A man child of John Deane's of Altrincham was still born 29th October 1653.

A man child of Robert Arstall of Hale fields was born dead January 26th, 1653, &c.

In 1653, during the Commonwealth period, there was a very stringent Act of Parliament passed, requiring marriages to take place before a Justice of the Peace. The form usually adopted was the following :—

Publication of banns of marriage was made in our parish church of Bowdon three several Lords days between John Yeates of Lime parish and Margaret Baxter of this parish, wh. days of publication were the 4th, the 11th and the 18th dayes of December in the year 1653, and were married the 23rd day of December within the same year before me.

Peter Brookes Esquire.

The following contains the first reference to any trade pursued in the district :—

> Publication of banns of marriage was made in our parish church of Bowdon three several Lords days betwixt Wm. Tippinge, of Hale, woollin webster (woollen weaver), and Katheren Hall, of Ashley, both of this parish of Bowdon, wch dayes of publication were the 22nd, 29th dayes of January, and first day of February, and noe objection being made but that they might lawfully proceed in marriage : and were married by me, Thomas Standley (Stanley), of Alderley, Esquire, one of the Justices of Peace for this County, the 6th day of February, 1653.

Proclamation was in some instances made, generally by the bellman, at the Cross in the Market Place. These proclamations usually read as follows :—

> Publication of banns was made in the Altrincham Market, within our Parish of Bowdon, three severall Market dayes betwixt Edward Woodall, of the parish of Ashton upon Mercey Bancke, and Anne Carrington, of this parish, which dayes of publication were the 15th, 22nd, and 29th dayes of August, in the year of our Lord God 1654, and were marryed the 16th day of September, in the year of our Lord God 1654, before
> Tho. Brereton, Esquire.

Some of the entries state that publication was made between the hours of eleven and two in the Market Place, but this does not appear prior to the year 1656 to have been a popular mode, as three-fourths of the proclamations were made in "our parish church." The majority of the marriages took place before Thomas Brereton, Esquire ; but it is interesting to note that on one or two occasions Colonel Henry Bradshaw, of Marple, brother to President Bradshaw, also officiated. In 1656 and 1657, the publications were, with few exceptions, made in the Altrincham Market Place, "at the close of the morning," or 12 o'clock. In 1658 they were made in solitary instances, but they are solemnized by the Vicar, James Watmough, "in the presence of numerous people." This elaborate style of entering marriages then ceases, except in the instances of the principal families of the district, when the details are given with some minuteness. The births at this period partake of the same character as the marriages in the extent and preciseness of the entries. The wife of the Vicar presented him with three or four interesting "olive branches," to all of whom due honour is accorded in the matter of registering. That the schoolmaster was also a married man and similarly situated, is proved by the following amongst the baptisms :—

Hanna, daughter of Peter Hurdes, schoolmaister, (August 24th, 1667).

The ages are not given, and very seldom the trades, but occasionally they crop up. Husbandmen are the most numerous, yeomen coming next in order. There were several websters or weavers in Bowdon (1657), and at a somewhat later date, blacksmiths, saddlers, gardeners, "joyuers," shoemakers, in Altrincham and the neighbourhood.

John Higginson, of Bowdon, innkeeper, was buried 24th day of Novr. 1657.

A poore woman web. was a stranger came by pass, buryed ye 9th day of November.

A poore ould woonman whose name was thought to be Steenson, January 12th, 1658.

A child that was born dead of Tho. Kinge, was buried 15th March, 1658.

Roger Shuttleworth, schoolmaister, buried 7th day of February (1659).

Thomas Brereton, Esquire, of Ashley, departed this life the 10th day of July, and was buried the 19th day of July, in the year of our Lord God, 1660.

Jane Drinkwater, of Hale, a poore woman, buryed 22nd October (1661).

Edward Leigh, of Altringham, a poore man, buried 23rd November (1661).

Mr. John Lightfoote, vicar of Bowdon, departed this lyfe ye 22th day of December, in ye yr. of our Lord, 1661.

Mrs. Margrett Vaudrey, of ye Bancke (Bank Hall), widow, was buryed in Carrington Chapel by leave and lycense of George Lord Delamer, by the interest of Samuel Vaudry, the son, June ye 24th, 1662.

Charles, son of John Houghton, Schoolmaister, Decr. ye 8th, 1662.

Robert Tippinge, of Bowdon, gent and steward to George, Lord Delamer, was buryed ye 21th day of ffebruary, 1662.

Isaac Tipping, son of Edward Tipping, of Hale, Dec. 22th, (1665).

William, son of John Hoyle, of Hale, was buryed Dec. ye 28th.

The two last mentioned Isaac Tipping and William Royle had not xtian buriall, theire friendes contemuinge it. Tho: Weston, Vic.

Wm. Tippinge, of Dunham, bayliffe to Lord Delamer, buryed March 23th, (1670).

Raphe Thomas, of Altringham, piper, buried September 12th, (1672).

Thomas Sanderson, clark of the church, buryed March ye 13th (1672).

" William Shuttleworth, servant to Francis Mosley, vicar, April 17th, (1673).

The two succeeding volumes of Registers are very small, volume III. containing baptisms from 1682 to 1702, and volume IV. marriages from 1683 to 1719. On the title page of volume III. there is a memorandum, dated August 29th, 1697, setting forth that :—

Richard Rogers, Wm. Coppock, Robert Leather and Isaac Eccles, churchwardens for the p'sh (parish) of Bowdon in the yeare 1690, did pay unto John Lawrinson, Wm. Simpson, Robert Leather and Isaac Eccles, churchwardens for the p'sh of Bowdon for the yeare 1693 the summe of six pounds eighteen shillings and sixpence (which they had in their hands) towards reimbursing them, wch was in full for all moneys they were out of purse in the yeare 1693. Witness my hand,

Jo : Hyde, Vic. of Bowdon.

The "baptizings," as they are now called, continue until the year 1683 in a most orderly manner, when there is a record of "John, son of ffrancis Newton, of Altringham, March ye 22th." Underneath this is written : "A brave boy ; long may hee live to God's glory." It is to be hoped that this pious wish was fulfilled. In July, 1696, the handwriting changes, and Altringham is spelled Althringham, just as though the clerk was a native of the sister isle. Almost simultaneously we have the first indication of dissent in an aggressive form in the parish.

1696.—Deborah, daughter of Robert Hankinson, of Ashley, was born July 13th and baptised July 28th, 1696, by Mr. Dernily, as is said by a note sent thereof to ye vicar.

John, son of George Warburton, of Hale, born Dec. 3th, 1696 and baptised Dec. 23th, 1996, by whom I don't know. Aron Warburton told mee of it.

1698.—Henry, son of Richard Green, of Altringham, apothecary, born November 27th, baptised Dec. 13th (1698).

William, s. of John Taylor, of Timpley, mason.

John, s. of Richard Millington, of Althringham, carpenter.

John, s. of James Whitehead, Baguley, weaver.

A female child of Wm. Norman, of Altrincham, sadler.

1699.—Josiah, s. of Robert Hankinson, of Ashley, born May 21th, and baptized June 1st ; Timothy, s. of Robert Hankinson, of Ashley, born May 21th, and baptized June 1st. They were twins. Both the aforesaid children were baptized at Robert Hankinson's house, by one Dernily, a dissenter, contrary to law, the house not being lycensed. He preaches at Ringey chappell, a chappell anciently belonging to the Church of England and under Bowdon Church.

Mary, d. of James Mosse, of Dunham, born July 12th, baptized July 19th by Mr. (Mr. this time) Dernily, the Nonconformist, contrary to law.

Wm. s. of Theo. Heald, of Ashley, baptized at Heald's house by Dernily, the dissenter, contrary to law.

Geo., s. of James Hardie, of Althringham, born Dec. 3th, and baptized Dec. 11th by Mr. Dernily, the dissenting minister, at Ringey.

These would be the "separatists" who were said to be about this time so numerous and troublesome in the parish.

Mr. Dernily's name then drops out of the Register, and so far as he is concerned the breast ecclesiastical ceases from troubling, and its conscience is at rest. How it fares from others later on will be seen. We proceed with more interesting extracts.

1699.—March 2nd, baptized John, s. of John Lupton, grocer, Altringham.

1700.—James, s. of James Hardy, alderman, of Altrincham.

This is the first reference to any one holding any official position in connection with the Corporation of the town.

1700.—Ann, d. of John Worsley, glacier ; Nathaniel, s. of Wm. Brownhill, of Dunham, born December 23rd, baptized January 6th, 1700 ; the father did not acquaint me with the birth or baptism till June 8th, 1701, being Whit Sunday. Mr. Yates baptized it unknown to me.—Jo. Hyde.

We now hark back to the burials in the same volume, several of which refer to the Booth family. There are one or two references to trades then being pursued in the district, notably that of malting at Altrincham. At the end of the volume, amongst the list of the stillborn children, is Margaret Hardey, Quaker, probably the same Margaret Hardey, widow, of Bowdon, who is referred to in the volume as having been "buryd at the

Quaker's burying place in Mobberley p'sh." Many of the people dying at Carrington and Partington were buried at Flixton, probably on account of its being more convenient than Bowdon.

We now take volume iv., which contains marriages from the year 1683 to 1719. There are one or two entries on the title page, amongst them one to the effect that—

"Peter Barber, of Agden, was married in Cartwright's land, beyond Limme."

The marriages begin to be noted as being solemnized by banns or by licence. The one following, however, was not in "either of these fashions."

Joseph Peirson and Sarah Hurlbut, of Ashley, marryed by Mr. Gooden (clandestinely), January 1th, 1697.

"James Coe, of Ashley, marryed to a woman in Lanc (Lancashire), sells meal at a meal house in Manchester, his father lives at Ashley, not marryed at Bowdon, but at Manchester as I am told.

A reticent individual was

Thomas Ogden, keeper, at Dunham, and Ann Moulston, marryed about Christmas, 1698, but he will not tell where nor by whom.

This reticency appears to become epidemic at this time, as subsequent entries show.

Isaac Rylands, of Hale, and Elizabeth Hankinson, marryed in July, in the year 1698, he will not tell when, where, or by whom; by Mr. Gooden.

This latter name looks as if it had been tacked on at a venture. Both the Hankinsons and the Rylands were rather troublesome dissenters at this period.

John Newton, of Hale, and Elizabeth Drinkwater, marryed in August 19th, 1699, at Sandbage (Sandbach), as I am told.

Ellin Warburton, of Dunham, and James Pauden, of Brownley Green, in Northenden parish, were marryed Septr., 1699, I know not wn., where, or by whom.

Roger Simpson, of Altringham, smith, and Mary Harrison, of Altringham, marryed (as is said) about Novr. 21, 1699, but do not tell when, where, or by whom. They were marryed, 'tis said, by Mr. John Brown, not in holy orders.

This Mr. Brown was a sort of Gretna Green gentleman who lived at Ashton-on-Mersey, and he united several couples in the bonds of holy matrimony "contrary to the statute in that case made and provided." These storms subsided, and for a long time marrying and giving in marriage proceeded in the orthodox fashion. Even the Rylands and the Hankinsons saw the error of their ways, and went to the Parish Church as in duty bound. There is also not the same loose style of entering, but it is difficult to withstand the conviction that this is rather ungallant :—

Richard Ardern and ye whoman from Prestbury parish, marryed Octr. 25th (1708).

Probably she had the same objection to giving her name as ladies are said to have to stating their age.

The most important entry we come to for many years then, is the record of the marriage of the Vicar :—

August 28th, 1717.—Mr. Peter Lancaster, vicar of Bowdon, and Mrs. Mary Edmonds, of this parish, were married at Bowdon Church, by Mr. Spencer, curate at Lymme, by licence from Mr. Allen, of Peover.

At the end of the volume is the following :—

October ye 20th, 1709.—At a parish meeting in Bowdon Church it was granted and agreed that Augustin Rawlins, parish clark, instead of gathering his wages wh. is one lay (rate) he is to have it gathered by ye church wardeus and collectors from henceforth.

This is signed by Matthew Wood, vicar, the churchwardens, and others present at the meeting, including Alderman John Higginson, who makes his mark, the said mark resembling the figure four made very awkwardly.

Volume v., which we take next in order, contains baptisms from 1702 to 1720, and burials from 1702 to 1717. It was provided at the charge of the parish, as testified to by "John Millatt, de Dains, of Carrington, George Timperley, of Timperley, George Leicester, of Hale, and Aaron Warburton, of Bowdon, churchwardens." The children baptised are those of a tanner at Hale, a flaxman, gunsmith, horse-jockey, mercer, glover, clothier, apothecary, brickmoulder, bricklayer, barber, basketmaker, butcher, cooper, flaxseller, baker, a whitesmith, at Carrington, and a miller at Dunham, which tend to show that 200 years ago this was a district of some importance.

There are several baptisms of illegitimate children, one of which must have been the offspring of a man of consequence, and must have held even the powers that be in awe. After the words detailing the usual particulars, there is—"Wch. she fathered upon Mr. G . . . . C . . . . ."

There are some children baptised by Mr. Waterhouse, who, like Mr. Dernily, was a dissenting thorn in the ecclesiastical side, and the fact is always precisely stated. In some cases he is "dissenting minister," in others "dissenting teacher," and he appears to have been in business in a large way. At Carrington, "Mr. Orrill," another dissenting teacher, was busy at this period.

Amongst the burials in June, 1703, there is that of—

Mr. Robert Whitehead, Curate of Bowdon.
April, 1708.—Ann Johnson, servant for 40 years at Dunham House.

In the year 1667, an Act of Parliament was passed for the encouragement of the woollen and paper manufactures in the kingdom. It enacted that no corpse should be buried in "shirt, sheet, shroud, or shift," but in woollen, and an affidavit made made within eight days of interment that the dead was not shrouded in linen. A penalty of £5 was incurred if the law was broken. These affidavits are regularly entered in the Bowdon Parish Registers as having been made, except in solitary instances, which were at once notified to the churchwardens. No specific entry of the enforcement of the Act appears until June, 1709, when there was--

"Alice, wife of Thomas Warburton, of Hale, buried in linnen contrary to Act of Parliament. He paid ye fine to ye churchwardens of Bowdon for ye use of ye poore."

Not many years afterwards, the fine of £5 was enforced in the case of—

"Mary Leigh, widow, Bowdon, buried in linnen. £2 10s. whereof went to the poor."

In 1728, Nicholas Waterhouse, of Bowdon, a dissenting teacher, "was buried in linnen," but there is no note made as to whether any fine was enforced. This famous Act was not repealed until 1814, and then not without some opposition.

Amongst other burials are :—

"1709, Dec.—Mary, wife of George Leicester, gouldsmith, of Altringham."

"1710, March.—James, son of Hen. Smith, of Altringham, Alderman."

1710, March 11th.—A still born child of William Coppock, of Hale, clandestinely buried about this time, notice given to ye churchwardens, and then Wm. Coppock pd. ye buriall fees and 2d. churching.—Wit: Tho. Birch.

1711, Dec.—Wm. Hesketh, of Altringham, Alderman.

1712, Dec.—John Pritchard, servant to Mr. Robert Orrell, Ashley, who drown'd himself.

1714.—Wm., son of John Royle, of Altringham, flaxman.

1716, May 9th.—Mr. Matthew Wood, Vicker of Bowdon.

Volume VI. contains baptisms from 1720 to 1738; weddings from 1719 to 1731; and burials from 1717 to 1738. We here find the first reference to another trade or calling in Altrincham and the vicinity not mentioned before, in the baptism of—

Wm., son of Wm. Garner, *fustian man*, and of Elizabeth, his wife, of Hale.

1722, Jan. 20th.—Mary, d. of Robert Leather, Alderman, of Altrincham, and of Hanna, his wife.

1722, Jan. 24th.—Richard, son of Richard Leigh, ale seller, Altrincham, and Elizabeth, his wife.

1723, Aug. 3.—Elizabeth, d. of John Swindells, turner, and Elizabeth, his wife, of Baguley.

1723, Aug. 10th.—Mary, d. of John Yates, bricklayer, and Deborah, his wife, of Baguley.

1723.—Henry, son of John Kinsey (barber), and of his wife, Elizabeth, of Altrincham.

1723, Aug. 30.—George, s. of Joseph Harding, fustian man, and of Elizabeth, his wife, at Altrincham.

There were several ale sellers in Altrincham at this period, and we once more notice that the dissenters began again to trouble their brethren in the church. Baptisms by dissenting teachers are often recorded—notably by Mr. Fletcher. There is also a Mr. Robinson mentioned as at Ringey or Ringway chapel. The practice of recording trades appears to have been most capricious. Sinderland, too, is for a great number of years spelled Sunderland.

Amongst the burials at this period was—

Joseph, son of Peter Melann, a Grecian, and of Mary, his wife.

One still more noteworthy occurred in 1727 in respect of Hannah, wife of Robert Orrill, of Hale,—

She was buried at her own desire without being brought into ye church or having prayer said over her at ye grave, being a most rigid dissenter.

On June 16th, in the same year,—

Robert Prasmore, a wayfayring man, from the Bishopric of Durham.

And—

On the same day, Farmery, son of Mr. Lawton, and of Ann, his wife. "This child was buried in the church without leave from me," says the vicar of that period, "or leave ask'd. Agt. wch. I protested at ye grave, tho. I did not refuse to bury ye corpse."

In 1734 there was interred "a travelling woman of the kingdom of Ireland, who died at Bollington." The marriages in the volume present few features of interest, one excepted, viz., that on Feb. 22nd, 1725-6 :—

James Hardey, teacher of a seperate (dissenting) congregation at Stockport, and Elizabeth Bentley, of Bowdon, spinster, by licence from Mr. Giles.

Volume VII. contains marriages from 1731 to 1754, and it is pleasing to observe that about the first-named period Bowdon was apparently a place to which those from a distance wishful to enter into the estate of holy matrimony resorted. At the end of the volume there is a list of the "briefs" collected in the year of our Lord, 1751 :—

	£	s.	d.
June 2nd, Shipston Church in com. Worcester Ch. £1,487,	00 :	06 :	06.
June 23rd, Knighton Church in com. Radnor Ch. £1,436	00 :	03 :	11.
July 21st, Netherseal Church, com. Leicester Ch. £2,138	00 :	04 :	11.
September 1st, Upton on Severn Ch. com. Worcest.Ch. £2,015	00 :	04 :	08.
Oct. 10th, Stamford Bridge Mill in com. Ebor (York) lost by fire, collected from house to house, Ch. £2,884	1 :	1 :	7½.

These "briefs" were letters patent issued by the Crown for various charitable objects, such as the rebuilding of churches destroyed by fire, or places desolated by a plague. They were usually read in the church during morning service, and a collection made ; but, as in one of the above instances, it was sometimes collected from house to house. Volume VIII. is a book of stupendous proportions, and brings down baptisms and burials to a comparatively recent period—1769. They are most uninteresting entries, but about this time Peggy, Betty, Kitty, and Molly were favourite names.

There are other volumes of Registers which are to a great extent similar to the preceding ones. One point only remains, and that is as to centenarians. Owing to the ages not being mentioned in the earlier records, it is impossible to say whether there were any or not. Altogether it cannot be said that the registers form a very useful study, but from preceding extracts it will be seen that they are not entirely devoid of interest.

It would not do to overlook the famous proverb, "Every man is not born to be Vicar of Bowdon." Sir Peter Leycester, who quoted it, appeared somewhat puzzled to account for its true meaning, although it is very much on a par with a great many other proverbs—self-evident. There are two reasons assigned for the proverb. The first is that in olden as well as in modern times, it was an appointment that might be sought for. It had a good stipend attached, was placed in the midst of a fertile and lovely country, and was as a rule fairly free from the interference of schismatic controversy such as existed among the neighbouring churches. The second is that Charles Jones, son of the then Vicar, was intended by his father, who had secured the Bishop's patronage, to succeed him on his decease, thus debarring anyone else from any chance of the appointment.

A short notice of some of the Vicars and Curates of Bowdon may be interesting. At the latter end of the reign of Henry VIII. Dus Willus Wright was serving the cure in the pay of Tho Roncorn or Runcorn, Vic.; Dus Henricus Tipping, a chantry priest, was paid by Ralph Massey; Dus Ric. Warburton by John Carrington; and Dus Johes Colior or Collier, was at Ringeye chapel. In 1569-70 there was an episcopal enquiry or visitation in Frodsham deanery, and under Bowdon, it says (what is decipherable)—

" . . . . Thome Spede our sworne, &c., saith they . . . . . paraphr and the first tome of homilies. They had no sermons their iij. yeres: he saith he did nev reade the declaration . . . . . saieth he nev had hit."

Of one we cannot speak with the credit which may have been deservedly due to both his predecessors and successors. This was Ralph Hough, who, according to a note in the edition of Ormerod, edited by Charles Helsby, Esq., "married Blanche, a widow in Peever or Peover, about 1585." "He lived with her about a year, then fled away from her after selling her goods, came back to her again, sold her goods, and ran away for good." A Vicar of Bowdon not mentioned in the list usually given, is — Smith. Walker, in his "Sufferings of the Clergy," states that he was sequestered on account of not complying with the solemn league and covenant, and he was turned out by a committee of Parliament without ever being heard.

During the temporary ascendancy of Presbyterianism in Cheshire in 1648, the ministers of the county, after the example of their brethren in London and other places, adopted and signed an attestation which had been drawn up by Mr. John Ley, "the present preacher at Astbury." It was entitled "An attestation to the testimony of our Reverend Brethren of the Province of London to the truth of Jesus Christ, and to our solemn league and covenant;" and was signed by "James Watmough, pastor of Bowdon," amongst others. The very air, however, seemed thick with controversy, and disturbances arose in his parish between Presbyterians and Independents or Separatists. The Act of Uniformity was passed in the year 1662, and it would appear that the Vicar of Bowdon conformed, thus saving himself from the fate of numerous other brethren. In 1689-90, John Peake, for refusing to take the oath of allegiance to King William III., was deprived of his living as a Non-juror. Many of the Vicars of Bowdon have been men of talent and erudition, and two or three have figured as authors of learned works, such as Wroe, Lancaster, &c.

It may not be inappropriate to give a brief notice of one whose memory will be long revered by the inhabitants,—we refer to the late Venerable Archdeacon Pollock, who died at Claughton, Birkenhead, on the 11th October, 1873; but whose mortal remains are laid under the shadow of the sacred edifice the restoration of which was due to his indefatigable efforts. He was appointed to the Vicarage of Bowdon in 1856, having previously, as the reader will have gathered already, laboured hard in the county, and also at Liverpool. On his appointment he set to work to make his parish what it ought to be. After organizing ample machinery for the immediate wants of his flock, his next endeavour was to get a school built at Hale Barns. He then undertook the much needed and truly Herculean work of rebuilding the Parish Church, and he had the pleasure, within four years of his appointment, of seeing a dilapidated edifice replaced by an entirely new fabric. He gave much active help and warm sympathy in the erection of St. John's Church, Ashley road. Another work was the building of a new Vicarage, the old one being at a distance from the Church at the foot of the hill in the vale. He was also the means of erecting the School Church, at

Ashley, and through his instrumentality the adjacent village of Dunham was accommodated with the pretty church dedicated to St. Mark. His next great undertaking was the building of new national schools, the old ones having become inadequate for the purpose intended. He was subsequently appointed Honorary Canon of Chester Cathedral, Rural Dean of Frodsham East, Archdeacon of Chester, and was presented by his University with the degree of D.D., in recognition of his early and distinguished scholarship. In both local and general work he was unwearied; he was mindful of all things great and small, and thought of all other interests before his own. He was also conspicuous, as is well known, for his eloquence and learning. His arduous labours had the effect of undermining his constitution; and, disregarding urgent warnings to take rest, he was struck down by parnlysis on 1st August, 1870, having preached his last sermon, on the re-opening of St. George's, Altrincham, in the month previous. A little more than three years afterwards he breathed his last. His funeral took place at Bowdon, on Thursday, 16th October, 1873, when the choir sang a hymn which he had himself composed, on the subject of "Lazarus." It is sublime and affecting in its simple pathos, and opens with the words :—

> Lord, if he sleep
> He shall do well!
> Why should we weep?
> Why should a knell,
> Dirging and deep,
> Over him swell,
> He shall do well.

An appropriate address was delivered by the Rev. Canon Falloon, of Liverpool. The funeral was attended by the clergy and ministers of other denominations, and the laity was largely and influentially represented.

The Ven. Archdeacon Gore, who succeeded him, is a graduate and late scholar of Trinity College, Dublin (1850), B.A. (sen. mod. math) 1853, Div. Test (First class) 1855, M.A. 1858. He was ordained Deacon in 1855, priest in 1856. He was preferred to the perpetual curacy of St. Luke's, Liverpool, in 1862, and in 1873 was presented to the Vicarage of Bowdon on the death of the Ven. Archdeacon Pollock. He was honorary Canon of Chester 1877 to 1879 chaplain to the late Bishop Jacobson 1877, Proctor for the Archdeaconry of Macclesfield 1884, Archdeacon of Macclesfield 1884-1893, and Canon residentiary of Chester Cathedral, 1893. In recognition of his high attainments, both as scholar and divine, he had in 1890 the degrees of B.D. and D.D. conferred upon him by the Senate of Trinity College, Dublin, of which he was appointed select preacher in 1891 and 1892. His latest appointment is Proctor of the Archdeaconry of Macclesfield. St. Peter's, Peel Causeway (for description of which see ecclesiastical Altrincham), in addition to the mission room in the Vale, the enlargement of the Parish Schools, &c., has been the outcome of the Archdeacon's special talent in organising and drawing round him all classes of his parishioners.

LIST OF THE VICARS OF BOWDON.
[COMPILED FROM VARIOUS SOURCES.]

Presented.
- 1210 Gillebt or Gilbert, Sacdos.
- ...... Ricardus de Aldcroft.
- 1309 Ranulphus de Torrald.
- 1362 Ricardus de Wever.
- 1369 Ricardus More.
- 1411 Thomas Spencer
- 1441 John Urmeston
- 1473 William Minshall.
- 1535 Mr. Thomas Runcorne.
- 1556 Johes Hanson, M.A.
- 1558 Adam Wood.
- 1562 Robert Vawdrey.
- 1582 Ralph Hough.
- 1587 Thomas Warburton.
- 1597 Henry Starkey.
- 1614 George Byrom.
- 1616 Robert Janny.
- 1628 Thomas Pagett (minister and preacher).
- 1647 — Joanes or Jones.

Presented.
- 1648 James Watmough.
- 1660 John Lightfoote.
- 1667 Thomas Weston.
- 1669-70 Francis Mosley.
- 1676 Charles Jones.
- 1661 (ante) Richard Wroe.
- 1689-90 James Peake.
- 1690 (16th Jan.) John Hyde, on privation of Jas. Peake.
- 1708 Matthew Wood.
- 1716 Peter Lancaster.
- 1763 Thomas Hopper.
- 1772 John Baldwin, LL.B.
- 1815 James Thomas Law, A.M.
- 1820 W. H. Galfridus Mann, A.M., exchanged with Jas. T. Law for Lichfield.
- 1856 William Pollock, D.D.
- 1873 Arthur Gore, D.D.

THE MIZE, OR OLD RATE AND ACREAGE.

Chapelries and Townships in the Parish of Bowdon.		A.	R.	P.	Value in 33rd year Henry VIII. reign. £ s. d.
Agden (one half)	T	670	0	0	0 2 9
Altrincham	C	520	0	0	0 10 9
Bollington (one half)	T	400	0	0	0 3 0
Bowdon	C	690	0	0	0 10 0
Baguley	T	2070	0	0	0 16 0
Carrington	C	2070	0	0	0 10 9
Dunham Massey	T	3710	0	0	0 8 0
Ashley	T	2390	0	0	1 7 4
Hale	T	3540	0	0	1 12 10
Ashton-upon-Mersey (one half)	T	670	0	0	0 7 0
Partington	T	1220	0	0	0 6 8
Timperley	T	1380	0	0	0 10 9

From the above townships there were formerly four churchwardens elected annually to manage the affairs of the church and to collect the rates, and as remuneration about £20 was allowed them to defray any little expenses that might occur during the execution of their office. The churchwardens are appointed by the trustees of the Earl of Stamford and Warrington.

The following is the table in the church of "Benefactions to the poor of Bowdon Parish, in lands per annum or sums of money, the interest for ever":—

1619, Dame Elizabeth Booth, relict of Sir William Booth, of Dunham Massey, Knt., £100. 1691, Edward Leigh, of Baguley, Esquire, £100 Mrs. Mary Booth, £5. 1714, William Chapman, of Hale, 2 acres of land; Thomas Brereton left to the poor of Ashley £20; Mrs. Francis Barlow, £10; Dame Meredith, £2. 1721, Rectr. de Croxden in com. Staff. left to the poor of Altrincham, £2. 1744, Oliver Bellefontaine gave to buy gilt plate for ye Communion table £105, also, for ye use of ye poor £11. 1766, Mr. Joseph Walton, £40. 1761, the Right Honorable Harry, Earl of Stamford, £52 : 10s. 1773, George Norman left to the poor of Altrincham £40; to the School, William Tipping, of Dunham, Gent., £10. 1722, Rev. John Ashton, £2. 1807, John Cooper, Esquire, conveyed to Trustees, a messuage and lands in Partington, containing altogether, Cheshire measure, in trust, 3a. 0r. 12p., for poor householders in Altrincham, of the age of 50 years and upwards. 1816, Mrs. Elizabeth Cooke, of Altrincham, left £50; Mrs. Sarah Cooke, of Altrincham, left £50. 1827, Mr. Robert Twamlow, of Altrincham, left £100.

CHAPTER V.

Altrincham 600 years ago—The ancient charter—Sanjam fair—Election of Mayor, form of oath and proclamation—The Court of Pye Powder—Importance of the Bellman—A Mayor's wisdom—The Earl's Christmas Box—Sayings regarding the Mayor—Election of burgesses—Progress of the trust and its disposal—List of Mayors—Abolition of Sanjam fair.

WITH the granting of a charter by the Baron of Dunham, upwards of 600 years ago, the town of Altrincham commenced its constitutional existence. At that time it was described as being nothing more than a small cluster of chimneyless cottages, whose occupants were bound to use the Lord's bakehouse of the place, with a wooden shed for its town hall.

The Cheshire people appear to have been greatly behind in the matter of architecture down to a comparatively recent period. Smith, in a Treatise on Cheshire, written about the year 1609, remarks that "In building and furniture of their houses, till of late years, they used the old manner of the Saxons. For they had their fire in the midst of the house, against a hob of clay, and their oxen under the same roof; but, within these forty years it is altogether altered, so that they have builded chimneys and furnished other parts of their house accordingly." This, it may be readily inferred, was a picture of the primitive state of the Altrincham people. Such were the comforts of "the good old times!"

Of the derivation of the name there does not appear to be any exposition. In ancient documents it is spelled "Altringham," and it is so pronounced to the present day, although by many of the inhabitants, old ones particularly, the "ing" is given as the sound in hinge, which is in all probability the truest pronunciation. As a fee of the barony of Dunham, Altrincham derived great privileges on receiving its charter. Serfdom was got rid of to a great extent, and freedom dawned for the burgesses of the place. The arbitrary power of the Lord, giving him complete control over the movements of his dependents was relaxed, and since that time Altrincham has possessed the oldest known form of justice in the land, namely, that of the Saxon Court Leet. The Hamon, of which we have already heard, received a concession from Edward the First, in the year 1290, of a market at Altrincham on Tuesdays, and a fair of three days' duration, upon which he granted a charter to his burgesses, of which a copy will be given hereafter. This charter is still preserved, and is the most historical and valuable document the town possesses. It was enclosed in a peculiarly shaped oak casket or box, two or three inches in diameter, fitted with an oval lid. The charter itself is a piece of parchment about ten inches by eight, yellow with age, and written in the quaint but beautiful monkish Latin of that period. Appended to it is the seal of Hamon de Massey or Macy, as it is there spelled which has however, been crushed and broken. Subsequently, Edward II., in the 12th year of his reign (1319), by letters patent erased the grant of Edward the First, of the fair named therein, and, in lieu thereof granted to Sir Hamon another fair, on the eve, feast, and morrow of St. James's day, yearly—which latter continued to be held under the well-known appellation of "Sanjam" fair up to April 25th, 1895, when it was abolished by the Home Secretary. There was also a fair held in April, but this was a comparatively modern one, as in 1734 there is an entry in the books of the Leet "that the first new fair that ever was kept, or held in the spring in Altrincham, was upon Thursday, 18th April, to which fair came very great choice of cattle."

It is believed to have been the practice since the charter of Hamon de Massey was granted, to elect a mayor annually under it ; but papers and documents proving the fact are only to be had for about 200 years past. The Mayor is elected at the autumnal

Court Leet of the trustees of the Lord of the Manor, the Earl of Stamford and Warrington, and a jury of the Leet of the borough, which consists of burgesses only, return by their verdict three persons for the Mayor, out of whom the Steward of the Court selects one, who is thereupon sworn by such Steward in this wise :—

You shall swear, well and truly to serve our sovereign lord the King (or Queen) and the lord of this franchise, in the office of Mayor of this boro', for one whole year, now next ensuing, or until another be sworn in your room ; you shall administer equal justice to all persons to the best of your judgment and power ; you shall diligently procure such things to be done as may lawfully and justly tend to the profit and commodity of this corporation, and shall support, uphold, and maintain the lawful customs, rights, liberties, and franchises thereof ; you shall, to the utmost of your power, endeavour to preserve the King's (or Queen's) peace within this borough, and that all misdemeanours and offences committed therein be duly punished ; and in all other things you shall faithfully and uprightly behave yourself, to the utmost quietness, benefit, worship, and credit of this borough and the inhabitants thereof. So help you God.

In former years, on each fair day in July and November, it was customary for a Court of " Pye Powder " to be held before the Steward of the Lord of the Leet and the Mayor in the Court House, which was styled the Court of Pye Powder of the Right Hon. the Earl, &c., holden for the Boro' of Altrincham before the Steward and the Mayor. At this Court none of the freeholders or their tenants attended, but the leasehold tenants of the Lord of the Leet, and their sub-tenants, and also the rack tenants were called to do suit and service. This pye powder or pie poudre, in English law is the Court of Dusty Foot, and its jurisdiction was established for cases arising at fairs and markets to do justice to the buyer and seller immediately on the spot. After the holding of the Court, the Mayor and the Steward proceeded to the Market Place, where the Bailiff (Crier of the Court) proclaimed the fair in the following terms :—

Oh yes ! Oh yes ! Oh yes ! Draw near and hear the King's (or Queen's) proclamation ! I, A—— B——, gentleman, Mayor of the Boro' and Corporation of Altrincham, in the name and on behalf of our Sovereign Lord the King (or Queen), and in the name and on behalf of the Right Honourable the Earl, &c., Lord of this boro' and the liberties thereof,

strictly chargeth and commandeth all manner of persons resorting to this fair that they do keep the peace during the continuance thereof, upon pain of forfeiting for every assault or affray five pounds, and their bodies to prison :

And that all manner of persons do forbear to carry any unlawful weapon or weapons, but that they leave the same at their respective lodgings upon pain of forfeiting the same weapons :

And that all manner of persons do forbear to buy, sell, or exchange any horses, mares, geldings, cows or other cattle in any stable or back yard, or any other place except in the open fair or market ;

And that all persons who bring any goods or cattle to sell above the price or value of 4½d. do pay the accustomed toll for the same upon pain of forfeiting the same goods ;

And that no town dweller do keep in or about their houses any goods or cattle to defraud the Lord of his toll upon pain of forfeiting for every such offence 6s. 8d. ;

And lastly, the said Mayor strictly commandeth all rogues, vagabonds, and other idle wandering persons who can give no just account of their repair hither, that they forthwith depart this fair and the liberties thereof, upon pain of such punishment as is by law appointed for such offenders. God bless the King (or Queen), the Lord of this borough, the Mayor, and all his (or her) Majesty's loyal subjects.

Courts Leet are also said to have held the same relative position to the sheriff's tourn or circuit, a court dating from the time of the Saxons, as the Petty Sessions now do to the Assizes or Quarter Sessions, and "were minor local courts of the same jurisdiction, but being limited to smaller districts." Their criminal jurisdiction, however, became limited in process of time, but they were predecessors of the modern Lighting Commissioners, Local Boards, Sanitary and other local authorities. The view of Frank Pledge, granted by the reigning Sovereign to a local Lord of the Manor, is an ancient custom by which every free born male of the age of 14, with certain exceptions, was called upon to give security that he would be loyal to his Sovereign and true to the latter's subjects, and a neighbour was bound to see that he was forthcoming when required. In case the youth did not answer, then the person in whose *frank pledge* he was, had to produce the the offender within a given period or "satisfy" the Court for his offence. The increase of population rendered this very difficult

J

to exercise in towns, and it fell into disuse, but in some places in Cheshire it was in operation within the past 30 years, and persons who had been summoned formally to the Court Leet with view of *Frank Pledge* have been fined for non-attendance, although it was well known these fines could not legally be enforced.

Some of the duties of the Court Leet were interesting. The stewards had to enquire if highways or footpaths had been stopped or hedged up which had been accustomed to lie open, and the jury had to "present" the person who shut it up, "for the King's subject must not bee stopped of his lawful passage to church, mill, or market." Common bridges which had been broken down were to be repaired by the parties responsible. "Also you shall inquire of (about) sleepers by day and walkers by night to steale and purloine other men's goods, and conies (rabbits) out of warrens, fish out of men's severall ponds or waters, hennes from henrouse (henroosts), or any other thing whatsover, for they are ill members in a commonwealth, and deserve punishment, therefore if you know any such, present them."

"Also you shall inquire of Eues droppers (Eves droppers) and those that are such as by night stand or lye harkening under walls or windows of other men's (dwellings), to heare what is said in another man's house, to the end to set debate and dissention betweene neighbors, therefore if you know any such, present them."

Evil members of a commonwealth were "forestallers," who tried to enhance the price of victuals to their own advantage before the sellers got them into the fair or market ; "regrators," those who purchased goods and sold them again in any market "within foure miles next adjoining thereunto;" and an "ingrosser" was one who got into his or her hands, corn growing in the fields, or butter, cheese, fish, &c., to the intent to sell the same again for profit. These offences were visited with severe penalties, and for the third offence persons were to be set upon the pillory, to lose all their goods and chattels, and " to bee imprisoned during the King's pleasure." Bakers were bound to make good and wholesome bread " for man's bodie, of sweet corn and not corrupted," to give proper weight ; whilst brewers and typlers were to make good and "wholesome" ale and beere, and not put out their signe or ale stake until their ales had been "asseyed" by the ale taster, "and then to sell and not before."

We have here also a reminder of a survival of these courts in the punishment of drunkenness. The orthodox fine of five shillings is well known, and here we have some guide to its origin. All drunkards were to be presented, and to pay "if they bee able for every time they bee drunke Vs (5s.) for the use of the poor of the parish," otherwise they were doomed to six hours in the stocks. An alehouse keeper was to lose XXs (20s.) for every pot of ale sold that was not a full quart, and Xs (10s.) for suffering any townsman to sit drinking in their houses except he be brought thither by a stranger, "and then hee may not stay there above one houre." There are also regulations concerning such as continually haunt taverns, and "such as sleep by day and watch by night, and eat and drink well and have nothing."

The officers of the borough formerly accompanied the Mayor and the Steward in a parade of the streets of the town, and these perambulations were supposed to extend to the boundaries of the borough. Some old verdicts contain orders of the Jury for all householders to attend the Mayor with halberts under fine for not so doing. The procession then must have had a formidable, as well as imposing appearance, and would, no doubt, embrace all sorts and conditions of men, from the Mayor, with the constables, market lookers, dog muzzlers, and ale tasters, down to the humble bellman.

The latter was a very important personage. The town books from an early period bear the stamp and impress of his valuable services ; for at a town's meeting held at the Court House, March 1st, 1796, it was ordered—

That it has been found by experience to be inconvenient to hold town's meetings without notice by the bell (bellman); therefore, in future, it is ordered that notice by the bell shall be given.

In the year 1699 a most important change took place in connection with the Mayoralty of the town, which was destined subsequently to render that office one of some responsibility to its occupants. Most people are acquainted with the story, which is to the effect that the then Earl offered to grant to the Mayor of Altrincham a yearly payment of £5, or land of the same yearly value, at his option, making at the same time a similar offer to the Mayor of Ashton-under-Lyne. The Mayor of the latter place took the money; but his brother of Altrincham thought, and thought rightly, that the property could not possibly deteriorate, and chose the land. The wisdom of the choice has been fully vindicated in modern times. The true version of the matter, however, is this :—

By an indenture dated the 25th November, 1699, made between the Right Hon. George Harry, the Earl of Warrington on the one part, and John Eccles, of Altrincham, shoemaker, then Mayor of the said boro' of Altrincham aforesaid on the other part, the said Earl, as well for the goodwill which he had and bore "to the then Mayor, aldermen (these, it is supposed, referred to the burgesses who had served the office of Mayor, the title being frequently recognised in the old verdicts) and burgesses of his boro' of Altrincham, and for the further and better defraying of the charges and expenses, which the Mayor of the boro' aforesaid, and his successors for the time being was and were likely to be at during his and their Mayoralty, as for divers other good causes and considerations moving him thereunto, did give, grant, bargain, and sell unto the said John Eccles, his executors, &c., certain lands, with liberty to take and hedge in and improve the same, for the term of 5,000 years, yielding and paying during the said term a rent of twelvepence upon Christmas Day in full"—a very handsome Christmas box certainly for an Earl! The deed further recites that this is to be only for the proper use and behoof of John Eccles and his successors in the office, subject to certain provisos, amongst them being neglecting or refusing to pay their rent, or neglecting to pay their proportionate shares of enclosing the lands; also for the re-entry of the Earl if the rent should be unpaid for ten days after it became due, being lawfully demanded, or if John Eccles should grant, bargain, or sell or convert the said premises, or any part thereof or profits thereof, in any wise contrary to the use and trust aforesaid.

Seventeen years afterwards, viz, in November, 1716, another grant of land was made in the same form from the said Earl to Charles Cresswell, then Mayor of the borough.

The Mayor's land, as it is called, was formerly waste, and was 13a. 1r. 26p., statute measure, and consisted of

	a.	r.	p.
Farther Moss Mayor Field	2	0	14
Nearer Moss Mayor Field	1	1	32
Thorley Moor	2	0	33
Higher Thorley Moor	1	1	29
Seamon's Moss Mayor Field	6	0	38
	13	1	26

It evidently formed a subject of notice at no very recent period, as at a public town's meeting held at the Court House, June 7th, 1796, it was ordered that Messrs. Worthington be authorized "to take such measures as they may think proper to procure an administration to be granted to Mr. James Gratrix, to empower him to take such legal acts as may be thought necessary, respecting the fields belonging to the Mayor." No record of any such proceedings having been taken appears; but in 1803 there is a "Memorandum," dated 8th October, which gives us some idea of the income then. It is as follows:—

Mayors field let to Mr. Rigby, at the yearly rent of £18,—who held it two years, and gave up possession (not willing to hold it longer) in the year 1796; holding it from February, 1794. It was in 1796 by public auction, at Bowling Green, let for 12 years to Mr. Gratrix, at the rent of £18 4s., which lease expires 1808; as, also, Mr. Geo. Lupton's lease of Mr. Taylor's Townsfield Garden, for 12 years, from 1796, expires year 1808, rent £3 3s. yearly. Then follows in a somewhat tremulous hand the signature, "Aaron Brundrett, Auctioneer."

Of the office and dignity of Mayor of this borough much has been said; and Webb, in his "Itinerary," written in 1621, speaks of Altrincham, "with its fine little market, and a town of no meaner government than the Mayor of an ancient institution to her principal officer;" while King, in describing the market towns of Cheshire, says, somewhat enviously, that although "Altrincham be none of the chiefest market towns, it hath a Mayor (Major), a weekly market, and yearly on St. James' a fair."

As there is a proverb attached to the Vicarage of Bowdon, there are one or two sayings which have contributed in no lesser degree to make the Mayoralty of Altrincham famous. In former times, the "honour" was much ridiculed, and it was said in an old rhyme:—

> The Mayor of Altrincham and the Mayor of Over,
> The one is a thatcher and the other a dauber.

Sir Walter Scott, too, in the forty-fifth chapter of his novel, "The Heart of Mid-Lothian," puts a peculiar apology into the mouth of the worthy dame mentioned therein. She has come down late to breakfast, and Sir Walter writes:—

The dame apologised to Captain Knockunder, as she was pleased to term their entertainer; "but as we say in Cheshire," she added, "'I was like the Mayor of Altrincham, who lies in bed whilst his breeches are mending,' for the girl did not bring up the right bundle to my room, till she had brought up all the others by mistake one after t'other. . . . Pray, may I be so bold as to ask if it is the fashion for you North country gentlemen to go to church in your petticoats, Captain Knockunder?"

"Captain of Knockdunder, Madam, if you please, for I knock under to no man; and in respect of my garb, I shall go to church as I am, at your service, Madam; for if I were to lie in bed like your Major what-d'ye-callum, till my breeches were mended, I might be there all my life, seeing I never had a pair of them on my person but twice in my life, which I am bound to remember, it being when the Duke brought his Duchess here, so I e'en borrowed the Minister's trews for the twa days his grace was pleased to stay, &c."

That this delicate Cheshire damsel and the ascetic rhymer somewhat libelled both the office and the many worthy gentlemen who have filled it there can be no doubt; for there is a long and goodly list of the best names in the place, amongst them those of Massey, and in 1758-9, that of the Honourable Booth Grey, son of the then Earl of Stamford. It was in removing the effects of the present Earl from Dunham Hall, some years ago, that a silver medal was found, which had evidently been struck in honour of his election. On one side is the inscription, "The Honourable Booth Grey, Mayor of Altrincham, 1759;" on the other, the coat of arms, with the motto, "A Ma Puissance" (According to my power). The Honourable Booth Grey was M.P. for Leicester in 1768, and Mayor at the age of 19. This was presented to the Mayor, Mr. John Astle Kelsall, in 1867-8, by whose representatives it was handed over to the Court Leet. It was made the basis of an official gold chain, being enclosed in a larger silver medal. On the links of the chain to which it is attached, are engraved the names of those Mayors who contributed to it. The chain itself is a beautiful specimen of the goldsmith's art, and was designed and executed by Mr. Eustace George Parker, himself Mayor in 1890.

One of its Mayors, so runs the tradition, was gifted with the grace of repartee excellent well. The Mayor of Over—for he and the Mayor of Altrincham are often coupled,—journeyed once upon a time to Manchester. He was somewhat proud, though he went on foot, and on arriving at Altrincham felt he would be all the better for a shave. The knight of steel and strop performed the operation most satisfactorily; and as his worship rose to depart, he said, rather grandiloquently, "You may tell your customers that you have had the honour of shaving the Mayor of Over." "And you," retorted the ready-witted fellow, "may tell yours that you have had the honour of being shaved by the Mayor of Altrincham." The rest can be better imagined than described.

It is singular that, while anciently the two were on such an unenviable footing of equality, the Mayor of Over, by prescriptive right, takes his seat as a magistrate both in his own borough and at Quarter Sessions, the Mayor of Altrincham does not appear either to have been invested with or exercised magisterial functions. That Mayors of the town when the charter was first granted did so is very probable indeed, but any active administration of justice by any of them has not been known.

The Court Leet was formerly all powerful in regulating and administering the affairs of the town. In order to do this with efficiency there were various officials appointed to assist the Mayor; the principal being—the constables, bailiffs, market lookers, burley or byelaw men, assessors, leather sealers, scavengers, swine lookers, common lookers, ale tasters, pump lookers, overseers, dog muzzlers, chimney lookers, and the bellman. These offices were not then sinecures, and all of them can be traced at work except the ale tasters—a feature greatly to the credit of the Altrincham publican one or two centuries ago. The chimney lookers on one occasion had George Twyford and Edward Cook each amerced in 1s. for neglecting to sweep their chimneys, which occasioned Edward Cook's to take fire; and a worthy Alderman, whose name is honourably associated with Altrincham (Alderman Cresswell) was ordered to "mussel" his dog in pain of 6s. 8d., which he, neglecting to do, had to pay, and was further fined 10s. The Overseers had Ann Grantham amerced in 10s. for entertaining vagrants contrary to Act of Parliament. The pump lookers saw that "no person washed potatoes at ye town's pump, or fetched water to degg straw, or set any barrel to be ledgined, or watered horses, or fetched water to make daub or mortar." The common lookers prevented persons gathering dung there, or "fleaing" the common, or "surcharging" it, or turning diseased animals on it. The swine lookers had Faith Brown amerced in 1s. for turning out one swine. The leather sealers had John Worthington, jun., fined in 3s. 4d. and William Ellam, of Lymm, in 6s. 8d., for selling leather not sufficiently tanned. The market lookers saw that butchers did not bring unmarketable meat, or the bakers give short weight in bread. In fact, the Court took care that the officers did their duty, or "pained" (fined) them for any omission. Thus the well-looker was amerced in 3s. 4d. "for neglecting his office about cleaning the town's well;" and the dog muzzlers in 12d. for not doing as they ought to have done. Concerning the Overseers, there is an entry 150 years ago, which states:—

We find heretofore yt ye Overseers of ye poor have been very neglectful in getting certificates from the interlopers, and for that reason wee doe order the sukceeding officers to take care for the future to get certificates of those that are in town yt have not given them, or those that may come in, if ye deny to remove them, on pain of 6s. 8d.

The previous Overseers had been fined 12d. each for their neglect. But if the Court saw the officers did their duty it also protected them in the doing of it, as we find James Berry "amerced in 3s. 4d. for insulting the market-lookers in the execution of their duty." Some particular persons gave a good deal of trouble, just as they do in the present day. Thus Faith (Ffaith) Brown was twice fined 1s. for gathering dung on the common, 2s. for twice turning out her pig, and another shilling for not paying or cleaning the well. Robert Leather, too, was well known at court: he was ordered to repair his ovens, to make a new and sufficient gate leading into the Town Field, to open his part of Timperley brook, was amerced in sixpence for ledgining his barrels at the town's pump, and lastly was fined 6s. 8d. for neglecting to brush his hedge and slance his ditch at Timperley. Hedges and ditches were the occasion of a variety of orders, parties being required to scour, ditch, slance, breast, and cleanse their ditches, and to fall, brush, fence, and back beat their hedges. "Muck," as it is always called, gave no small amount of employment to the Court. Widow Norman was told not to bring hers any further than the stumps from her stable on pain of 6s. 8d., James Robinson was twice told to keep his within his wall in his fold, while everybody was forbidden to lay "swine muck," or "little house muck" in the bank for the future. Mary Janson, for committing a great nuisance in this respect, was fined 10s., and was ordered to lay no more in the public street on pain of £01 00s. 0d. The houses were mostly thatched with straw, and there were sundry regulations respecting "straw for

K

thatching." Such straw was not to be wet in the highway, and great danger arising from the thatch taking fire, many persons were fined for not having their chimneys duly cleaned. George Twyford was ordered to make up a dangerous hole in the end of his brewhouse, on pain of 6s. 8d., and the smith was to prevent sparks passing out of his smithy under the comparatively heavy penalty of £01 00s. 0d. The bakers were ordered not to lay their heath, gorse, or other fuel, within sixty yards of any house, barn, or outbuilding, and to quench their hot ashes under similarly heavy "pains." The public bakehouse was an important institution, which was maintained until a recent period. The Court regulated the time of "setting in" and "drawing," the former at seven o'clock in the morning from May to Michaelmas, and eight o'clock from Michaelmas to May, also at such other times as "that the inhabitants may have their puddings, pyes, and other eatables out of the oven precisely at 12 o'clock," and "draw for supper by six o'th' clock in the evening," an hour which will be considered rather early in these days. James Tipping, the baker, repeatedly kept the lieges of Altrincham waiting for their dinners, and no doubt this was the case in reference to suppers—for he was frequently fined. The pecuniary affairs of the town were well guarded, the officers being often amerced for not producing their accounts to the assessor for inspection. A most important feature of the work of the Court was the preservation of footpaths and the repairing of highways, as several of the entries at different periods show.

Whereas the styles have lately been took up and the footway stopt leading from Charles Cresswell's, Wellfield at Sandiway Head, and so from thence leading through the upper end of John Smith's higher field, purchased of Mr. John Eccles, which has been an *immemorial footroad.* We agree and order that the several owners of the fields through which the footroad did heretofore lead, to fix good and sufficient styles through their several closes or fields in pain of each £1.

In 1738, it was agreed and ordered :—

That George Norman and William Royle do take down their several styles leading from Altrincham to Bowdon Church, and in lieu thereof do place stumps and rails for the better ease and convenience of Churchpeople and other passengers, and that within one month from this time on pain of 6s. 8d.

This is quite sufficient to show that the Court was a most important one, and fulfilled duties very much after the fashion of a Corporation in modern times.

The ancient custom in regard to the election of burgesses is still carried out. These burgesses are all freeholders within the borough, but must be elected by the Jury of the Court Leet before they can be said to be fully qualified. For many years the Jury returned one freeholder as burgess at each Court Leet, who thereupon usually paid a fine towards the expenses of the dinner of the Mayor, Steward, Jury, Constables, &c., partaken of after the Court had discharged the very onerous duties devolving upon it. This habit of inflicting a fine was not an ancient custom, as this election of burgesses was not carried out with such regularity 100 or 120 years ago ; and the Jury only elected one or two as they thought proper, and no mention of a fine or other expenses to be paid is shown by them. It is certain, however, that it was long the custom for the Lord of the leet to present to the company at the dinner, a certain sum towards the expenses of the same and the fines paid by new burgesses were added, the remainder being paid equally by the persons present, with the exception of the constables, for whom the Mayor paid, as well as for himself. No one can possibly remember when the custom originated, not even " the oldest inhabitant."

Occasions have been known when a newly-elected burgess has declined to pay the customary fine ; and no persuasion, not even that of the "ballivo" of the ancient charter, which is supposed to mean the bailiff returned by the Jury, who executed their precepts, and the warrants of the steward for levying all fines and amercements imposed by them, could induce him to part ; consequently, this money has been lost to the company. It is said that in the year 1820, and for several years afterwards, the Mayor gave no dinners, but only a certain sum towards the expenses of the Court Leet dinners, the rest of the funds being expended in lighting and watching the town. The practice of the Mayor giving these dinners is, however, an institution which cannot have existed from the granting of the charter, as he had no public funds to meet the expenses prior to the grants already mentioned, nor indeed until the lands comprised in the lease became productive. The date at which they are fixed as having commenced is 1749 or 1759, and about that time each burgess gave one shilling towards the expenses of such dinner.

With the progress of the town, the value of the Mayor's land correspondingly increased. Up to 1863, it had for many years been vested in a trustee, upon trust for the Mayors for the time being of the borough, during their respective mayoralties, and was leased for farming purposes; the rents, then amounting to £70 10s., being received and expended by the Mayor at his discretion. This discretion for a long time was not wisely exercised, and public opinion was on more than one occasion strongly expressed. It was alluded to many years previously at the Government Inquiry prior to the formation of the Local Board of Health; and Mr. Rawlinson, who held it, states in his appendix that he fully concurred in the recommendations relative to the Mayor's property. Mr. Joynson and others named the subject, and expressed an opinion that if the rental obtained from the land could be laid out for public purposes, much good might result to the inhabitants and the ratepayers generally. Mr. E. Joynson stated "they had reason to believe that Lord Stamford, whose ancestors left the property in question, to the Mayor and Burgesses, would have no objection to its being made available for the improvement of the town;" and Mr. I. Turton added that "the income from the land was at present of no use whatever, for it was spent in eating and drinking." Some remarks on the improvement of Altrincham, which were then drawn up for local use and information, pointed out that the town was suffering, as Manchester did for at least a century, from having outgrown the feudal usages and regulations under which it had hitherto been governed, and also that the main qualification which the Jurors of the Leet sought for in a Mayor-elect was that he should be disposed to disburse largely of this fund in the

SCOLDS' BRIDLES.

IN THE WARRINGTON MUSEUM. (FORMERLY AT CARRINGTON)

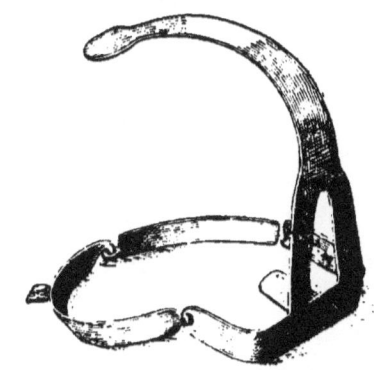

FORMERLY AT ALTRINCHAM. (LOST).

shape of good dinners and drinking bouts. Some of the Burgesses who did not approve of this mode of spending the money, did not attend the Court Leet or its dinners. It is pleasant to have to record that of late years there has been an absence of that license which formerly prevailed, and Mayors have vied with each other in publicly and privately helping on local objects, by subscriptions from the funds at their disposal. Efforts have also been made to add greater dignity to the transactions of the Court Leet, and perhaps by none more so than Mr. Edward Neild, who held the office in 1875-6. During his term he presented two splendid chairs for the use of the Court. They are constructed out of solid oak grown in Dunham Park. They are in the Jacobean style of the 16th century, from designs by Bernard Smith, of London, and therefore harmonize to some extent with the antiquity of the Court to which they are presented. The principal chair stands about seven feet high, and the other, which is not quite so elaborate, though not less tasteful in its design, is six feet. The principals of both are splendid specimens of turnery, and the carving is not less massive and imposing. In the back of the chairs is a shield artistically placed on a green ground, bearing the coat of arms of the town, with the motto in gilt letters "Altrincham en avant." Underneath, on a brass plate, is the inscription : "Presented to the Court Leet of the Borough of Altrincham, by Edward Neild, Mayor, 1875-6." They are upholstered in leather in olive and gold of antique pattern, and the panels are also decorated in the same manner. The back of the second chair is ornamented with the coat of arms of the Earl of Stamford and Warrington, in silver and blue, surmounted with a coronet, and the motto in gilt letters, "A ma puissance." A handsome lamp, formerly in the old Market Place, bore the legend "Pierson, Mayor, 1851-1852," and celebrates the memory of a good man and a worthy citizen in his day and generation.

Returning once more to the economic consideration of the subject, it was mainly owing to the efforts of Mr. W. Devereux

Nicholls, a former Mayor, that this trust was put on a satisfactory footing, legally speaking. He spent the whole of his mayoral income in accomplishing the object; and in his representation he pointed out that it was obvious that some parts of the land were eligible for building purposes, and that the income would be much increased if they could be leased for long terms. It had also been for many years considered that the rents might be much more advantageously applied than in the manner before detailed, and that the inclination of the Burgesses was very strong towards such an appropriation. This, Mr. Nicholls did not do with a view to decreasing the dignity of the office; and suggestions were made that the Mayor for the time being should receive a definite and sufficient sum for the due maintenance of his office, and the remainder be applied for some public purpose, as the Mayor for the time being and a committee of Burgesses to be chosen by themselves might determine.

There were, however, many difficulties raised to this course; but the object Mr. Nicholls had in view was ultimately gained, and with the consent of the Lord of the Manor and the Charity Commissioners, the following gentlemen were elected by the burgesses trustees of what has since been legally termed "The Mayor's Land Charity":—Messrs. James Street (Mayor), J. Howard, James Southern, Mark Pierson, C. Balshaw, S. Barratt, J. Renshaw, and J. A. Kelsall. Of these Mr. James Southern only survives.

Various inquiries have since been held under the auspices of the Charity Commissioners, which have changed completely the old order of things in connection with the Mayor's Land Charity. The report of the Commissioners of 1876, states that the Corporation of Altrincham has no municipal function, and that the Mayor elected at the Court Leet has no Magisterial Jurisdiction. Nothing in the Municipal Corporations' Act of 1883, however, prevented the holding of the Court Leet in the ordinary way, and the election of the Mayor as heretofore, but it specially provided that such Mayor should not have magisterial, municipal, or other jurisdiction. The ancient Corporation was dissolved in 1888, and by a scheme formulated by the Commissioners, the sum of £45 was made payable to the Mayor, "to be applied by him in his discretion during his term of office for some public purpose or purposes in the township of Altrincham." The balance was to be applied by the Trustees in subscriptions or donations in aid of the funds of any "Free Library, Museum, Reading Room, Dispensary, Infirmary, Hospital or Convalescent Home, or any Technical School in Altrincham." The Charity Commissioners further directed that the Mayor's gold chain of office, the chairs presented by Mr. Edward Neild, the scales, the brank or scold's bridle, weights and measures used by the market-lookers, the three silver-headed constables' staves, and the bell used by the town crier, should remain in the custody of the Mayor, the Chairman of the Local Board, and the Chairman of the new Board of Trustees of the Mayor's Land Charity until a Free Library is provided.

The present income of the Charity is, from chief rents £296 13s. 6d., from nursery grounds, 6a. 1r. 13p., £45 ; total £341 13s. 6d. The nett income is about £325, and deducting the £45 payable to the Mayor, leaves a sum of £280 at the disposal of the Trustees for one or other of the purposes stipulated for in the Act. From 1891 to 1895, inclusive, they have given to the Altrincham Hospital and Dispensary £480, and £850 to the Altrincham Free Library. The Trustees in 1896 were Messrs. Newton (Chairman), Davenport, Siddeley, Hamilton, Bowen, Steen, Percival, Boyd, and the Mayor for the time being.

TRANSLATION OF CHARTER OF HAMON MASSEY.

To ALL FAITHFUL PEOPLE OF CHRIST, that shall see or hear this present CHARTER, HAMON MASSEY, LORD OF DUNHAM, SENDS GREETING everlasting in the Lord : KNOW YE, that I have given, and by this my present Charter for me and my heirs confirm, to my Burgesses of Altrincham, that my Town of Altrincham be a Free Borough, and that my Burgesses of the same Borough shall have a *Guild Mercatory* in the same Borough, with all liberties and free customs unto such manner of

Guild belonging, according to the custom of the Borough of Macclesfield; and that they shall be quit through all my lands, as well by water as by land, of toll, passage, pontage, stallage, lastage, and all other servile customs. Also I have granted unto my said Burgesses, common of pasture, turbary and bruary, within the limits of Dunham, Altrincham, and Timperley, saving unto me and my heirs our improvements, and saving to me and my heirs the inclosure of Sunderland, at our free will without the contradiction of any person, whensoever we shall think fit, to enclose the same, so that my aforesaid Burgesses may have common of pasture always and everywhere for all their cattle within the bounds of Sunderland, so long as the aforesaid place of Sunderland shall not be enclosed; saving to me and my heirs in all the time of pannage in the aforesaid Sunderland so that in that time we may have power at our will to fence in Sunderland aforesaid, without the contradiction of any persons. And when Sunderland aforesaid shall be enclosed, my said Burgesses shall have their common up to the Hay of Sunderland aforesaid, and not beyond. It is also my will that all my Burgesses who shall have hogs in the time of pannage in my said Borough either after the feast of St. James and the time of pannage, shall give a right toll when they pasture within the aforesaid commons, and they shall not go from the said Borough with their hogs in the time of pannage. Also, I have granted to my aforesaid Burgesses housebote and haybote in all the woods of the aforesaid places (except my hays and enclosed woods). And also I do grant to my aforesaid Burgesses that they shall not be impleaded out of the portmote of the aforesaid Borough, nor shall they be interfered with out of their Borough on account of trespasses done within the Borough, and if any of them becomes liable for any offence he shall be amerced by his peers, and that according to the degree of his offence. I will also that my Burgesses shall grind all their corn growing upon the land of Altrincham, or expended in the same town, at my mills, for the eighteenth of the full measure. I grant also that my said Burgesses may make unto themselves Presidents and Bailiffs by the Common Council of me or of my Bailiffs and of themselves; and that no plea shall be holden or determined in the said Borough but before me or my Bailiff; and that every Burgess shall hold his several burgage of two perches of land in breadth and five in length, with one whole acre of land in the field, for twelve pence, to be paid to me and my heirs yearly. at three times of the year by equal portions, that is to say: at the Nativity of St. John the Baptist, the Feast of All Saints, and the Annunciation of the Blessed Mary; freely, quietly, peaceably, and wholly, with all the liberties aforesaid; and that every Burgess may sell, alien, give or assign by will, his burgage to any person or persons whomsoever he will (except to the officers of our lord the King and religious men) without the contradiction of any person or persons, saving to me and my heirs our free bakehouse in the same Borough. I truly, the aforesaid Hamon, and my heirs, will for ever warrant the aforesaid Burgages and the acres of land thereunto adjoining, and all the liberties above written, unto my said Burgesses and their heirs and assigns against all people. In witness whereof I have set my seal to this present Charter, these being witnesses:

> Sir Reginald de Grey (then Justice of Chester); Humphrey of Beauchamp, Richard of Massey, Knights; Gilbert of Aston; Thomas of Actone (or Agden); Hugh of Baggelegh; Matthew of Hale; Henry of Dunham; John of Bowdon; and others.

The above is the best translation of the charter which has been made, but it must be remembered that there are numerous others in existence. In some instances it is addressed to all "Shriften people," and charter is called pax and wrytynge, the expression varying with the period at which such translation was made. Passage is egress and regress; tollage is toll paid for standing in the markets and fairs; lastage is liberty to set out standings in the markets and fairs; turbary is liberty to get turf or turves; bruary, heath, furze, or briars; pannage, which is sometimes given as farmage, pession, and passion, is the time when hogs feed on acorns and stubble; housebote is the necessary timber for repairing houses and out-houses; baybote or haybold, wood for hedges; heyes, glades, and places for game; the free bakehouse was a place to which the inhabitants were bound to resort. In some instances president has been translated borough reeve, and there is an expression in one regarding the grain grown at Altrincham, or expended in the town, "or sold at an inn in the same town."

The exact date of the granting of the charter has not been ascertained, but authorities concur in fixing the year 1290. The Justice of Chester at that period was Sir Reginald de Grey, who continued to hold that important office until 1300; but as one Ricardus de Massey acted in his absence for some years, 1290 may be safely assumed to be the year in which the Altrincham Charter was granted.

There are many differences in the wording of the translations in addition to those already mentioned. The name of Massey is

82   ALTRINCHAM AND BOWDON.

given on both seal and charter as Macy. It has since been rendered in various ways—Macie, Macey, Mascie, Mascy, Massie, Massy, &c. No doubt, in connection with other old Cheshire names and the numerous changes in orthography connected therewith, it suggested the somewhat ill-natured though celebrated rhyme that in this county—

> Leghs are as numerous as fleas,
> And Masseys as asses.

LIST OF MAYORS OF THE BOROUGH OF ALTRINCHAM
FROM 1452 TO 1896.

1452 Edward Massey	1632 George Birch	1661 John Paulden
1483 Richard Massey	1633 Richard Brereton	1662 William Rowlinson
1547 Roger Booth	1634 Richard Brereton	1663 James Doe
1552 John Ryle	1635 Jeffery Coe	1664 George Birch
1555 John Morris	1636 George Vaudrey	1665 George Parker
1556 John Ryle	1637 Lawrence Leicester	1666 John Coe
1557 John Ryle	1638 Richard Wright	1667 James Brookes
1558 Ralph Massey	1639 George Ashton	1668 George Aldcroft
1559 Ralph Massey	1640 Robert Lingard	1669 George Hardey
1560 William Ardron	1641 William Hesketh	1670 William Leicester
1561 George Newton	1642 William Rowlinson	1671 George Vaudrey
1562 George Newton	1643 Henry Cartwright	1672 Richard Wright
1563 George Newton	1644 Henry Cartwright	1673 George Cook
1565 Ralph Massey, senior	1645 George Parker	1674 Robert Lingard
1614 William Rawlinson	1646 John Bent	1675 George Parker
1616 Alexander Vaudrey	1647 George Birch	1676 Thomas Doe
1618 Robert Linguard	1648 William Leicester	1677 John Ashley
1619 Richard Brereton	1649 George Vaudrey	1678 Henry Hesketh
1620 Edward Bent	1650 Richard Brereton	1679 William Delves
1621 Randle Wright	1651 Richard Brereton	1680 Richard Wright
1622 George Birch	1652 Richard Brereton	1681 George Birch
1623 William Rowlandson	1653 Henry Bradshaw	1682 Henry Smith
1624 William Hesketh	1654 Richard Wright	1683 James Brookes
1626 William Hesketh	1655 Peter Parker	1684 John Burgess
1627 Robert Parker	1656 John Ashley	1685 James Ashley
1628 Robert Lingard	1657 Robert Hesketh	1686 Thomas Hesketh
1629 James Leycester	1658 Thomas Hesketh	1687 Joseph Pierson
1630 Randle Wright	1659 Henry Smith	1688 George Hardey
1631 Peter Rowlinson	1660 Robert Lingard	1689 John Leather

1690 George Parker	1731 Richard Leigh	1771 William Taylor
1691 Jeffrey Stockley	1732 John Birch	1772 George Cooke
1692 Robert Lingard	1733 James Fletcher	1773 Isaac Worthington junr.
1693 Robert Leicester	1734 George Smith	1774 John Ratcliffe
1694 Timothy Taylor	1735 George Warburton	1775 John Derbyshire
1695 William Hesketh	1736 George Royle	1776 George Lupton
1696 Henry Smith	1737 Henry Smith	1777 William Howard
1697 James Hardey	1738 John Worthington	1778 Thomas Duncalf
1698 George Alcroft	1739 Aaron Eccles	1779 Edward Darbyshire
1699 John Eccles	1740 Joshua Grantham	1780 John Austin
1700 Jeremiah Brundrett	1741 Thomas Royle	1781 William Pooks
1701 George Birch	1742 John Smith	1782 Vernon Poole
1702 George Leicester	1743 Richard Neild	1783 Oswald Leicester
1703 William Grantham	1744 Robert Frith	1784 John Clough
1704 John Bent	1745 George Ashton	1785 Charles Poole
1705 William Higginson	1746 George Burgess	1786 Robert Mills
1706 John Higginson	1747 Benjamin Irlam	1787 John Eccles
1707 Robert Ashley	1748 John Leigh	1788 Robert Leicester
1708 George Smith	1749 Richard Royle	1789 James Staples
1709 James Warburton	1750 George Twyford	1790 Aaron Brundrett
1710 John Smith	1751 Joseph Grantham	1791 Thomas Howard
1711 Edward Garnett	1752 George Robinson	1792 James Walthew
1712 John Cooke	1753 Peter Bailey	1793 Timothy Brownell, jr.
1713 Thomas Royle	1754 Thomas Royle	1794 James Gratrix
1714 Robert Lupton	1755 James Wainwright	1795 William Parkinson
1715 Robert Frith	1756 Samuel Lamb	1796 John Atherton
1716 Charles Cresswell	1757 Richard Crouchley	1797 Samuel Howard
1717 Robert Leather	1758 The Honble. Booth Grey	1798 Samuel Hardey
1718 John Ashley	1759 Isaac Shaw	1799 George Burgess
1719 James Hardey	1760 Nathaniel Priestner	1800 George Worthington
1720 Richard Royle	1761 Charles Cresswell	1801 Peter Leicester
1721 James Robinson	1762 Robert Ashley	1802 Samuel Walker
1722 Samuel Holt	1763 Edward Cooke	1803 William Ashley
1723 John Smith	1764 John Birch	1804 William Smith
1724 George Hardey	1765 Thomas Moore	1805 Thomas Royle
1725 Joshua Grantham	1766 William Rigby	1806 John Postles
1726 William Leicester	1767 Thomas Warburton	1807 Thomas Carter
1727 Fernando Laughton	1768 William Leicester	1808 Abner Partington
1728 Richard Berry	1769 John Walthew	1809 William Royle
1729 William Taylor	1770 William Parkinson junr.	1810 Thomas Darbyshire
1730 William Royle		1811 John Mitchell

1812 Samuel Hope	1841 Joseph Bruckshaw	1871 Joseph Gaskarth
1813 John Austin	1842 William Collier	1872 Matthew Fowden
1814 Isaac Davenport	1843 William Collier	1873 John Shelmerdine Mort
1815 John Mitchell	1844 William Renshaw	
1816 John Barratt	1845 James Royle	1874 Samuel Burgess
1817 William Ashley	1846 James Matthews	1875 Edward Neild
1818 John Drinkwater	1847 Joseph Hall	1876 William Greenwood
1819 Joshua Ashcroft	1848 George Massey	1877 William Greenwood
1820 Samuel Bruckshaw	1849 Richard Broadbent	1878 John Siddeley
1821 Samuel Renshaw	1850 Richard Broadbent	1879 Joseph Gaskarth
1822 Timothy Brownell	1851 Mark Pierson	1880 James Byrom
1823 Samuel Street	1852 Mark Pierson	1881 George Smith
1824 Samuel Clarke	1853 George Berry	1882 Henry Balshaw
1825 John Faulkner	1854 Samuel Barratt	1883 Henry Balshaw
1826 John Hope	1855 John Davenport	1884 Ben Riley
1827 Richard Irlam Grantham	1856 William D. Nicholls	1885 George Bowen
	1857 William D. Nicholls	1886 Joseph Gaskarth
1828 John Clarke	1858 John Mort	1887 James Hamilton
1829 John Adshead	1859 John Mort	1888 Wm. Griffin, Alderman of Manchester
1830 Nathaniel Pass	1860 John Howard	
1831 Robert Shelmerdine	1861 Charles Balshaw	1889 Eustace G. Parker
1832 John Lupton	1862 James Street	1890 Joel Foden
1833 Charles Poole	1863 Thomas Balshaw	1891 Wm. Agar Renshaw
1834 Richard Poole	1864 Samuel Delves	1892 John Dale
1835 Isaac Harrop	1865 Samuel Delves	1893 William Griffin
1836 Isaac Harrop	1866 Samuel Delves	1894 William Griffin
1837 William Hamilton	1867 John Astle Kelsall	1895 David Morrison
1838 Isaac Gaskarth	1868 James Southern	1896 Frederick Raymond Barber Lindsell
1839 Joseph Arstall	1869 Humphrey Davies	
1840 Isaac Gaskarth	1870 Joseph Gaskarth	

CHAPTER VI.

A retrospect—Sundry lawsuits—The first Booth of Dunham Massey; his supposed death at the Battle of Blore Heath—A Booth knighted by Queen Elizabeth—Interesting wills—Dame Booth's Charity—Contributions to the defence of the Kingdom—Dr. Dee's reference to Sir George Booth—Purchase of the town of Warrington; the instructions thereon—Death of William Booth.

A BRIEF resumé is necessary before proceeding further. It will be in the recollection of the reader that the last Baron of Dunham sold the reversion of his estates in this neighbourhood to Oliver Ingham, Justice of Chester. At the time of Hamon's death, however, Oliver was abroad, having been appointed Steward of Gascony by the King. As has often been the case in modern times, the death of an individual, even of mean degree, has given rise to much legal contention. In this respect history only repeats itself; for it was about the year 1341 that "great suits" took place concerning the Barony of Dunham. It was only natural that the descendants of the barons on the female side should think that they were, in the absence of such a notable individual as the aforesaid Oliver, entitled to those broad acres, which constituted a most enviable possession. Richard Fitton, and the heirs of the other sisters, says Leycester, entered into the Manor of Dunham; but, by the King's command, Hamon Masci, of Tatton (afterwards the first Masci of Rixton) came and turned them out. The dispute was not settled until Henry, Duke of Lancaster, bought out the rights of all concerned, and with princely liberality gave it to Roger Lestraunge, or Strange, Lord of Knocking, who was descended from Oliver Ingham by marriage, and by whose descendants it was held for some time afterwards.

Up to this period no mention was made of the Booths in connection with Dunham Massey, and it was not until the reign of Henry V. that they acquired a footing in this district. The name Booth is derived from the Anglo-Saxon word Both, a seat, or chief mansion house, more usually a village. In the year 1402, Richard de Venables, heir to the estate of Le Bolyn, was drowned accidentally in the river Bollin, and by this event, his two sisters, Alice and Dulcia, or Douce, became co-heiresses. These lands were held in trust until Dulcia came of age. She was married to Robert del Bothe, or Booth, a younger son of Sir John del Bothe, Barton, near Manchester, "the Monday after the invention of the Holy Cross," in the tenth year of the reign of Henry IV. (1409), at which time she was only nine years of age. Twelve years afterwards the whole of the manors and estates were divided, Styal and Dean Row, and the mills on the river Bollin, with other lands in the County, principally in West Cheshire, falling to her share. By what has been described as a complicated series of events, this Robert del Bothe seated himself ultimately at Dunham Massey. He challenged his right to a portion of the land in this manor, which he contended ought to descend to him as one of the heirs by marriage through the Fittons and Venables from the last Baron of Dunham. Once having put his hand to the plough he did not look back, and ultimately it was agreed in the year 1433 between the holders of the barony, viz., Sir Thomas Stanley and William Chauntrell, sergeant-at-law, that one half of the lands, rents, and services in Dunham, Hale, and Altrincham, should be given him. Thus, in brief, was laid the foundation of a family which is generally agreed to have been one of the most distinguished and influential in Cheshire.

This Sir Robert had a goodly number of sons and daughters, amongst them John Booth, afterwards Bishop of Exeter, and Warden of Manchester College. He and his eldest son, William, were made Sheriffs of Cheshire for both their lives in the year 1443; and Leycester remarks that this is all the more note-

worthy, "as being the first patent for life which he could meet with in the county." That he took a prominent part in public affairs is often noticed in contemporary documents, and for his services he had an annuity of £10 per annum granted by Henry VI. The time of his death, however, appears to be involved in much obscurity. Leycester says he lived in the reign of Henry IV., Henry V., and seems to have died about the 29th year of the reign of Henry VI. Another authority (Dr. Ormerod) suggests that he was on the King's side in the battle of Blore Heath in 1459— which battle is well known to have been singularly calamitous to the gentry of Cheshire. It has remained for another antiquarian, Mr. Earwaker, by his painstaking research, to throw a great deal of additional light on the subject. Dr. Ormerod gives as his authority the monument in Wilmslow Church, to the memory of Sir Robert and Douce, his wife; but his rendering of the inscription is shown to have been caused by a misreading, and his remark that "it possesses considerable interest, and is the only inscription now remaining in the county relating to any of the warriors who fell at Blore Heath," threatens, says Mr. Earwaker "to become a popular local error," from its having been so frequently repeated. The description which he gives of the brass is also much more complete, and possesses the utmost interest for this district. This handsome brass still exists, but in a much worn state, and has lost the greater part of its inscription, and one of its canopies. It is, however, the finest yet left in Cheshire. Sir Robert is represented in the plate armour worn in the middle of the 15th century, his head uncovered, showing the short cut hair, his feet adorned with the knightly spurs, resting on a greyhound, and his sword lying across his body. In his right hand he grasps that of his wife Douce, who lies on his left side. She is habited in a tightly fitting dress, seen beneath a long heavy mantle, which is fastened by two brooches across the chest. Her flowing hair reaches down nearly to her waist, and is confined at the top of the head by a narrow fillet or circlet, probably enriched with jewels. Her little pet dog is represented at her feet lying on the folds of the mantle. Over each of these figures was a handsome canopy, that over the lady now only remaining. There were the shields on which the arms of Booth, Fitton, Masey, and Thornton were quartered, and round the edges of the tomb, in Latin, was the following inscription :—

> Here lies the body of Sir Robert del Bouthe Knight, formerley lord of Bolyn, Thornetou and Dunham, who died in the feast of Saint Edith the Virgin (Septr. 16) in the year of our Lord 1460; and the body of Douce, wife of the said Robert del Bouthe, who died on the morrow of the feast of St. Tecla the Virgin (Sepr. 23) in the year of our Lord 1453, on whose souls may God be merciful. Amen.

This account receives corroboration to some extent from another source. The Rev. Charles Boutell, in his work on "Monumental Brasses," gives a written description, as also an engraving of the tomb in question. He says that the height of the effigy in the original was three feet. The double canopy is entirely destroyed, as also the greater part of the border legend.

In the absence of the document recording the inquisition post mortem, this must now be regarded as conclusive testimony as to the date of his death.

Sir Robert was succeeded by his son William, who, in the year 1442, married Matilda, daughter of John Dutton, of Dutton, Esquire, and had issue, George, son and heir, and also other sons and daughters. He died on April 6th, 1477, leaving certain lands in trust to provide a chaplain to pray for the health of his soul and that of his ancestors and descendants, in a Chantry Chapel which he desired to be built in Bowdon Church for that purpose; this was afterwards built, and was said from its spaciousness "to be a faire Chappelle." In his inquisition post mortem, or inquest after death, which was taken at "Knottesford," before Thomas Wolton, Escheator, and a local jury, it is stated that he died seised of certain lands, and that he had conceded to him lands in Altryncham, &c. His wife, Matilda, married for her second husband Sir William Brereton, Knight.

George Booth, Esquire, was 32 years of age when he was declared his father's heir. He married Catherine, daughter and heiress of Robert de Montford, lord of Bescote, Staffordshire. It has been stated that his illustrious father-in-law was descended from Charlemagne, Emperor of the Romans, and David, King of Scotland, and that he was heir by his great grandmother to the ancient family of Clinton, of Colchester. By this marriage large estates were brought to the family. By her he had issue two sons and three daughters. He died the Sunday before the Annunciation of the Blessed Virgin Mary, March 25th, 1484. In his will he desired that his body should be buried "in the new Chapel of St. Mary of Bawdon." Katherine, who survived her husband, re-married. She died on the 7th December, 1498.

At the time of his father's death, William, the next heir, was 10 years of age. On attaining his majority in 1494, the necessary proof of age was made. In about four years afterwards he was knighted. He was twice married, his first wife being Margaret, daughter and co-heiress of Sir Thomas Ashton, of Ashton-under-Lyne; by her he had two sons, the heir being named George. The manor of Ashton-under-Lyne and other large inheritances in Lancashire passed by this marriage into the Booth family. His second wife was Ellen, the daughter of Sir John Montgomery, of Throwley, Staffordshire, and by her he had issue seven sons and daughters. In one of the windows of Wilmslow Church there was formerly heraldic stained glass, representing Sir William Booth, wearing a tabard of arms, and kneeling with six sons behind him, and his wife Ellen, also kneeling, with five daughters behind her. There was an inscription in Latin, desiring prayers for the souls of Sir William, and Ellen his wife, and for the souls of their children, who caused a window to be made in the year 1526.

The inquest after death, taken at Altrincham, before Sir Ralph Egerton, Knight, November 30th, 1519, recites the lands he was possessed of and that he died the Wednesday before the

Feast of St. Martin the Bishop (November 11th), last past (1519), and that George Bothe was son and next heir, and of the age of 29 years.

George, the fifth owner of Dunham, married Elizabeth, daughter of Sir Thomas Boteler or Butler, of Bewsey, the scene of a tragedy the remembrance of which is preserved by tradition, when a Butler was ruthlessly murdered by a relative. By her he was blessed with several "olive branches"; and one of his daughters, Ellen, was married to John Carrington, of Carrington, Esquire; and another, Dorothy, to Robert Tatton, of Wythenshawe, Esquire. He died on the 25th October, 1531, his eldest son, George, being then 15 years of age. In his will he states:—

I, George Bothe, of Donnham Massie, Esquire, &c., bequeath my body to be buried in Jhesus Chappell at Bowdon churche, among myn ancestors. Alsoe, I give to ye prior of Birkenhed my best horse to praye for me; also at Birkenhed aforesayd ten shillings to say a trentall of masses for my soule; also I give to ye prior and ye freires at Wariugton ten shillings to say a trentall of masses for my soule. Item to ye same prior of Warington towards ye gildying of our Ladie iij^s iiij^d (3s. 4d.) Also I will that my best gown of velvet and my best dublet shall be made in two vestements, and ye one of ye sayd vestements to be given to ye said chappell of Jhesus at Bowdon church, and ye other vestement to remene in ye chappell of Dunnham for ever. Also I give unto George Bothe, my son and heire apparent, my cheine of gold and my signet of gold as heire lomes.

Also it is my will that my chaplen, Sir John Percivall, or some other discrete prist, shall say masse, praye, and do devyn service for my soule and myn ancestors and all Xten (Christian) souls by ye space of vij (7) yeres nexte after my decese, and he to have for his salarie yerely iij^{li} xiij^s iiij^d (£3 13s. 4d.) And whereas I by my dede indented berying date ye xviijth day of Julie ye xxiij yere of Kyng Henre ye viijth have infeoffed my brother in law John Massie of Podington esquire, John Carryngton of Carryngton esquire, William Meyre of Meyre esquire, Richard Legh of High Legh esquire &c. in my manor of Dunham Massie and in all my messuages, lands, tenements, rents and services in Dunham Massie, Stayley, Bolyn, Deyn Roe, Stiall and Wilmeslowe, in trust, &c. as by the same dede indented more plenly doth appear.

Also I bequeth for ye makyng of ye side ile of ye Church of Bowdon at such time as it shall be taken down five marks of money.

His son George, who succeeded him, also contracted an early marriage, having at the age of 16 espoused Elizabeth, daughter of Sir Edmund Trafford, of Trafford, Lancashire, by whom he had

EARL AND COUNTESS OF STAMFORD.

issue William, son and heir, and three daughters. He was one of the gentlemen who received a letter from the Queen (Jane Seymour) dispersing the joyful news through the kingdom of the birth of Edward VI. in 1537.

The letter was in these words :—

By the Quene.

Trusty and wel-biloved, we grete youe well. And for asmuche as by the inestimable goodness and grace of Almighty God, we be delivered and brought in childbed of a Prince, conceyved in most lawful matrimonie between my Lord the King's Majestye and us, doubting not but that for the love and affection which ye beare unto us, and to the commyn wealth [common wealth] of this realme, the knowledge thereof shuld be joyeous and glad tydings unto youe, we have thought good to certiffie to you of the same. To thintent (the intent) ye might not only rendre unto God condigne thanks and praise for soo gret a benefit, but also pray for the long continuance and preservation of the same here in this lief, to the honor of God, joye and pleasor of my lord the king, and us, and the universall weale, quiet and tranquillyty of this hole realm. Gevyn under our signet, at my Lord's manor of Hampton cort, the xii day of October, [1537.]

To our trusty and welbiloved
GEORGE BOTH Esq.

He died in 1543, aged 28 years. His widow Elizabeth, survived him, and was twice re-married, firstly to James Done, of Utkinton, and secondly to Thomas Fitton, of Siddington. He appears to have made Wilmslow his place of residence, and in his will he desired to be buried there. His raised altar tomb, bearing his arms and initials, with those of his wife, remained in the Booth Chapel for a long period, but was destroyed at the restoration of the church in 1863.

His son and heir, William Booth, Esquire, was but three years of age on succeeding to his father's ample estates in 1546, and was ward to Henry VIII. He married Elizabeth, daughter of Sir John Warburton, of Arley, and had a family of seven sons and six daughters. One of his sons, Robert, distinguished himself as a soldier in Holland. In 1571 he was made Sheriff of Chester, and seven years afterwards had the honour of knighthood conferred upon him by the virgin Queen. He died on the 28th

November, 1579, and was buried at Bowdon on December 8th following, so that he does not appear to have long survived the honours bestowed upon him. His will is a most interesting one. He bequeaths to his wife "the chain of gold," which he last brought with him from London, weighing about xxx[li.] another small chain, a carcanet of gold, one pair of bracelets of gold, two suits of borders of gold, one single border of gold, one tablet of gold, with all the rings she was accustomed to wear, and certain small buttons of gold, enamelled black and white, three little gilt bowls, with his third salt cellar, and all the husbandry stuff at Stayley Hall. To his son George (his heir) he leaves all the rest of his plate (reserving one dozen of spoons "of the worser sort," which he gave to his wife), his best chain of gold with his signet, and all his apparel, with all his gold buttons except those before given to his wife. "To William Duncalf, my cast of flawcons (falcons), my baie trotting nagge and my setting spaniells." To his well-beloved mother "my sealinge ring, usuallie wore on my little finger;" to his brother-in-law, Davenport, all his hounds; to his cousin, William Tatton, George Brereton (Ashley), and Edmund Joddrell, all his fighting cocks and hens; to his sisters Davenport, Chauntrell, and Done, each a gold ring; and to his brother-in-law, Mr. John Done, his best baie nagge and his pied horse, then at Stayley Hall; to his daughter-in-law, Jane Bothe (married to his son George, then a minor), a black ambling nag that was Mr. Carrington's, and also a gold brooch; to his brother-in-law Mr. Peter Warburton, his best gray nag that he himself was accustomed to ride upon, and also his lute; to his brother-in-law Mr. George Warburton, a young coal-black nag; to Mr. Vicar, of Rochdale, iiij[li.]; to William Leigh, his long black cloak; to George Holme his best pair of virginalls, &c.

His wife, dame Elizabeth, survived him for the long period of 49 years, and appears to have distinguished herself by her widely diffused charity. In 1620 she granted to the Mayor and citizens of Chester the sum of £400 upon trust for ever, the interest of which at five per cent. per annum, is to be annually paid out by them in certain sums, £5 of which is handed over to the overseers of Bowdon parish, amongst others, to be expended in weekly instalments in purchasing loaves of bread to be distributed weekly, on every Sunday, for ever, immediately after morning prayer in the Parish Church, to 24 poor aged people. It is divided over several parishes, and the distribution continues to be made.

George Booth, the second surviving son of the preceding, lived in those critical times when the Protestantism of this country first rested on a firm foundation ; when, as one writer has eloquently put it, Englishmen performed those brilliant and glorious naval exploits, especially the destruction of the Spanish Armada, which are unsurpassed in our naval annals ; when the majesty of English prose was formed by the hand of Hooker ; when the harmony of English verse flowed from the lips of Spenser ; when the drama, the surest proof of advanced civilization, had its first beginnings, and was perfected by the immortal genius of Shakespeare ; while Bacon opened up a new method of philosophy, whose practical fruits we may be said even now to gather. Born on October 20th, 1566, Sir George was, on the death of his father, still a minor, and was made a ward of Queen Elizabeth. He was married in 1577 to Jane, daughter and heiress of John Carrington, he being 11 and his wife 15 years old at the time. She was an orphan, her father having died only the month previously. She died without issue, and he obtained, by suit, possession of the land of Carrington. His second wife was Catherine, daughter of Sir Edmund Anderson, Chief Justice of the Common Pleas, and by her he had a large family. He was, like all Englishmen of the period, seized with the contagion of patriotism, and contributed liberally, as also did his mother, towards the armaments which were raised for the defence of the kingdom. He was Sheriff of Chester for the first time in 1597, and he is referred to by the gifted, but eccentric Dr. Dee, the then Warden of Manchester College, who records in his diary that he received a "viset" from Sir George, who had no doubt just been knighted by the Queen, and that "after some few words of discourse," he agreed to stand by the arbitrement of Mr. Homfrey Damport or Davenport, "a Cownsaylor of Gray's Inne," concerning two or three tenements in his occupying in Dunham Massey. He also mentions a second "viset" he had from Sir George, who "sayed he wold yeld to me what he wold not yeld to the bisshop nor any other," thereby showing that the worthy doctor stood high in his estimation. Sir George was created a baronet by patent bearing date May 22nd, 1611, in the ninth year of the reign of James I., being the tenth person who was created a baronet after the institution of that order. To entitle him to this honour he was amply possessed of all material requisites. Webb, in his "Itinerary," speaks of the beautiful seat of Dunham, at that time "never more graced than in the present possessor, upon whom, and his most worthy son, William Booth, Esquire, the world hath deservedly set great love and affection, himself bearing a chief sway in the great commands of regiments in the country, and his son already giving proof of that wisdom and moderation in government which have adorned his ancestors before him."

Of the eldest son William, mentioned above, it becomes necessary to speak more at length, as his opening acts, conspicuous for great ability, gave promise of a brilliant future. It was by his efforts that the family acquired possession of Warrington. The instructions which he gave to his stewards on that occasion are remarkable, as being probably the last instance of an appeal being made on the old principle of feudal benevolence to the tenantry for pecuniary aid. The sum which was to be paid for Warrington to Thomas Ireland, Esquire, of Bewsey, was £7,000, and in his instructions William wishes the tenantry to be called together, the amount to be paid signified to them, in order that by their assistance he and his father might be enabled to finish the purchase. It was an opportunity for the tenants to show their loves, such as might never probably occur again, and the "desire" was for three years' rent, which, if they would give, neither he nor his father would require any more rents or gifts of them for their two lives. Failing this, "they might provoke him to 'sharpe courses.'" Other landlords in Cheshire and Lancashire, he reminded them, had recently demanded three years' rent only for spending money which had been readily granted, and from the fact of the purchase being rumoured about the country, if the tenantry forsook them in this extremity it would cause much disgrace. The purchase was afterwards completed. William did not live more than seven or eight years after this great event, but died on the 26th April, 1636, in the lifetime of his father. He had married Vere, second daughter and co-heiress of Sir Thomas Egerton, eldest son of Lord Chancellor Egerton, and she bore him five sons and two daughters. Thomas, the eldest, died at Chester at the age of 12. Consequently, George Booth, the second son, succeeded to the baronetage on the death of his grandfather, who attained the ripe age of 86, October 24th, 1652.

This Sir George was conspicuous in the political theatre during the civil disturbances of the seventeenth century, and a sketch of his life and actions may well form the subject of a separate chapter.

CHAPTER VII.

Birth of Sir George Booth, first Lord Delamer —Description of Sir William Brereton — Indictment against Sir George; his part in attempting to pacify the county—Its failure—The siege of Nantwich—Spirited defence—Defeat of the Royalists—Sir George elected member for Cheshire; his exclusion by Colonel Pride's purge— Royalist attempts at a Restoration—Sir George's celebrated rising— The battle of Winnington—His betrayal and arrest; his committal to the Tower—Release and re-election --His improvements at Dunham—Description of the old mansion —His death.

AT the period of the birth of Sir George Booth, in 1622, those aspirations for constitutional liberty inherent in a commercial nation were beginning to animate the mass of the people, and find vent in the House of Commons. Those aspirations, repressed for the nonce by an untoward display of regal prerogative, only burst out with greater violence at a subsequent period. It is not to be wondered at that the Booth family ranged themselves on the side of the people, and from this fact the grandfather of Sir George was looked upon as the chief corner stone of the Puritan or Presbyterian party in Cheshire. The word Puritan must not, however, be misunderstood. There were Puritans of various political complexions in those days, and ranked deservedly in the first grade were those who were in favour of maintaining the highest principles of civil liberty, apart from religious doctrine—not those sour, narrow-minded bigots usually associated with the word, and which are popularly thought to be such in the present day. The part which the Booths of Dunham Massey were called upon to take was one fraught with danger and perplexity, but one which few have succeeded in carrying out with greater honour, and this at a time, too, when England had never before showed so many instances of courage, ability, and virtue.

In illustration of this, there appears the following quaint notice of Sir George's grandfather in Ricraft's Worthies:—

And next to this religious and faithful Lesley, is Sir George Booth, the leader of Cheshire, who, when the troubles first began, stood up for his country, exciting his tenants so to do, promising them that had leases of their lands from him that if any such did suffer in person or goods he would make them recompense, and if any had lease by life and should be slaine, the life of his wife, child, or friend, should be put in his stead, a brave religious resolution, which, if all the gentry that had adhered to the Parliament had done the like, the warres could never have lasted so long. But this religious brave Booth thought it not enough so to doe, but took a place of command himself, and was very active and courageous for the preservation of his country, did many gallant exploits which I hope hereafter to mention at large, and at present give him this character—free, brave, godly brave Booth, the flower of Cheshire.

When the signal of open discord and civil strife was given in August, 1642, Sir George Booth, and Sir William Brereton, who was described by his enemies "as a notable man at a thanksgiving dinner, having long teeth and a prodigious stomach," were the only two Cheshire gentlemen mentioned by name in the first order for arming the county and securing the magazines and equipments of the Royalists. The battle of Edge Hill took place in October of the same year, and soon after a great Session or Assizes was held at Chester, where bills of indictment were preferred before the Judges against Sir George Booth and hundreds of others for high treason in taking up arms and adhering to Parliament in the war : but this indictment they would not see fit to appear in person to answer. In the following year (1643), that internal peace was necessary for the good of the country was greatly felt; and in July a meeting of the principal persons in the county was held at Bunbury. They appeared to be pretty equally divided between King and Parliament, and a treaty of pacification was then drawn up, which was signed by Sir George, on behalf of the Parliamentarians, and by Lord Kilmorey, Sir Harry Mainwaring and others, for the Royalists. This measure, however, appears to have been particularly distasteful to Parliament, who considered it of such importance as to immediately render it null and void, so far as they were concerned, by a special ordinance.

Military preparations were on this rupture pushed on vigorously by both sides, and Nantwich, which was esteemed an important garrison, was taken possession of by Parliament. The Royalists, whose head quarters were at Chester, made several unsuccessful attempts to get possession of the town, and in the severe siege by Lord Byron in January, 1644, Sir George acted a most prominent part. The privations endured by the garrison were extreme; and when the town was greatly harassed, Lord Byron sent a message asking him to yield the town into his hands, as they were in a low and desperate condition. To this Sir George sent a spirited refusal, in which he said that though they might be termed traitors and hypocrites, God in his own good time would show their unstained and unspotted loyalty towards His Majesty as well as their sincerity in all their privations.

There is a prophetic ring about these words. Sir George was evidently animated by the highest feelings of love of country; and events in the latter part of his life strongly confirm this. Other papers were also sent to the commander by various parties, amongst them one from Captain Sandford or Handford, a man "very lavish of ink and big words."

The suspense in which Sir George and his companions in arms were kept was soon to be removed by very unexpected means. The rising of the Weaver caused the Royalists to withdraw, and the "plat" which they had placed over the river was swept away. This was taken advantage of by the townsmen and soldiers; and on the same day the Royalists were defeated by the combined forces of Sir William Brereton and General Fairfax, and they retreated to Chester.

In 1646 the celebrated fortress of Beeston was ordered to be dismantled, and Sir George was on the commission which sat at Warrington for this purpose. Two years afterwards, years pregnant with eventful history, Parliament was invaded, and the celebrated Pride's purge was applied. Sir George was one of those members excluded on that occasion; and at a subsequent meeting in Westminster Hall he headed a deputation to the House demanding equal liberty to sit. This, however, as is well known, was not granted.

In 1650 he was on the commission of the peace for the county, and instructions were afterwards issued when the Commonwealth was fully assured, directing the Sheriff, in conjunction with Peter Warburton, Sir George, and others, to meet on certain days to enquire into conspiracies and secret meetings, to disarm Papists or disaffected persons that had appeared such by their actions and words, or corresponded with Charles Stuart, son of the late King, and to "observe" strangers resorting to the County of Chester. By this tribunal ten persons were condemned, and five executed. He was again elected a member for the county in 1654, and it was this Parliament which showed such little sign of submission to Cromwell's commands that they were dismissed in January, 1655. In the succeeding Parliament of 1656, the county again honoured him with a renewal of well-merited confidence.

His views appeared for some time past to have been undergoing a vital change. The reasons which caused Sir George to become as active a partisan of the exiled Stuart as he had formerly been of Parliament are, no doubt, to be found in the disgust engendered by the high-handed proceedings of Cromwell, the position taken by the Independents, who now regarded their former superiors, the Presbyterians, with contempt, and his exclusion from the House by Pride's purge. The Royalists made many attempts at Restoration, and in some of them Sir George does not appear to have been at all backward in asserting his changed principles. An old Royalist song of the period says :—

> Young Mainwaring fell by the side of hys sire,
> Stout Booth was revenged for him there ;
> For the foe left his grim trunkless head in the myre,
> By the sword of old Dunham's young heir.

The union between the Presbyterians and the Royalists gave additional impetus to the cause in which Sir George was embarked. In July, 1659, Sir George proceeded to Manchester, and after holding a conference with the Presbyterians and the Cavaliers returned to Warrington and fixed a rising for the 1st of August. Sir George also entered into correspondence with the Earl of Derby and Lord Kilmorey, and such of the gentry of Lancashire and Cheshire as desired to assist in the deliberations for restoring the monarchy were allowed to do so. These plans were, however, revealed to the prevailing powers, and the risings in other counties were suppressed. That of Sir George was only destined for a feeble continuance. A few of his followers in their jubilancy plundered some of the houses of the Cromwellians; but this action, on their part, was strongly condemned by Sir George. As showing the great affection still felt for him by many of his old acquaintances, one of those who had suffered from the exuberant handling of his followers, a relative of President Bradshaw, wrote, warning him that all the other counties in England were quiet but Cheshire. Still he persisted in his enterprise, notwithstanding that he complained that he had been falsely deserted by a large number of the "best in England" who had promised him assistance.

Pushing on to Chester, which city he took, though the Castle held out, he and his forces rendezvoused at Rowton Heath. An old tract of the period says that Sir George invited the gentry of those parts to meet him, when he declared "he was for a free parliament and *a single person*, which proved effectual with the malecontented party, and divers sparks appearing in this great flame." It appears they had above 3,000 horse and foot, well mounted and armed, "with drums beating, and colours flying, and trumpets sounding;" and after they were drawn up on the Heath, Col. Brooke and Col. Blackburne divided the horse and foot into several bodies, "placing them in sundry warlike figures and postures, after which Sir George made a speech showing the grounds and reasons of their present engagements and undertakings."

This speech or declaration had great effect in rousing the

drooping spirits of his party. Not being able to get possession of the Castle, he set off with a portion of his forces in the direction of York; but the rapid approach of Lambert from Ireland compelled him to return to his former position at Chester, Clarendon remarking that Sir George went to meet him with his natural impetuosity.

His misfortunes now appeared to be at their height. On the 19th August the decisive battle of Winnington was fought, resulting in the complete defeat of Sir George's troops, and his own ultimate capture. The troops of the Royalists were quartered at Northwich, while Lambert's were at Weaverham. The two armies, on this eventful day, came into action amongst the enclosures at Hartford. The horse were unable to act, and the Royalists "retired uninjured from hedge to hedge, and passed the bridge without any other loss," says Lambert, "than that of reputation, and discouragement in meeting with those whom they found of equal courage, but engaged in a better (?) cause." The Royalists now endeavoured to secure the bridge, which would have given them a great advantage, seeing that at this point the river was unfordable, the bridge narrow, and flanked with a strong ditch at the far end, and a high hill which no horse could pass otherwise than along the side in a narrow path. Those who are familiar with the picturesque road which formerly approached Winnington Bridge will be fully able to realize the disadvantages our ancestors stood at in the way of locomotion, compared with our steam and telegraphic times.

This coign of vantage was not long held by the flagging Royalists. "After three good volleys," says Lambert, "the horse passing the bridge together with the foot, charged the horse of the Royalists, which advanced to cover the retreat." Sir George Booth's infantry retired in good order, following their colours up the hill, and protected by the gallantry of the cavalry. Lambert gives due praise and honour to the English valour of his adversaries, and states that within a quarter of a mile the Royalists halted to give battle, but were a second time routed, although disputing "the place very gallantly, both parties showing themselves like Englishmen." Such is the description of the battle of Winnington, taken from an old tract of the period ; and contemporary historians agree in describing it as very decisive. Sir George escaped with great difficulty, and disguising himself as a gentlewoman, left the scene of action. He was, however, betrayed, having acted his part very badly ; and was taken at Newport Pagnell, in Buckinghamshire, where he was riding on a pillion in the disguise mentioned. He was committed to the Tower. The proceedings of this period awakened national comment, and several tracts were published relative thereto. One of them, in particular, purports to give a dialogue which occurred in the Tower between Sir George and an imaginary individual named Sir John Presbyter, in the course of which Sir George expresses his great repentance at having been connected with the parsons in any way, and uses strong language concerning them.

His confinement in the Tower was not of long duration, General Monk having declared for a full and free Parliament in which the nation would be thoroughly represented, the excluded members and Sir George were released from the sequestration under which they had laboured. In 1660, the Long Parliament was dissolved ; and what was called the Convention Parliament, from its not being regularly summoned, was held. Of this Parliament Sir George was elected a member, and the commission for the Restoration having been made, and carried amidst general acclamation, he had the happiness of being the first of the twelve members elected to carry to King Charles the Second the answer of the House to His Majesty's celebrated declaration of Breda.

Honours were now showered upon Sir George. In the same year, the sum of £20,000 was on the point of being voted to him as a reward for his services and great sufferings, when he in his place in the House requested, with a high-souled patriotism, which only those acquainted with the manners of the time can fully appreciate, that it should not be more than half that amount; which was accordingly granted by the Commons on August 2nd, and confirmed by the Lords the day following. As a reward from the Crown, he was ennobled by the title of Baron Delamer, of Dunham Massey, the patent bearing date April 20th, 1661, and at the same time he had the liberty to propose six gentlemen to receive the honour of Knighthood, and two others for the dignity of Baronet.

During his eventful life, Sir George appears to have found ample time to devote to domestic matters. According to one old writer, he greatly improved the Manor house of Dunham Massey by building the north side thereof answerable to the opposite part, surrounded it with "a large outward court, with brick wall and a faire gate of stone," and made a domestic chapel on the south side of the house. It was then, as shown on the illustration, what Dr. Ormerod has described as "a large quadrangular pile, with gables within and without. The gables within the court were indented and scalloped, and large transome windows introduced. The exterior front appears to have been finished at a later period, with pilasters and ornaments in imitation of the Italian style of architecture, and large octagonal turrets were placed at the corners. It stood within gardens laid out in the stiff taste of the time, and surrounded by an ample moat, in one angle of which is drawn a large circular mound, with a summer house on the top of it, supposed to be the site of the Norman keep tower." The noble avenue of beeches was in its swaddling clothes, so to speak, being surrounded with large wooden guards, while the landscape is destitute of that sylvan beauty which is the admiration, and justly so, of modern times. He was twice married; firstly, to Catherine, the daughter of Theophilus Fiennes, Earl of Lincoln, who died in childbirth, leaving an only daughter, Vere Booth; and secondly, to Elizabeth, daughter of Henry Grey, Earl of Stamford, by whom he had seven sons and six daughters, and who died in 1690 at Oldfield Hall.

Sir George died August 8th, 1684, and was buried at Bowdon

on the 9th September with great solemnity ; on which occasion Mr. Cawdrey, a Presbyterian minister, preached. The Latin inscription to his memory was written by William Andrews, who had been for thirty years his faithful domestic servant, and whose remains were deposited, at his own request, in the same tomb as his master. Clarendon describes Sir George as being of one of the best fortunes and interests in Cheshire, then said to be the "seed plot of gentilitie;" but his deeds, more than all, entitle his memory to be held in veneration and esteem by his fellow-countrymen.

CHAPTER VIII.

The second Lord Delamer ; his popularity ; his advocacy of the people's rights—Court jealousy - His committal to the Tower on three occasions ; his remarkable trial at Westminster Hall ; his eloquent defence and justification ; his retirement to his seat in Cheshire ; his support of the Prince of Orange ; his subsequent honourable career and death.

HENRY, Lord Delamer, second son and heir of the preceding nobleman, was born on the 13th January, 1651, and succeeded to the peerage on the death of his father. He had been elected member of parliament for the County during the father's lifetime, and was appointed to the high office of Custos Rotulorum in 1673. He married Mary, daughter and sole heiress of Sir James Langham, Bart., of Cotters Brook, Northamptonshire. She died in 1690-1, leaving him with four sons and two daughters. He was distinguished at an early period of his career by his ardent advocacy of those liberties which were overshadowed and threatened with extinction by the movements of the papists. He was particularly anxious for the passing of the famous Bill of Exclusion, for which Lord Russell, on the morning of his execution, sent him a kindly message of respect and thanks.

He also made great exertions for securing the purity of Parliaments ; in instituting inquiries into the corruption of the judges, and in recommending the punishment of such as might be guilty. For his part in promoting the Bill of Exclusion he incurred the animosity of the Duke of York, and the Duke's influence on the facile King was no doubt increased by the fact of the sympathy of this nobleman with the Duke of Monmouth. In fact, his name had been returned by the Court spies as one of the Cheshire gentlemen who attended Monmouth when he visited Dunham in 1682. He was deposed from his public positions of trust, and just before the death of Charles II. committed a prisoner to the Tower. He was released, after an incarceration of several months, without any formal accusation being made against him. Soon after the accession of the Duke of York, as King James II., to the throne, he was committed to the Tower under somewhat similar circumstances, but was released on bail. This system of petty persecution was still further carried out, and a third time he was committed. It was the last straw which broke the camel's back. The Lords, anxious for the consolidation of those ancient safeguards which had received such severe shocks in previous reigns, interfered on his remonstrance, or rather petition, by a demand from the Sovereign why he was absent from his attendance in the House. Newcome, in his diary, speaks of the unexpected prorogations of Parliament which took place at this period, and tremblingly awaited the issue of these things, if possible, to rescue Lord Delamer. Matters were thus brought to a crisis, and he was put on his trial on a charge of high treason, " the violent and inhuman " Jefferies being appointed Judge. Fortunately, he had the right of being tried by a jury of his peers, and although Parliament was then existing by prorogation, he was not tried by the whole House, but by 27 specially summoned for that purpose.

This remarkable trial took place in Westminster Hall, on January 14th, 1685, his Lordship the previous day having only completed his 34th year. The formalities of the opening of the Court were gone through with much solemnity. Sir Edward Lutwich, one of His Majesty's Serjeants-at-Law, and Chief Justice, put in his writ and return, which were read *in hæc verba*, and the Lieutenant of the Tower delivered in his precept, and also brought his prisoner to the bar.

The following Peers then answered to their names, each making a reverence to the Lord High Steward :—Lawrence, Earl of Rochester, Lord High Treasurer of England ; Robert, Earl of Sunderland, Lord President of His Majesty's Privy Council; Henry, Duke of Norfolk, Earl Marshal of England ; Charles, Duke of Somerset ; Henry, Duke of Grafton ; Henry, Duke of Beaufort,

Lord President of Wales; John, Earl of Mulgrave, Lord Chamberlain of His Majesty's Household; Aubrey, Earl of Oxford; Charles, Earl of Shrewsbury; Theophilus, Earl of Huntingdon; Thomas, Earl of Pembroke; John, Earl of Bridgewater; Henry, Earl of Peterborough; Robert, Earl of Scarsdale; William, Earl of Craven; Lewis, Earl of Faversham; George, Earl of Berkeley; Daniel, Earl of Nottingham; Thomas, Earl of Plimouth; Thomas, Viscount Falconberge; Francis, Viscount Newport, Treasurer of His Majesty's Houshold; Robert, Lord Ferrars; Vere Essex, Lord Cromwell; William, Lord Maynard, Comptroller of His Majesty's Household; George, Lord Dartmoor, Master General of His Majesty's Ordnance; Sidney, Lord Godolphin; John, Lord Churchill.

Three of the Peers called, viz., James, Duke of Ormond, Lord Steward of His Majesty's Household; Christopher, Duke of Albemarle; and Richard, Earl of Burlington, did not answer to their names.

Then the Lord High Steward addressed himself to the Lord Delamer, the prisoner at the bar in this manner: My Lord Delamer, the King being acquainted that you stand accused of high treason, not by common report or hearsay, but by a bill of indictment found against you by gentlemen of great quality and known integrity within the County Palatine of Chester, the place of your residence, has thought it necessary, in tenderness to you, as well as justice to himself, to order you a speedy trial. My Lord, if you know yourself innocent, in the name of God do not despond, for you may be assured of fair and patient hearing, and in proper time free liberty to make your full defence; and I am sure you cannot but be well convinced that my noble lords that are here your peers to try you will be as desirous and ready to acquit you, if you appear to be innocent, as they will to convict you if you be guilty; but, my Lord, if you are conscious to yourself that you are guilty of this heinous crime, give glory to God and make amends to His vicegerent, the King, by a plain and full discovery of your guilt, and do not by any obstinate persisting in the denial of it provoke the just indignation of your Prince, who has made it appear to the world that his inclinations are rather to show mercy than to inflict punishment. My Lord, attend with patience and hear the bill of indictment which has been found against you read. Read the bill of indictment to my Lord.

Clerk of Court.—Henry, Baron of Delamer, hold up thy hand.

Lord Delamer.— My Lord, I humbly beg your grace would please to answer me one question, whether a peer of England be obliged by the laws of this land to hold his hand up at the bar as a commoner must do; and I ask your Grace the rather, because in my Lord Stafford's case it was allowed to be a privilege of the peers not to hold up their hands.

Lord High Steward.—My Lords, this being a matter of the privilege of the peerage, it is not fit for me to determine it one way or the other; but I think I may acquaint your lordships that in point of law, if you are satisfied this is the person indicted, the holding or not holding up of the hand is but a formality that does not signify much either way.

Lord Delamer.—I humbly pray your Grace's direction in one thing farther; whether I must address myself to your Grace when I would speak, or to your Grace with the rest of these noble lords, my peers.

Lord High Steward.—You must direct what you have to say to me, my Lord.

Lord Delamer.—I beg your Grace would please to satisfy me whether your Grace be one of my judges in concurrence with the rest of the Lords.

Lord High Steward.—No, my Lord, I am Judge of the Court, but none of your triers. Go on.

The Clerk of Court then read a formidable indictment to the effect that Henry, Baron Delamer, stood indicted in the County Palatine of Chester, by the name of Henry, Baron of De la Mer of Mere, in the City and County of Chester, for that he, as a false traitor against the most illustrious and most excellent Prince James the Second, by the grace of God, of England, Scotland France, and Ireland, King; his natural lord, not having the fear of God in his heart, nor weighing the duty of his allegiance, but being moved and seduced by the instigation of the devil, the cordial love and true duty and natural obedience which a true and faithful subject of our said Lord the King ought of right to bear : did plot against the tranquility of the kingdom, &c., &c.

At the request of his Lordship, the indictment was read a second time, whereupon he raised the point that his cause was one which should be wholly determined in the House of Peers, but not elsewhere, as in cases formerly brought ; and that as he could not be tried during the continuance of Parliament, except in the said House of Peers, he pleaded that he was not bound to make any further answer. He disclaimed any distrust of their Lordships, and added, "I cannot hope to stand before any more just or noble, nor can I wish to stand before any others : but you will pardon me if I insist upon it, because I apprehend it a right and a privilege due to the peerage of England, which as it is against the duty of every peer to betray or forego, so it is not in the power of anyone or more to waive it or give it up without the consent of the whole body of peers, every one of them being equally interested."

Attorney-General Sawyer urged that there was very little in the plea under the circumstances, whereupon Lord Delamer asked to have counsel to put his plea into form and argue it.

Judge Jefferies ruled against him, and after some further legal wrangling on the question of privilege, he was formally charged and pleaded "not guilty," agreeing at the same time to be tried by "God and his peers."

The Serjeant-at-Arms having made proclamation, the Judge gave his charge to the Peers. The indictment was opened by Sir Thomas Jenner, one of His Majesty's Serjeants-at-law and Recorder of the City of London.

P

The Attorney-General, in the course of a long speech, explained that the prisoner stood indicted for conspiring the death of His Majesty, and in order thereunto to raise rebellion in the Kingdom. Cheshire was one of the stages where the rebellion was principally to be acted, that preparatory to it great riotous assemblies and tumultuous gatherings were set on foot by the conspirators, and that the late Duke of Monmouth looked upon Cheshire as one of his chief supports, and my Lord Delamer as his principal assistant there.

Lord Howard of Eskrigge was first called, but he gave no evidence concerning the prisoner. Lord Grey, who said he had been subpœnaed by both sides, also did not know anything of his own knowledge against him, but said that Lord Delamer was to be applied to in connection with Monmouth's rising. This was confirmed by Nathaniel Wade, Richard Goodenough, Jones, and Story. Jones was sent to give notice to Lord Delamer (amongst other persons) of this rising, the latter stating that he heard the Duke of Monmouth say that his great dependence was upon Lord Delamer and his friends in Cheshire: but that he was afraid he had failed him or betrayed him, or some such word, and that he could have been supplied otherwise but placed his dependency upon them. Vaux and Edlin swore that Lord Delamer left town under the name of Brown, and that he went into Cheshire to see a sick child. Tracey, Paunceford, and Thomas Babington deposed to the fact that Lord Delamer was constantly known as Brown in that business by his party. One of these, however, admitted in cross-examination there was "a discourse" about a Mr. Vermuyden going in the name of Brown. Hope was called to prove the frequent journeys into Cheshire to stir up the people there, and that Lord Delamer had said " he feared there would be many bloody noses before the business was at an end."

The most formidable witness, and one on whom the prosecution relied, was Thomas Saxon, a tradesman of Middlewich, who sought to persuade the Jury that he had been specially sent for to the house of Lord Delamer, at Mere (Dunham); and in the presence of two or three gentlemen whom he named, the question of Monmouth's rebellion was discussed, and Saxon was selected, he being acquainted with the common people, to spread insurrection amongst them. He equivocated grossly in his evidence, and was asked by the noble prisoner the name of the messenger who came for him; but this he said he did not know.

As a great deal had been said, Lord Delamer asked for an adjournment, but this the Judge would not permit. He then proceeded with his defence, and in the course of an eloquent address said he could with great comfort and satisfaction say that those crimes wherewith he was charged were not only strangers to his thoughts, but also to what had been his constant principle and practice. He also said that few had more heartily conformed to the practices of the Church, and urged, (and it must be admitted with some truth) that there was little or no legal evidence affecting him, and ridiculed the idea that the particulars of such an important adventure should be communicated by him to a perfect stranger. He called several witnesses to speak to the ill-repute of Saxon. A witness named Hall said that Saxon had forged a note to obtain money from him.

The Lord High Steward acknowledged that the objection carried a great deal of weight, and if fully made out would prove him to be "a very ill man indeed."

Francis Ling said that Saxon had received money in the name of Mrs. Wilbraham, and Richard Shaw also said he had been guilty of receiving money which was not his own. Peter Hough said he should have given him a bond for £7, but by trusting him he found it was only made out for £6. Edward Wilkinson had been more illused still. He said Saxon hired a horse from him for three days at twelvepence a day, but he had neither seen horse nor money since Saxon took it.

William Wright said he had had some dealings with him, and never found him to perfect his word in anything. He added,

"I met him one evening, after evening prayer, and said to him, Thomas Saxon, if I cared no more for keeping my word than thou dost, it were no matter if I were hanged, for to be sure if thy mouth open thy tongue lyes; and he turned away from me and would not answer me a word; and since that he owed me some money, and when I asked him for it he told me if I did trouble him for money it should be worse for me, whereof all the town knows as well as I that I cannot set him forth in words as bad as he is."

Lord Delamer called several other witnesses in this way, and also to prove that he was not at Mere at the time deposed to by witnesses for the prosecution.

Mr. John Edmonds, sworn, said: On the 5th of May my Lord Delamer did me the honour to come to my house, and he stayed there a little while and desired me to be a witness of his taking possession upon a lease of my Lord Bishop of Chester, and we went into the house which is next to mine, and there he took possession.

The Lord High Steward.—Where is your house?

Mr. Edmonds.—At Boden, in Cheshire.

Mr. Henry was called and sworn.

Lord Delamer.—Pray will you give his Grace and my Lords an account whether you were not an attorney and delivered me possession upon the lease of my Lord Bishop of Chester.

Mr. Henry.—My Lord, I was attorney by appointment, and the 5th May last I delivered possession to my Lord Delamer at one of the most remarkable places of the land that belonged to that lease of the Bishop.

Lord Delamer hoped that this was a satisfactory reason for his going down at the time, the Bishop being ill, and the lease worth £6,000 or £7,000. The next occasion he had to speak to was the 27th May. He said, "I had taken up the resolution before to go and see my child, which was not well, but I had not taken my journey so soon nor with such privacy but that I had notice that there was a warrant out to apprehend me, and knowing the inconvenience of lying in prison I was very willing to keep as long out of custody as I could, and therefore I went out of the way and under a borrowed name."

At his request his Lordship's mother, who sat by him at the bar during the trial, was examined. She said that this child of his was more than ordinarily "pretious" (precious) to him in regard it was born to him at that time "when he was an innocent honest man (as he was then a prisoner in the Tower for high treason) above two years ago, and she thought it had increased his affection to that child that God had given to him when he was in that affliction." While he was at Dunham, her daughter sent word that it had pleased God to visit his eldest son in London with a grievous distemper, and thereupon he made all the haste he could back.

Witnesses were called to prove that persons said by Saxon to have been present on a given date were in London at the time, and, altogether, conclusive evidence was forthcoming to show that his testimony was not at all of a reliable character. Amongst these witnesses were two brothers of the noble prisoner. In the course of some further remarks he denied that he ever wrote or sent any message, or had had any correspondence for three years past with the Duke of Monmouth. He pointed out circumstances in the evidence for the prosecution not borne out by facts, and concluded by reminding their Lordships that the eyes of the nation were upon their proceedings that day. "Your Lordships are now judging the cause of every man in England that shall happen to come under like circumstances with myself hereafter: for accordingly as you judge me now, just so will inferior courts be directed to give their judgments in like cases in time to come. Your Lordships know very well that blood once spilled can never be gathered up again, and therefore, unless the case be very clear against me, you will not, I am sure, hazard the shedding of my blood upon doubtful evidence. God Almighty is a God of mercy and equity. Our law, the law of England, is a law of equity and mercy, and both God and the law require from your Lordships tenderness in all cases of life and death ; and if it should be indifferent or doubtful to your Lordships (which upon proofs that I have made I cannot believe it can be) whether I am innocent or guilty, both God and the law require you to acquit me. My Lords, I leave myself, my case, and the consequences of it with your Lordships, and I pray the All-wise, the Almighty God, to direct you in your determination."

No wonder after such an eloquent appeal, Lord Churchill, the spokesman of the Jury, should declare upon his honour, with uncovered head, and hand upon his breast, that the noble prisoner was not guilty. Lord Delamer retired to his seat at Dunham, and abstained for the time being from any active participation in public affairs. Scarcely three years passed away, however, ere the Prince of Orange, afterwards William III., arrived in England. Lord Delamer then expressed himself as feeling that the deliverance of the nation must be worked by force or miracle, and that as it would be presumption to expect the latter, he very wisely levied a large force of men. On the 16th December, 1688, he took up arms in Cheshire. He convoked his tenants, called upon them to stand by him, and promised that if they fell in the cause their leases should be renewed to their children, and exhorted everyone who had a good horse either to take field, or to provide a substitute. He appeared at Manchester with 50 men armed and mounted, and his force had trebled before he reached Bowdon Downs. So says Macaulay. He soon afterwards joined the Prince of Orange, and his forces. On the arrival of the Prince at Windsor, he despatched Lord Delamer, the Marquis of Halifax, and the Earl of Shrewsbury, with a message to King James, commanding him to quit the Palace. His Majesty was in bed at the time of their arrival, it being one o'clock in the morning, but they were introduced to him by the Earl of Middleton, then Secretary of State. This has been justly described as a remarkable instance of the vicissitudes of fortune. By one writer it is spoken of as an instance of Divine retribution. Here was a subject whom he had seen arraigned, not three years before as a culprit at the bar, appearing now with an order, which would have the effect of virtually dethroning him. To his honour it is recorded that the generous conduct he displayed on that occasion made such an impression on the fallen Sovereign that after his retreat into France he said the Lord Delamer, whom he had illused, had treated him with much more respect than the other two Lords to whom he had been kind, and from whom he might better have expected it.

With this reign ended that great crisis in English history - the struggle between King and people ; and the people, led by those whose patriotism was above reproach, triumphed.

Amongst the leaders was Lord Delamer, and as a result, he was now very fully rewarded. He was made a Privy Councillor in February, 1689, which office he held for life ; in the following April he was made Chancellor and Under Treasurer of the Exchequer, and subsequently Lord-Lieutenant of the County of Chester, and Custos Rotulorum. In 1690, he was created Earl of Warrington, in acknowledgment of his peculiar services, and a pension of £2,000 per annum was settled upon him. This was only paid for the first half-year, and the arrears are stated in a list of King William's debts, drawn up by Queen Anne. Many minor honours were also conferred upon him, amongst them the Mayoralty of the ancient City of Chester, in 1691.

His Lordship's works were published in the year 1694, being edited from his own MS, by J. Dela Heuze, tutor to his son, afterwards Earl of Warrington.

A review of his writings would absorb too much of our space. It may, therefore, be sufficient to record some of his sayings and opinions. His language, particularly against the Papists, as they were termed, is marked in some places by great extravagance and warmth of tone, perhaps permissable by the circumstances in which he had been placed. The country, too, was unsettled, and

although not out of place then, it would sound oddly now to hear
a justice of Chester haranguing the Grand Jury to give information of any plot, if they were acquainted with it, for dethroning
the reigning monarch. Most of the charges take a strong political
tinge, but in others are suggested a consideration of domestic
matters. We are admitted by them to a peep at the manners and
customs of that age. In one of his speeches, when Earl of
Warrington, he encourages the magistrates to strictly inform
themselves of such as offend in the matter of swearing, "the
horrible prophanation of God's name," and give them the punishment which their offence deserved. He also harangues at length
against the sin of drunkenness, that till then this vice was not
grown to considerable size.

He was as a patriot proud of the government of his country
under William III., and praised it as beyond all others. He
shows that while all manner of taxes and impositions are laid
upon the people at the will and pleasure of the King, in England
they could not be taxed but by their own consent in Parliament.
Although the King had the sole power of making peace and war,
" the sinews of war," meaning the money, were with the people,
and the people were not bound to support every war that the
King might engage in ; " for methinks it's all the reason in the
" world that a man should be satisfied with the *cause* before he
" part with his money ; and I think that man is very unworthy of
" honour to serve his country in Parliament who shall give away
" the people's money for any other thing, but what shall be
" effectually for the *good* and *advantage* of the people and nation."
There are few who will not admit that his Lordship's words,
spoken nearly 200 years ago, hold good in the present day.

The prayers which his Lordship used in his family bear the
mark of close application, and breathe a truly devotional and
earnest spirit throughout. Although he did not die " in a good
old age, full of days," he possessed " both riches and honour."
His death took place in London, on January 2nd, 1693, on the
same memorable day on which eight years before his trial had

been. His funeral sermon was preached in Bowdon Parish Church by the Rev. Richard Wroe, Warden of Manchester Cathedral. On his monument in the same Church is inscribed a record of his life in brief, which is well worthy the attentive perusal of all interested "in perpetuating the remembrance of so much virtue till that great day come wherein it shall be openly rewarded," For in these words concludes the epitaph which a reverent son inscribed to a noble father.

CHAPTER IX.

The House of Dunham, continued—The Second Earl of Warrington; his character and literary attainments—The union of the House of Dunham with that of Stamford—The Honourable Booth Grey— "Domestic happiness, a family picture"—The revival of the lapsed titles of Baron Delamer and Earl of Warrington—A Romance of the Peerage.

AFTER the great political crisis through which the house of Dunham had passed, it may easily be imagined that the quiet repose of a country gentleman's life would be most compatible with the feelings of the heir succeeding to its now consolidated honours. It is, therefore, to his many literary works, completed in periods of uninterrupted leisure, that we are most indebted for the character of George, the second Earl of Warrington. He was the second son of the first Lord Delamer, and was born on the 2nd of May, 1675. He was married in 1702, to Mary, eldest daughter and co-heiress of John Oldbury, of London, merchant, by his second wife Mary, daughter and co-heiress of Thomas Bohun, Esq., of Dartmouth, and descended from the ancient Earls of Hereford. The issue of this marriage was an only daughter named Mary, who was born about the year 1703. His Lordship died August 2nd, 1758, and was laid in the tomb of his ancestors at Bowdon, having passed the allotted "span" of life by 13 years. Amongst his contributions to contemporary literature, was "Considerations on the Institution of Marriage;" a letter to the writer on "The present State of the Republic of Letters," in which he vindicated his father from some of the reflections cast upon him by Burnet in the "History of his Own Times," and which seem to have been copied more or less by the great historian, Macaulay. With his decease, the Earldom of Warrington became extinct, and the barony of Delamer descended to his first cousin, Nathaniel Booth, of Hampstead, Esquire.

An event had, however, occurred before this, which had marked an epoch in the history of this noble house. Mary, the only daughter and sole heiress to the estates of her father, had married in 1736, the Right Honorable Harry Grey, Earl of Stamford. This family, according to Collins, "has been the most ancient, the most widespread, and most illustrious in the English peerage, the house of Stamford being derived from the most illustrious branch of it." Lord Stamford was thus descended from the first Lord Grey of Groby, the grandfather of the first Earl of Stamford, who was distinguished in 1628 by his efforts in the ranks of the Parliamentarians, and who was nephew of the great Duke of Suffolk, the father of Lady Jane Grey. There are few who have not noticed the prominent part the Greys have played in history ; and what schoolboy has not melted at the touching recital of the execution of the unfortunate lady, whose little attempt at Queendom was attended with such fatal results ? He was thus placed at the head of the younger branch of the house of Tudor, whose claim to the throne of England rested rather on the despotic will of Henry VIII., than on the inherent right which belonged in failure of direct inheritance to the Scottish branch of the same Royal line. To this may be added the fact that the family, on both sides, is of Norman origin, and was first summoned to Parliament in 1446 in the person of Lord Ferrers of Groby, whose elder daughter-in-law, Elizabeth, became the wife of Edward IV.

Lord and Lady Stamford had a family of three sons and two daughters. The eldest, George Harry, succeeded to the earldom ; the second, Lady Mary, who assisted the Princess Augusta in supporting Queen Charlotte's train at her coronation in 1761, and who married, 24th February, 1761, the Honourable George West, second son of the Earl Delawar, died March 1st, 1783. The third son, the Hon. Booth Grey, was born August 15th, 1740 : he was admitted a nobleman of Queen's College, Cambridge. He was one of the Mayors of Altrincham, and was member for Leicester 1768-1774. He died on the 4th March, 1802. His Lordship died at Enville Hall, June 24th, 1768, and was succeeded by his eldest son, George Harry, the fifth Earl of Stamford, born October 1st, 1737.

In a curious work published about the latter end of 1700, entitled "Characteristic Strictures or Remarks," is a sketch of the family of this Earl. It is headed "Domestic happiness, a family picture," and proceeds: "What satisfaction must a sentimental artist experience when he has only one unhappy countenance to copy in so numerous a family, especially as the varied features which express felicity will free his performance from the imputation of sameness? The piece not only comprehends the parents and their posterity, but the brother and sister of the principal figure. The junior members of the family are of too tender an age to be distinguished by features that prognosticate either tempers or manners, except the eldest youth (Lord Grey) who is the very picture of his father, and in neither of whose features is there a fault. The father is a perfect example of integrity, filial affection, and tender husband; and the mother, from her prudent, virtuous and sweet tempered disposition, every way worthy of so honourable a mate. Two brothers make up the group (the Hon. Booth Grey and the Hon. John Grey). The elder on a distant view seems of a morose and sour temper; but when you examine the features more closely you are agreeably disappointed to find those of sullenness not only expand with freeness, but discover themselves to be the strongest signification of a solid understanding. The younger is in every point of view a pleasant, lively, generous figure, that seems to give spirit to the whole society." This quaint picture is only a reflex of a certain school of criticism which obtained at that period. The "unhappy countenance" referred to is that of Lady Mary West, and is probably an allusion to her death, which would have taken place a short time previously. The fifth Earl was elected Knight of the Shire for the county of Stafford, 1761, and at the coronation of George III., was one of the six eldest sons of peers who supported the King's train. His lordship, on the 20th May, 1763, married Lady Henrietta Cavendish Bentinck, second daughter to William, the late Duke of Portland, and had issue four sons and six daughters. He was created Baron Delamer and Earl of Warrington, thus reviving the lapsed titles of his ancestors; and in addition to his other offices, was Lord Lieutenant and custos Rotulorum of the County of Chester. He died in 1819 at Dunham, and was buried at Bowdon. He was succeeded by his eldest son, George Harry Grey, Earl of Stamford and Warrington, born October 31st, 1765, married December 23rd, 1797, to Henrietta Charlotte Elizabeth Charteris, eldest daughter of Francis, Lord Elcho, and had issue two sons and three daughters. He died at Enville Hall, Staffordshire, April 27th, 1845, and was buried at Bowdon. George Harry, Lord Grey, his eldest son, died November, 1837, in the lifetime of his father.

With the death of George Harry, the seventh Earl, in January, 1883, the Barony of de la Mer and the Earldom of Warrington became extinct. The Earldom of Stamford and the Barony of Grey of Groby devolved upon his kinsman, the Rev. Harry Grey, whose remarkable career in South Africa formed a veritable romance of the peerage. In May, 1893, the House of Lords Committee of Privileges sat. Counsel said the history of the eighth Earl presented undoubtedly some curious features. He was a clergyman, and in 1844 he married, at Tiverton, as his first wife, a person called Susan Gayden, who was in a humble situation of life, and with whom he lived for some years. In 1854 or 1855 he separated from her, and left England for the Cape, where he resided continuously until his death in 1890. There was no issue of that marriage, and Susan Gayden died in 1869. In 1872, Harry Grey, as the eighth Earl then was, married at Wynberg a woman named Annie Macnamara, who was also in a comparatively humble situation of life, and who died in 1872, there being no issue of that marriage either. At the time of the death of Annie Macnamara there was living in the house as a servant a woman of colour named Martha Solomon, and it would seem that Harry Grey subsequently cohabited with her, with the result that two illegitimate children were born—namely, a son, John, in 1877, and a daughter, Frances, in 1879. In December,

1880, Harry Grey married this woman, and counsel believed it was a matter of common knowledge that, according to the Roman-Dutch law which prevailed at the Cape, the effect of that marriage was to legitimise there the offspring previously born. Subsequently to the marriage there was only one child, a girl, who was born in July, 1881, and she was, he would submit, the only legitimate issue for the purpose of succession in this country to this peerage. The eighth Earl succeeded to the peerage in 1883, and from that time onwards, being well aware of his position and rights, he treated the two children born before his marriage with Martha Solomon as illegitimate children, and recognised both by his pedigree, which he signed, and also by instructions for his will that he regarded William Grey, his nephew, as his inevitable successor in the title if no male issue was subsequently born to him. No male issue was born, and when he died in 1890 the title would have descended to John, his next brother, if he had been alive. He died in 1868, and William, the next brother, died in 1872, and he was the father of William Grey, who claimed the Earldom.

Formal evidence was put in as to the creation of the peerage and the issuing of a writ of summons to the eighth Earl to sit in the House of Lords, but he did not avail himself of the privilege. Evidence of the death of Susan Gayden and Annie Macnamara, as also of the marriage with Martha Solomon (who remarried in 1892, Pieter Pieterse, of Wellington, Cape Colony) was given. Mr. E. J. Moore, attorney-at-law, practising at Capetown, produced a certified copy of the will of the eighth Earl. A certain portion of the property was left to one Emma Grey, his natural daughter by a woman named Collins. The witness became acquainted with the late Earl shortly after the death of the seventh Earl in 1883, and from 1887 to the time of his death he was his private secretary. They frequently discussed the affairs of the family, and on many occasions the late Earl referred to Mr. William Grey as the person who would succeed him in the Earldom of Stamford.

The Rev. F. B. Moore, rector of Constantia, near Wynberg, stated that he first became acquainted with the late Earl about 1864 or 1865. He was curate of the parish when the late Earl married Annie Macnamara in 1872, and from that time to the time of her death in 1874 he saw them frequently. There were no children of that marriage. He knew the woman Solomon or Simon quite well. She was a servant in the house for about two months prior to Annie Macnamara's death, and after that event she continued to live in the house. The children, John, Frances, and Mary, were born to her, John in 1877, Frances in 1879, and Mary on the 25th July, 1881. This woman Solomon and the late Earl were married on the 6th December, 1880. With reference to these children and the inheritance of the peerage, he said, "Of course none of my children can ever inherit the peerage." The woman Solomon had previously cohabited with a man named Simon, and had had two sons, so that she was called Solomon or Simon indifferently.

Conclusive evidence was called to show that the eighth Earl always looked upon Mr. William Grey as heir presumptive to the Earldom, and evidence having been given as to the death of his father, and also the birth of the claimant,

The Lord Chancellor moved that their Lordships report that petitioner had made out his claim to the peerage. There was no question of fact to raise any doubt in their Lordships' mind. Personally, he felt that it was in some sense a hardship upon the parties, on account of the expensive nature of the inquiry which had been cast upon them, but looking to the South African incidents it was impossible that he could of his own motion have certified that the claimant had established his claim without proof.

The motion was unanimously agreed to.

William Grey was born April 18th, 1850, at Newfoundland. He was adjudged to be the ninth Earl and also Baron Grey of Groby by the Committee of Privileges above referred to. He was educated at Bradfield, and graduated at Exeter College, Oxford, where he took his B.A. degree in 1872, and M.A. in 1875. He was formerly Professor of Classics and Philosophy at Codrington College, Barbadoes. On his return to England he was admitted into the Order of Diocesan Readers by the Bishop of London, 1891, and his work in the East End of the Metropolis is now well known and highly appreciated. He was married, April 18th, 1895, to Miss Elizabeth Louisa Penelope Theobald, third daughter of the Rev. Charles Theobald, Rector of Lasham, Hants., and Rural Dean of Alton. Their union has been blessed with a son and heir, who takes rank as the eleventh Baron Grey of Groby, born October 27th, 1896.

CHAPTER X.

The Maceys of Altrincham—A rebellious subject—The Bowdon family—Disposal of lands—Some old district names—Bowdon free school—Guy Fawkes at Altrincham—A witty Bowdon Curate—The advance on Manchester by Lord Strange—The Unicorn Hotel three hundred years ago—An Altrincham landlord and landlady of the olden time—Sir Peter Leycester's description of the town in 1666—The story of the "Bloody Field"—Adam Martindale at Dunham; his duties there—Bowdon Dissenters troublesome—Dick Turpin; his exploits at Newbridge Hollow and Hoo Green—Prince Charlie's troops at Altrincham.

THE house of Macey, or Massey, which settled at Dunham, in course of time had numerous branches, so much so as to give rise to the uncomplimentary proverb already quoted in these pages. There is no doubt, however, that their connection with Altrincham is as ancient as it is honourable. We find them coming into prominence in troublous times of Richard II., and they appear to have held the town by military service for a long period. In 1397 it is recorded that William Massey was the lessee of the King of the beadlery of the Hundred of Bucklow, for the year, at the sum of £7. 6s. 8d., he taking by his lease all the pleas and profits of all the townships within the aforesaid hundred, and in that year he also received a grant from the King of an annuity during pleasure of one hundred shillings. He was evidently a favourite with the King; and as a zealous supporter must have made his power felt, for in the General Act of Pardon which Henry IV. issued in the opening portion of his reign, he was specially exempted on account of his adherence to the fallen monarch. His offence was not probably very severely visited; as in the year 1399, a William Macey, probably one and the same person, was given a protection on his departure for Ireland to do service for the King.

About the year 1400, for reasons best known to himself, a Massey assumed the local name of Bowdon, and the Bowdon family has been traced by the Lysons down to the reign of Elizabeth. It held a fourth part of the lands in the township until Urian Bowdon, in 1565, sold to William Booth of Dunham Massey, Esquire, certain portions of land in Bowdon, as also in Hale and Dunham. In 1569, Thomas Vawdrey, of Bowdon, and George his son, sold several parcels of land to Hugh Crosby, of Over Whitley, who, in turn, sold them to Sir George Booth at a later period for £220. These parcels were in the several holdings of Thomas Vawdrey, Robert Massie, Thos. Nelde (or Neild) and Alice Hardey. William Brereton, in the reign of James I., became, by purchase from Sir Thomas Holcroft, owner of one fourth of the lands in the township; but these, as also all the others, have long since passed by gift, sale or lease to the present Earl of Stamford.

The foregoing reference to names prevalent three or four centuries ago will make the reader curious to know more. There are allusions to a family of Oldfield, no doubt a branch of the Massey family, who assumed that name, and from plea rolls relating to a few of the lesser holdings in Altrincham, it is shown that in the 22nd year of Edward III., Emma, wife of John Howell, was against Robert Drake, of Altrincham, for a dower of three messuages and three acres of land; that in the 19th of Henry VII., Edward Walker conveyed to Thomas Deyne, and Margery, his wife, the fee simple of three burgages of land, "of which one was situated between the burgage of Edward Massey, and that late of Richard Chadurton, of Tympyrly, called Flaxyarde, and two burgages called Tayntre Crofts in the same town;" that in the 13th year of Henry VIII, Stephen Atkynson was against Thomas Massy, son and heir of Robert Massy, for the recovery of two messuages, five burgages, ten acres of land, one meadow, and one dove cote. The names of Birche, Coppok, Royle, Bekke or Beck, Neuton or Newton, Kyncy, &c., are also to be found. In Dunham Massey there were Heskeths, Ashtons,

Hazlehursts, Johnsons, &c., and we believe their descendants are to be found there. The allusion to the Flaxyarde shows that the manufacture of linen was an old Altrincham industry, quite as much as woollen was at a later period.

A Free School was founded at Bowdon about the beginning of the year 1600. In 1640 a "presentment" was made to the Commissioners for Pious Uses, against Mr. Richard Vawdrey, of the Banck, gentleman, for denying to pay £4 per annum, left by his grandfather, for the schoolmaster of Bowdon. It is said, in Gastrell's *Notitia Cestriensis*, that although he may have been presented, the endowment was not made by his grandfather, but by Edward Janny, of Manchester, merchant, who, in 1553, devised certain lands to his "kynseman, Robert Vawdrey, to keep a ffre scole at Bowdon, to instruct youthe in vertue and lernynge." This Robert Vawdrey was one of the executors, and it may probably have led to his being spoken of as the founder. Janny, the testator, had the advowson and lease of the vicarage of Bowdon, for a term, and this he also devised to Robert Vawdrey, whose family held it for several years. The schoolhouse was rebuilt at the expense of the parish in 1670, again in 1806, and up to a recent period served for the purpose of teaching the young ideas of the neighbourhood, when, on the new National Schools being built, it was converted into a showroom for furniture, &c.

James, Lord Strange, who by succession became 7th Lord Derby, marched from Warrington early on 23rd September, 1642, with the whole of the force that he had assembled, 400 horse, 200 dragoons, 2,000 foot, with 10 large guns. The greater portion of this muster the Earl commanded in person, and had with him Sir Gilbert Hoghton, Sir Alex. Radcliffe, Sir Gilbert Gerard, Capt. Windebank, Mr. Farington of Worden, Mr. Tarbock, and several others. They marched along the left bank of the Mersey to Ashton, where they were detained at the ford by an accident to the wheel of one of the gun carriages. Clarendon, in his "History of the Rebellion," describes the Earl's pikemen as having no breastplates, a few of the musketeers had swords, the front rank of the horse were fully armed, the rear rank carried axes in lieu of carbines. On the side of the Parliament among the many neighbouring gentlemen who assisted to defend Manchester was Captain John Booth, of Dunham. To him was entrusted the defence of the Mill Gate; during the night following the second day of the siege he commanded a company of 50 musketeers in a sortie, when the head-quarters of the Earl, Alport Lodge, was set on fire. On Friday, September 30th, by the King's express orders, the siege was raised. This assault upon Manchester was the first outbreak of the great civil war. Captain John Booth, of Dunham, was the son of Sir William Booth; he married a daughter of Mr. Thomas Prestwich, of Hulme, and died in 1644.

We read in one of Harrison Ainsworth's novels that Guy Fawkes was carried through Altrincham, on his way to Ordsall Hall, after having been wounded "in a little affair" at Malpas. This was not long before he attempted that horrible enterprise which will ever make his name memorable to the small boys of the land. If the enterprise was horrible it has been embalmed in still more horrible verse. It was done by a worthy parish clerk, who had an insatiable desire to distinguish himself; and on one occasion, when service was being celebrated for providential deliverance from this plot of plots, he fairly electrified the congregation by giving out the following verse:—

> This is the day that *was* the night,
> When wicked men *conspire*,
> To blow the Houses of Parliament up,
> With g-u-n-pow-*dire*.

It is unnecessary to say that this parish clerk was not connected with Bowdon; but it may be mentioned that a witty curate once gave a most remarkable certificate of publication of banns. A worthy couple had been "asked," as the local phrase has it; and the Vicar of Wilmslow, where the woman lived, had the following addressed to him:—

MARKET PLACE, ALTRINCHAM DEC. 1ST, 1745.—PRINCE CHAS. EDWA'D'S VANGUARD DEMANDING QUARTERS.

> John —— and Jane Cooper were,
> Thrice in my church announced this year
> To tie the knot of beauty.
> So John and Jane I trust hereby,
> May without shame together lye,
> When you have done your duty.
>
> Jenks, Curate of Bowdon Church.

It is to be hoped that the Wilmslow Vicar did his duty, as well as Mr. Jenks, and that this worthy couple lived a long and happy life in the married state.

In May, 1644, Prince Rupert had a rendezvous for his army on Bowdon Downs. According to a Royalist, William Davenport, of Bramhall, "he marcht up to Cheadle, where the parliaments forces ran away." In May, 1648, at a meeting of the Lieutenancy, held at Bowdon, "it was resolved that three regiments, consisting each of 600 men strong, should be raised;" but the country people as a rule refused to join. With the Downs is associated the story of the "bloody field," the scene of a combat between Sir Samuel Daniel, of Tabley, and Captain Robert Ratcliffe, of Ordsall Hall. A brawl had ensued at a party; and, according to an old rhyme:—

> The next day Robert out a shooting went,
> And still his mind upon revenge was bent;
> By accident he met Sir Samuel
> On Bowdon Downs, for so the people tell;
> And fight he would, and one of them should die,
> Ere they did part, and that immediately.
> Sir Samuel says, "I see how discord ends,
> I never thought but sleep had made us friends."
> "No parley, now," says Robert, "fight I will,
> Or with my gun I here now will you kill."
> "Well," says Sir Samuel, "if to fight I must,
> My sword is not the sword I wish to trust."
> Then fight they did, and on the sandy downs
> Rash Robert fell, covered with blood and wounds.

He was buried at Northenden, and the inscription on his gravestone states that he was "of illustrious descent, of comely appearance, pious towards God, and unfailing in His worship; loyal to the King faithful to his friends, courteous to all, and a vigorous combatant. But the age being unworthy of such a hero, and heaven permitting it, he perished, strange to say, in a sword fight in the presence of a few spectators, . . . on the 20th of February, in the year of our Lord, 1685, in the 30th year of his age."

It is a matter for surmise whether Guy Fawkes, after having been wounded in the "little affair" at Malpas, stopped at that ancient and still celebrated hostelry, the Unicorn, to refresh the inner man. Most probably he did, and drowned the sense of his injuries in libations of choicest canary. At all events the Unicorn stood at Altrincham for centuries on very nearly the same site; but if we are to believe the traditions which have come down to us, it was then a very different place to what it is now. It was a delightfully rural roadside "public," environed with a profusion of vegetation; and a purling stream, of which there is now only a mere trace, flowed past until it joined the brook which has its rise on Hale Moss, and which fed the lake and moat at the Hall of Dunham. Subsequently, this stream turned the water wheel by which the landlord of the old original Unicorn eked out his livelihood; but the wheel is hushed, the stream has long since disappeared, and an advancing civilization has caused a structure more in accordance with the wants of the age to be erected in its place.

It is also believed that Sir Walter Scott, in his "Peveril of the Peak," has given the name of the Cat and the Fiddle to the Unicorn, when he speaks of Julian Peveril's journey from Liverpool to his ancestral home in Derbyshire. The picture which the great novelist draws of that period is an excellent one. Sir Walter says :—

At length near Altringham, a halt became unavoidable, and a place of refreshment presented itself in the shape of a small cluster of cottages, the best of which united the characters of an alehouse and a mill, where the sign of the Cat (the landlord's faithful ally in defence of his meal sacks), hooted high as Grimalkin in the fairy tale, and playing on the fiddle for the more grace, announced that John Whitecraft united the two honest occupations of landlord and miller; and, doubtless, took toll from the public in both capacities. Such a place promised a traveller who journeyed incognito, safer, if not better accommodation than he was likely to meet with in more frequented inns; and at the door of the Cat and Fiddle, Julian halted accordingly.

In the succeeding chapter, the narrative is continued, and the manner in which the jolly miller and his wife manage the business is humorously depicted.

If the great Scotch novelist had read the quaint description given of the town by Peter Leycester, who says in 1666, "there are so many cottages erected here by permission of the Lords of Dunham Massey that it has now become a nest of beggars;" he could not have been nearer the mark. While this character is given to Altrincham, Bowdon bore a very different one; and at a somewhat later period, it is spoken of as "one of the most remarkable places in the land." Sir Peter mentions that in the rental of Dunham Massey in 1402, there were about forty freeholders or charterers in Altrincham, the rest of the tenants not above eighteen in number being tenants at will. He also speaks of the increasing value of land and other commodities; and adds that at the period at which he wrote there were above twenty charterers, which would tend to show that the number of tenants at will had increased, while the number of freeholders had diminished. Of these holdings, Robert Parker's, of Oldfield Hall, Altrincham, gentleman, was of the greatest value; next to which was that belonging to William Leycester, of Hale Lowe, gentleman. The rest were very small parcels, "not worth the reckoning up."

Adam Martindale, one of the many puritan divines who experienced the sad effects of the long political tempest of the seventeenth century, found an asylum at Dunham on his ejectment from the living of Rostherne, under the Act of Uniformity of 1662. He was a prominent character of that period, and his avowed hatred of superstitious customs, as he thought, brought him into most unpleasant collision with his parishioners. In his autobiography, he gives us one or two glimpses of Bowdon, which show that it was not entirely free from the religious bickerings and theological hair-splittings of the period. The Quakers, as they were then called, really had sound reason for "quaking" sometimes. The "Separatists," as the Dissenters were termed, were numerous and troublesome in the parish, and being a fierce ecclesiastical champion, Martindale informs us that he was engaged in "a paper scuffle" with their teacher, much in the same way no doubt that newspaper controversialists cut each other up now-a-days. He tells us that in 1663, the Bishop of Chester, Dr. Hall, preached fiercely against non-conformists at Bowdon, and as one that had a notable faculty of extracting salt water out of pumice upon the words, *We are not ignorant of his devices*, 2 Corinthians ii. 11., made even the most harmless practices of the non-conformists, "devices of Sathan, soe farre as his Episcopall authoritie would authenticate such doctrine." At Dunham he devoted himself to study, in which he was greatly assisted by Lord Delamer, who gave him many excellent books, lent him his choicest manuscripts, and "imparted freely any knowledge he had, which was as useful as anything else."

While chaplain here his salary was £40 per annum, and his employment, "besides accompanying my Lord abroad, was family duty twice a day, which after dinner was a short prayer, a chapter and a more solemn prayer, and before supper, the like ; only a psalme or part of one after a chapter. When it was my Lord's pleasure that the Lord's day or any of the King's days should be kept at home, I officiated, and when on the Lord's day we went to Bowdon, I catechised in the evening, and expounded the catechism in a doctrinal and practical way, so as it was as of much pains for me, and as profitable to the auditors as though I had preached." A pleasant picture truly of family life at Dunham, two centuries ago

From "pulpit to prig" is a great step downwards, but it is the one we now take. Knutsford can boast of a highwayman of some celebrity "born and bred" within its limits. Altrincham cannot; at all events there has not been one of the "gentlemen of the road" who was proud of the place of his nativity, and who has made for himself name and fame in history by his so-called exploits. As a very efficient substitute we find the renowned Turpin—for he has got "renown" in "Rookwood" (though his life shows him to have been both blackleg and coward)—often taking up his quarters in the neighbourhood and levying illegal toll on travellers. The scene of his adventures was principally New Bridge Hollow. "What!" no doubt exclaim readers acquainted with the magnificent road to Chester, "how could a man pounce out on anyone and rob him there?" Wait a little, my impetuous friend. There was no wide road then. It was an apology for one; in fact, a mere bridle-path, and then, as now, primroses and wild flowers bloomed in bewildering profusion around. The river was not spanned by a bridge, but forded at a convenient and shallow point. Flanked on each side by tall trees and umbrageous foliage, the poet of to-day can draw inspiration therefrom for his glowing pages; but then, when dangers were thought to be hidden behind every tree, the aspect of the road to most travellers would be stripped of its picturesqueness. On one occasion the daring Dick had a narrow escape from paying the extreme penalty of the law for a robbery committed in the hollow, and this escape was attributable, it is said, to the legendary speed of "Black Bess." A lawyer was travelling from Chester to Manchester, when he was attacked by Dick, and relieved of his cash. Turning the head of Black Bess, he put her to her extreme speed, and on arriving at the Kilton, Hoo Green, he accosted the hostler with "Holloa! what o'clock is it, my cockolorum, eh?" With a view to receiving a speedy reply, he accompanied the question with a sharp blow on the shoulder, and, singular to say, he got the required answer. We use the word "singular," because a modern knight, "of more breeches than brains," would have replied with a torrent of well-selected Billingsgate, and summoned him before a magistrate, with a view to having him fined. As it was, Dick strolled calmly on to the green, where a number of country gentlemen were playing bowls, taking care, of course, to remark about the time. An investigation into the circumstances took place, and Dick found out the advantages to be derived from what Samuel Weller's "paternal parient" in "Pickwick," chose to call a "halibi." The groom was called, and as the difference between the time of the robbery and Dick's appearance in the inn yard was so small, only a few minutes, although the distance from the place was over three miles, the magistrates discharged him, under the impression that no horse could carry him in the time that Black Bess did. Turpin appears to have gloried in the feat that he then accomplished, for it is made the subject of a song, which is given in "Rookwood."

It was in 1745 that Altrincham had a visit from the forces of Prince Charles Edward, prior to the disaster at Culloden. It was on Sunday morning early, December 1st, 1745, that a detachment from Manchester marched into Altrincham. There was snow upon the ground, and we can well imagine, as depicted in our illustration, the provost marshal demanding from the bewildered landlord of the "Red Lion" quarters for the men who are just marching in with the Prince's colours flying, while the local watch looks unconcernedly on, for the common people were indifferent on the principle of "Fight dog! Fight bear!" without taking part themselves if they could help it, "but feeling very angry with the Pretender for coming to disturb the peace of the Kingdom." As the troops marched into Altrincham, a resident, standing at the top of Well Lane, now Victoria Street, was informed by a "braw highlander" that he must give up his brogues or boots. Might was right, and the Altrincham man was forcibly deprived of his "understandings." A remarkable revenge appears to have been taken. There were many desertions, and as the troop marched from Altrincham the then host of the Bleeding Wolf (where local tradition asserts the last wolf was killed in England) sallied out, pulled one of the rebel troopers from his horse and slew him with his own sword. Singularly enough this sword remained in the possession of a local family, and was carried for generations in the demonstrations of the local Lodge of Oddfellows. At Sale the Scotchmen did little damage, but it is recorded that they stole the Rector's horses, which were at pasture on Sale Moor.

CHAPTER XI.

Indications of growth and enterprise—The cutting of the Bridgewater Canal—A few figures—Manufacture of woollen and cotton yarn—Obsolete punishments: penance, cucking stool, scold's bridle, public whippings in the Altrincham Market-place—Executions for burglaries at Bowdon—A man hanged for poaching near Altrincham—The ancient custom of souling—The entertaining play of St. George and the Dragon—Wassailing and Christmas carols—The barley hump and Dunham ale—The lions of Dunham—Altrincham races—Dunham Parks and the Hall—De Quincy's description of Altrincham.

THE first indication of an era of enterprise in this district was the cutting of the Bridgewater Canal, which commenced about the year 1760, and its opening six years or so afterwards gave a great impetus to the town of Altrincham. In 1778 there were in the town 185 houses, which taken at the usual average of five persons to a house would give 925 inhabitants. In 1801, this number had increased to 340 houses, occupied by 346 families, numbering 1,692 souls. There were then three large factories for the manufacture of woollen and cotton yarn, as also a mill for bobbin turning, which were worked by water power. Two of these mills were situated on the north-west side of the town, near the present Altrincham station. The dam or reservoir was only a few yards down Stamford Road, and was fed by a stream which flowed hard by. Up to a recent period this dam remained; but it is now filled up, and streets, notably Mill Street, occupy its site. An old map of the town shows that at this time the houses were clustered about the Market-place and the Unicorn. Within fifty or sixty yards on the Dunham side were hedgerows and trees of the most approved agricultural type. Dunham Lane, as it was then called, was scarcely a cow road, and had not even the semblance of a footpath. The social customs of the inhabitants were quite as primitive as its appearance.

Readers of history are familiar with the penance which the unfortunate Jane Shore did in St. Paul's, before the people, three or four centuries ago. They would be surprised to hear that this form of doing penance—not so much from a religious as from a legal point of view—was carried out at Bowdon not 150 years since. Women of light character, or those who had been guilty of spreading scandal, were the subjects. A white sheet was kept at the Parish Church, the condemned woman was enveloped in it, marched along the aisles of the sacred edifice; after which she had purged her offence. One of the last, or about the last who did penance was clever enough to make a witty, though very indecent rhyme of the circumstance. A much more ancient and common form of punishment was the cucking stool—a field formerly existing in Altrincham called Cuckstool field. This instrument is described in Doomsday Book as *cathedra stercoris*. Scolds, cheating bakers or brewers, and other petty offenders, were led to this stool and immersed over head and ears *in stercore*, or stinking water. The "brydle for a curste queane" was fixed in the mouth of the delinquent, and tied behind with ribbons. When the punishment of the cucking stool was relaxed, the scold's bridle appears only to have been used, and the Altrincham Corporation is credited with being possessed of a "branck," or iron bridle, of the most simple form known. Brushfield, who has written a work on the Obsolete Punishments of this county, says :—

It is the most rudely constructed, primitive-looking, scold's bridle I have yet seen; the workmanship is so rough as to lead one to suppose it must have been made by some very ordinary blacksmith: in form it is somewhat similar to the Oxford example; the gag is a plain flat piece of iron, the hook is fastened at the back by a plain hook and staple, and there is a separate hook for the leading chain. (Fancy, ye gods! leading a woman with a chain, like a bear!)

Listen, again :—

No compensation whatever exists for the adaptation of the instrument to heads of different sizes, and as the bridle is a very small one, a great deal of additional " scolding " must have been caused during the endeavour to fix it to any large head. The ascending portion terminated in an enlarged flat extremity, the base of which appears as if constructed for the purpose of attaching a cord to secure it more firmly to the head. The gentleman to whom I am indebted for the loan of this specimen (Mr. Mort, of Altrincham) informs me that he saw it used upon an old (?) woman, about 35 years ago, who appears to have been a regular virago, and who, apparently, abused her more peaceable neighbours, more particularly two very inoffensive people on each side of her own dwelling. All means were tried in vain, and as a last resource she was ordered to be bridled and led through the town. When the instrument was fixed to her head, she refused to walk; the authorities were, however, so determined to make her a public example, and carry out the punishment, that they ordered her to be wheeled through the town. She was accordingly placed in a barrow, and, escorted by a great mob, was wheeled through the principal streets round the market place, and thence to her own home. It may be as well to mention that this punishment was attended with the most salutary results, as she ever afterwards kept a civil and respectful tongue in her head.

Our country cousins at Carrington were far ahead of us in this respect. Their "branck," which is now in the Warrington Museum, is designed with greater attention to mechanical details. Its "gag" is much more neatly formed; it has three rings to which the hook or chain may be attached, and it is made with an adjustment for the difference in the sizes of people's heads. Probably it was in greater request at Carrington, and therefore greater anxiety was manifested lest it should produce needless "scolding," and thus increase the ill it was intended to cure.

The spectacle of men being publicly whipped for trivial offences was common, and, generally, the punishment was inflicted on the unfortunate culprits on market days.

In April, 1801, the town was thrown into a state of excitement in consequence of some opposition to the public whipping of one Thomas Owen. The subject was discussed at a town's meeting in July, "convened by publick advertizement and by the bellman, by order of the constables," when it was—

> Resolved unanimously, that the constables be and are directed at the expense of the town, to prosecute William Coppock, and such other person or persons as can be discovered to have beaten the horse in the cart when Thos. Owen was to have been whipped, in Altrincham, on the 28th of April last, pursuant to the sentence of the Court of Quarter Sessions, held at Chester in and for this county, on the 21st day of April last.

It may be inferred from this that Mr. Owen had a large number of friends who were bent on preventing the infliction of the prescribed punishment; as on that occasion the horse block at the Unicorn was so seriously damaged that upwards of thirteen shillings had to be spent by the town on its repair.

On one occasion, probably the last, two men were whipped, one after the other. One of them, after having received his portion, begged, with a self-abnegation and gallantry worthy of all praise, that he might receive his companion's lashes, as he was sure he was unable to bear the punishment. No wonder that with men made of such sterling stuff, Wellington won Waterloo. No wonder that their descendants conquered at Inkermann, and clove through the Russian hosts at Balaclava! The old spirit still lives. It is manifested daily in thousands of humble homes in our land; but its humbleness is its truest nobility, and there are numbers who are unconsciously saying by their actions, to that angel who is inscribing it in a book of gold,

I pray thee, then,
Write me as one who loves his fellow-men.

The dark record of this portion of "the good old times" is not yet complete. Executions were common, and it is not unusual to read in the papers of the period blood-curdling narratives of the wholesale way in which our fellow creatures were launched into eternity. For instance, on September 25th, 1819, there were executed at Chester, Samuel Hooley and John Johnson (a man of colour), for burglary at Bowdon. In April, 1820, Thomas Miller was executed for burglary at Bowdon. Some ten or fifteen years after, a man named Henshaw was executed for poaching near Altrincham. This caused an intense sensation throughout the whole district, and is still remembered by a large number of the older inhabitants.

A much pleasanter theme is afforded by an examination of some of the old amusements, such, for instance, as "souling" on All Soul's Eve, which is not, however, kept up as it used to be forty years ago. The observance is referred to Catholic times, and is undoubtedly one of great antiquity. Some of the songs which are sung by the "soulers," are peculiar, and there is an unaccountable play upon words. One of them opens :—

> Soul day, Soul day, Saul,
> One for Peter, two for Paul,
> Three for Him that made us all.
> An apple, a pear, a plum or a cherry,
> Anything that will make us all merry.
> Put your hand into your pocket and pull out your keys,
> Go down into the cellar and bring up what you please ;
> A glass of your wine, or a cup of your beer,
> And we'll never come souling till this time next year.
> We are a pack of merry boys all of one mind,
> We have come souling for what we can find.
> Soul, soul, sole of my shoe,
> If you have no apples money will do ;
> Up with your kettle, and down with your pan,
> Give us an answer and let us begone.

Of course this is all very well, and no doubt very laudable so far as the men and boys of a single village go; but when it comes to providing for those of a large town, split-up into numerous gangs, it must be admitted that souling is a custom "more honoured in the breach than the observance." A more enjoyable and artistic amusement is the "Peace Egg," or "St. George's annual play for the amusement of youth," which is supposed to have an entirely Cheshire origin, St. George, representing in some people's ideas, the Baron of Chester. If this be the case, it now obtains little in the county of its nativity ; but in Yorkshire it flourishes amazingly.

The practice of "wassailing amongst the leaves so green " has almost died out ; but the singing of carols at Christmas time flourishes in its pristine power, and oftentimes unfortunate Christians are called upon to awake at most unseasonable hours.

Who in this neighbourhood does not remember or has not heard of the "barley hump" and Dunham ale ? The latter was given on stated occasions to all comers, and its potency was often evidenced in those who partook too freely of it. But round the "barley hump" cling the tenderest memories, and men and

T

women, whose locks are now silvered with age, remember the time, when as rosy-faced boys and girls they scampered over the breezy downs to Dunham Hall, for this hump, which was a piece of barley bread a few inches square, good and wholesome, hard nearly as a board, but not proof against the assaults of a vigorous appetite. The schools of the neighbourhood were turned out at a given hour, and an exciting race for the Hall began. It was first come, first served. The boys were ranged on one side, and the girls on the other, and down the human avenue, a barrow filled with these "humps" was wheeled, and a piece given to each child. Sometimes, the number of little visitors was so great that the supply ran short, and those who had not yet eaten theirs had to divide with their less fortunate brethren. Having had their treat—for such it was always looked upon—they betook themselves to their homes, joyful with anticipation of another turn at the "barley hump." The "Lions" of Dunham, have even a "tradition" associated with them. They are well known to visitors, and were once looked upon with awe by the juvenile natives. In fact, it is implicitly believed, by lovers especially, that at the hour of midnight, when the spirits of the departed are attacked with restlessness, these "lions" raise up one paw, and put down the other, remaining in this position for twenty-four hours, until a change is again considered desirable!

Race meetings formerly flourished at Altrincham, but were many years since discontinued, except at rare intervals, and then they were stripped of their ancient glory. Race-field, now covered with stately mansions, serves to perpetuate the fact, but the principal races were held on Hale Moss. An old newspaper, published in 1753, contains an advertisement announcing that the races would be held on the 11th day of July of that year, " on a good course," and that no person would be allowed to sell liquor on the Common who had not subscribed two-and-sixpence to the said races. In this respect the old does not appear to differ from the new, however much people may be inclined to lament the decadence of modern horseracing.

A word may now be said of the Parks at Dunham, both of which have formed appropriate subjects alike for the brush of the painter, and the pen of the poet. In what is called the Old Park, the beech avenue, which leads to the Hall, is a most imposing object. Of the present mansion, which replaced its predecessor, a description of which has already appeared in these pages, little need be said, except that it is a large quadrangular brick building, and was built in 1730. The collection of family plate was of a most extensive and valuable character, and there was also a number of family and other portraits by various eminent masters.

A fitting conclusion to this chapter may be found in the reference to Altrincham made by Thomas De Quincy, whose fame in connection with every department of literature is well known. In his autobiographical sketches, he describes the circumstances under which he left Manchester to travel to Chester, and he says that on his route (this would be about the year 1814), the first town that he reached, to the best of his remembrance, was Altrincham, colloquially *Awtrigem.* He goes on :—

"When a child, three years old, and suffering from whooping cough, I had been carried for a change of air to different places on the Lancashire coast; and in order to benefit by as large a compass as possible of varying atmospheres, I and my nurse had been made to rest for the first night of our tour, at this cheerful little town of Altrincham. On the next morning, which ushered in a most dazzling day in July, I rose earlier than my nurse fully approved; but in no long time she had found it advisable to follow my example; and, after putting me through my morning's drill of ablutions and the Lord's prayer, no sooner had she fully arranged my petticoats than she lifted me up in her arms, threw open the window, and let me suddenly look down upon the gayest scene I ever beheld, viz., the little market-place of Altrincham at eight o'clock in the morning. It happened to be the market day; and I, who till then had never consciously been in any town whatever, was equally astonished and delighted by the novel gaity of the scene. Fruits, such as can be had in

July, and flowers were scattered about in profusion; even the stalls of the butchers, from their brilliant cleanliness, appeared attractive; and the bonny young women of Altrincham were all trooping about in caps and aprons coquettishly disposed. The general hilarity of the scene at this early hour, with the low murmurings of pleasurable conversation and laughter that rose up like a fountain to the open window, left so profound an impression upon me that I never lost it. All this occurred, as I have said, about eight o'clock on a superb July morning. Exactly at that time in the morning, exactly such another heavenly day in July, did I leave Manchester, at six a.m., naturally enough finding myself in the centre of the Altrincham market-place. There were the same fruits and flowers; the same bonny young women trooping up and down in the same (no, not the same) coquettish bonnets; everything was apparently the same; perhaps the window of my bedroom was still open, only my nurse and I were not looking out; for, alas! on recollection, fourteen years precisely had passed since then. Breakfast time, however, is always a cheerful stage in the day; if a man can forget his cares at any season it is then—and after a walk of seven miles it is doubly so. I felt it at the time, and have therefore stopped to notice it as a singular coincidence, that twice, and by the merest accident, I should find myself precisely as the clocks on a July morning were all striking eight, drawing inspiration and pleasurable feelings from the sights and sounds in the little market-place of Altrincham."

The "bonny young women" were not, however, sufficiently attractive to keep the youthful De Quincy from pursuing his journey. Most of them will by this time have passed away; but their descendants will read with interest of the manners of their grandmothers and great-grandmothers in days gone by.

CHAPTER XII.

Ecclesiastical Altrincham: The Wesleyan Methodist Churches—Wesley's visits to Altrincham—St. George's Church; its Schools, &c.— An Altrincham Centenarian—The Unitarians; their early history; description of the new Chapel in Dunham Road—The Methodist New Connexion— The Independents or Congregationalists, with some notices of their Pastors and Work—St. Margaret's, Dunham Massey—St. John's—The Old Downs Chapel—The Primitive Methodists—St. Peter's, Peel Causeway, &c.

WHEN John Wesley, with a lofty enthusiasm which made the whole world his parish, introduced a new leaven of religious fervour throughout the land, Altrincham was among the many towns he visited. It is one of the first places mentioned in his famous Journal; and it would appear that the date of his first visit was 1738, which is prior to the formation of the first Wesleyan Society in London. In 1751 he again came to the town, and preached under a pear-tree in Mr. Priestner's garden on Oldfield Brow. He also preached in Church Street, near the site of St. George's, and in other parts of the town. The nucleus of a "church" was thus formed; but it was not until the 17th February, 1788, that the old chapel in Chapel-walk, or Chapel Road, was opened by the Rev. Thomas Taylor, even then an eminent Methodist minister. The Church of England Service was read on that occasion; Abner Partington, a name well known in the annals of Altrincham, and who was probably one of its Mayors subsequently, officiating as clerk. It is also interesting to state that Altrincham was one of the first chapels settled under the celebrated deed poll, in which they are legally specified to be "The conference of the people called Methodists." It was more than two years after the chapel was opened that Mr. Wesley preached in Altrincham, about twelve months before his death. In his Journal he describes the devout and earnest demeanour of the crowd both inside and outside the chapel, and expresses a hope that henceforth the Altrincham people will be less "furious" than they have been. Mr. Wesley, when he preached at Altrincham for the last time called the building a chapel, and not a "house," as was his wont. Nearly eighty years afterwards the elegant structure in Bank Street was built, and many were the regrets felt, especially amongst the old supporters of the Methodist cause, at leaving what had been their spiritual home for so long a period. This chapel is in the Byzantine style of architecture, and was erected from the plans of Mr. C. O. Ellison, of Liverpool. Liberal aid for its erection was given by both Churchmen and Dissenters, and to some extent it was looked upon as a town movement. The foundation stone was laid on the 22nd March, 1865, and it was opened on the 10th of May, in the year following. Its main frontage is to Bank Street, and is of freestone with a campanile at one of the angles Its interior is of majestic proportions, and the moulding of the arches is most imposing. There is accommodation on the ground floor for 600 people, and 200 in a good gallery across the end of the building. This gallery is so arranged that it can be continued, if found necessary hereafter, along the sides of the chapel, giving accommodation to 260 additional or in all over 1,000 persons. The organ was removed from the old chapel, and built into the new, with additions and improvements; the cost of this, over £100, being raised by Mr. John Balshaw who for a long period acted as organist. The total cost of the chapel was above £5,000 A capacious lecture hall has been erected adjoining the chapel.

An offshoot of the old chapel was made in the erection of a rather cramped edifice off Stamford Road, Bowdon, which, although no doubt quite adequate at the time for the wants of the congregation was not at all calculated to meet the Bowdon of the future. Its arrangements, including its high-backed pews, did not at all accord with modern ideas of religious worship, and strenuous efforts were made years ago to provide increased accommodation of another character. It could not be said that those efforts were crowned with the success they deserved at the time. So far back as May, 1874, the foundation or memorial stones of the new chapel were laid by Mrs. William Billing, Mrs. John L. Barker, and Miss Mewburn. The position

BOWDON WESLEYAN CHAPEL.

selected is on the brow of the gently sloping hill, which may be said to constitute Bowdon proper, and is close to an ancient footpath now widened out into a thoroughfare leading from the Downs to Stamford Road. The designs were by Mr. W. H. Brakspear, of Manchester, and the style the pure English Gothic of the 13th century. It has accommodation for 700 persons on the ground floor, and for 200 more by the erection of galleries in the transepts. The splendid traditions of this energetic body are well sustained in the chapels and schools erected at Broadheath and the various villages round Altrincham and district.

We now come to St. George's Church, of which, so far as its architecture is[or was]concerned, not even its warmest friends could boast. By one writer it was styled the ugliest church within seven miles of Manchester Exchange; but probably he did not look at home, as within a stone's throw of that place is to be found St. Ann's, which might be placed in the same category as the one he so mercilessly criticised. Moreover, we must remember that the period at which it was built was not one in which the fine arts were fostered or the æsthetic tastes of the people developed to the extent they are now-a-days. Public taste in matters of church architecture was at a very low ebb indeed. The clustering ivy with which it was overgrown, prior to rebuilding, gave it to some degree an appearance of beauty.

It was built as a Chapel of Ease to Bowdon, in 1799, by subscription, and in 1809 it is stated in the returns of the Bishop of Chester to the Governor of Queen Anne's Bounty to be a curacy, not augmented or charged, of the annual value of £91 13s. 6d., arising from dividend of stock, seat rents, and surplice fees. Its first minister was the Rev. Oswald Leicester, an Altrincham man, and he continued in the office for upwards of thirty years. He was the son of a well-to-do shopkeeper in the town, and from his childhood was very religiously disposed. He attended the Wesleyan Chapel, and was greatly influenced by a Mr. Samuel Bradburn then stationed here. He would in all probability have joined this body, had not his father taken the matter into his own hands, and had him educated and trained as a clergyman. The church was three times enlarged, first in 1858, when 198 additional sittings were obtained at the west end; in 1871, when 268 sittings were added at the east end, at a cost of £1,000; thus providing accommodation for 1,180 persons.

REV. GEORGE LONDON.

The east window was erected to the memory of Samuel and Ann Hardey, her parents, George Hardey, her brother, and James Holland, her husband, by Sarah Holland, A.D. 1861.

On a brass let into the wall underneath is an inscription :—

This memorial window was accompanied by an offering of £1,000 for the additional endowment of this church, and £200 to be invested, and the interest given in bread to the poor attending Divine worship there:n.

Other stained glass windows are to the memory of Ann, daughter of the Rev. Oswald Leicester, the first incumbent; to Catherine Gardom, to Samuel Barratt, to John Astle Kelsall and his wife Ann Kelsall, to Thomas and Elizabeth Blease, and their daughter, Amelia Mottershead; to Rachael Blease, to Georgina Isabella London, "by the congregation of St. George's Church, as a tribute of their affection and esteem for their pastor, the Rev. George London, and to mark the completion of his 25 years' increasing and warm-hearted labours amongst them, 1884," and also to the Rev. George London, 34 years vicar of the parish. The latest additions are those by F. R. B. Lindsell, Esq., to the memory of his two children, and in remembrance of a deep and bitter bereavement which evoked the greatest sympathy of the inhabitants of the whole parish.

The inscriptions on the gravestones do not present many novel features; but one on the first clerk of the church, George Samuel Drinkwater, who filled the post for 33 years, thus records the virtues of his wife :—

> She was——
> But words are wanting to say what,
> Think what a wife should be, and she was that.

She left him, so it is said, an annuity of £50 a year; hence this extraordinary eulogy.

St. George's remained a chapel of ease from 1799 to 1860, when it was made into a district church. In 1868, it was formed into a separate parish, of which the Rev. George London, who was presented in 1859, was made vicar. It has been endowed by a grant from Queen Anne's Bounty of £1,000, and up to 1859 had an income of £150 per annum. This was increased in 1861 by a gift of £1,000 from Mrs. Holland, of Sandiway House, as already indicated. Connected with the church are flourishing day and Sunday schoo's, the latter being established in 1783, before the church was built. The first day or national school was erected to commemorate the fiftieth year of the reign of George III., and from this circumstance received the name of the Jubilee school. It was cramped and ill adapted for the required purpose; but singular to say, it continued to be used for 50 years, and thus celebrated its own as well as King George's jubilee. The present spacious schools were erected in 1860, and have since had to be enlarged to meet the increasing requirements of the neighbourhood.

The Sunday School of St. George's is reputed to be the oldest in the county, having been founded in 1783 by the Rev. Oswald Leicester, long before the church was built. There are now flourishing branches at Oakfield Road and Broadheath, where also is a neat daughter church dedicated to St. Alban, which will, however, soon be too small for this rapidly growing end of the parish. At the time of writing these lines, an earnest appeal has been made by the vicar, the Rev. M. Lutener, for funds to rebuild the nave of the church, and thus carry out the expressed wish of his revered predecessor when the new chancel was built in 1886, that this might be considered as the beginning of the great work of giving to Altrincham a parish church worthy of the town. Messrs. Paley and Austin, the eminent church architects, presented a report, strongly advising the building of a new nave without galleries, and the opening out of the west end of the church, retaining the tower and chancel and east and west walls of the nave. The total sum required is about £5,000, to which already there has been a liberal response. The church on its completion will accommodate 788 worshippers on the ground floor, as against 757 on the present ground floor and galleries combined. In concluding his appeal the vicar points out that it can only be done by an earnest effort for a great and exceptional purpose. "Let us make up our minds," he adds, "to do this work enthusiastically, and thoroughly, and quickly ; let us erect for our Centenary Memorial a monument that we shall in after years be proud of ; let us give to Altrincham a Parish Church worthy of the town, and to God a gift of which each one of us can honestly say—" My offering has cost me *some* self-sacrifice." Let it be the offering, not of a few, but of us all. Each Churchman and Churchwoman in the Parish should be able to feel of our Church—" I helped to build it."

The register, which begins with the present century, contains the names of one centenarian Catherine Holt, of Altrincham, who was buried June 30th, 1813, aged 103.

LIST OF THE MINISTERS OR CLERGY OF ST. GEORGE'S CHURCH :—

1799.	The Rev.	Oswald Leicester.
1832.	,, ,,	George Ranking.
1834.	,, ,,	Wilmot Cave Brown Cave.
1843.	,, ,,	Francis Orton, D.C.L.
1856.	,, ,,	John B. Honnywill.
1858.	,, ,,	George London.
1894.	,, ,,	W. Maurice Bonner Lutener.

Not one of the Dissenting bodies in Altrincham possesses a history so eventful or interesting as the Unitarians. The Altrincham chapel is an offshoot of the old congregation at Hale, which at irregular intervals for a long period had possession of the church at Ringway or Ringey. Ringway was then the "debateable ground" of dissent, and the battles ecclesiastical which were waged upon it were both fast and furious.

"In Hale," writes Sir Peter Leycester in 1666, "is an hamlet called Ringey, wherein is situated a chappel of ease (far from being an easy one to hold, by the way), called Ringey Chappel ; within the parish of Bowdon, of which I have little to say save that it was much frequented in the late wars by schismatical ministers, and as it were a receptacle for nonconformists, in which dissolute times every pragmatical and illiterate person, as the humour served, stepped into the pulpit without any lawful calling thereunto, or licence of authority."

For a very long period this chapel remained in the hands of the Dissenters, and from certain notices which have been made of it in various documents, would appear to have been under the protection of the powerful families of Booth and Crewe, who were at that time strongly favourable to the then Presbyterian cause. It was here that William Dearnily, who is so disrespectfully alluded to in the Bowdon Parish Register, ministered. He was ordained at Knutsford in 1692, on which occasion Matthew Henry was present. He died in May, 1701, and in the Cheshire Minute Book he is described "as a person of great worth, of very

THE OLD CHURCH RINGWAY

good natural parts, a considerable scholar, of sober and moderate principles, and a blameless and exemplary conversation." The present Hale chapel was erected in 1723, during the ministry of Mr. Waterhouse, who, being dispossessed of Ringway chapel, took along with him the bulk of the congregation. There is a tradition that Mr. Waterhouse was forcibly expelled from Ringway by a Mr. Assheton, then resident at Ashley Hall. The version given is that about the year 1721, John Crewe, Esq., of Crewe Hall, inherited the Lordship of Ringway, and declared his intention of restoring it to the established Church. The scene which followed savours more of a public-house than a place of worship. Presuming upon Mr. Crewe's connivance, this resident at Ashley Hall, who seldom went to a place of worship, and who was reputed to have been a man of very dissolute habits, went to the chapel one Sunday, attended by a number of servants, seized Mr. Waterhouse by the collar, pulled him from the pulpit, and bundled out both him and the congregation, "bag and baggage." Having accomplished this operation to his own satisfaction, he locked the doors, and no doubt on his way to Ashley Hall was jubilant over this gentlemanly (?) action. The dissenters, however, entered again the week following, and continued in it without molestation until a clergyman licensed by the Bishop of Chester took possession of it. His behaviour on going to his new cure was in striking contrast to that of his lay brother of Ashley Hall. On the Sunday when he first came, the dissenters had begun their worship, but instead of displaying his muscular Christianity, he bade them proceed with the service, and remained a devout hearer to the end. He took possession of the place in form in the afternoon. Mr. Waterhouse afterwards preached in a barn at the Ashes farm, near the chapel, till a dissenting meeting house was erected; but he did not live long to enjoy it, as he died in 1754. Canon Raines, in his notes to *Gastrell's Notitia* states that there is a bell at Ringway, with G. B. upon it; the initials of Sir George Booth. In 1747, the minister of this chapel was the Rev. Hugh Worthington, jun., and from a diary of Mr. Isaac Worthington, of Altrincham, it appears he was minister of Hale chapel from 1748 to 1767. Mr. Isaac Worthington took great interest in the affairs of this chapel, and in 1769 he went to Stockport and engaged Mr. Harrop to come to Hale. Mr. Harrop continued in it for forty-six years, during thirty-seven of which he held the chapel at Sale conjointly with that at Hale. He resigned his charge in 1816, at the age of seventy. He lived for twenty-one years after, and went down to the grave at the venerable age of ninety-one, beloved and honoured by all who knew him. In

1816, the Rev. William Jevons was invited to undertake the pastoral charge of the united Presbyterian societies in Hale and Altrincham, but he only held the position for about three years. The old chapel in Shaw's Lane, Altrincham, lately used as the Salvation barracks, which was built about this period, has long been given up ; and on the closing of the burial ground, the remains of the "rude forefathers of the hamlet" were taken up and removed to Hale. In the pretty chapel in Dunham Road, there is a good congregation, and the descendants of Mr. Isaac Worthington still take a deep interest in the cause. It was opened on Wednesday, December 18th, 1872, on which occasion the Rev. Charles Beard, of Liverpool, preached. It is enclosed on two sides by a stone wall, in which a handsome covered stone gateway leads by a flight of steps to the porch on the south side, which forms the principal entrance to the chapel. The interior consists of a nave fifty-seven feet long, and one aisle to the north, separated from it by five arches with granite shafts, making a total width of thirty-seven feet. The east end is apsidal, with carved wood pulpit and reading desk, and communion table, all upon a raised dais.

The exterior of the building is plain, but substantial, being faced with brick, and stone dressings round the entrance doorway and windows, the heads of which are filled with geometric tracery. The west end has two gables, and the roof is carried round the east end, having a large cross at the apex of the apse. The chapel is fitted with pitch pine seats for about 225 adults and 40 children. An aisle 4ft. 6in. in width leads down the centre of the nave, and a passage 3ft. 6in. in width along the north side of the chapel.

The cover of the communion table, beautifully embroidered in needlework, was presented to the chapel by Miss Nicholson, daughter of the late Mr. Robert Nicholson, of Bowdon. The three apse windows are filled with stained glass, illustrating by means of flowers, the emblems of Faith, Hope and Charity. They were the gift of Mr. and Mrs. James Worthington, of Sale

Hall. The large west window of three lights and the double lights, which extend along both sides of the chapel, are filled with plain diamond quarries. The edifice was erected from the designs of Mr. Thomas Worthington, of Manchester.

The Methodist New Connexion erected a fairly sized chapel in George Street about the year 1821. At one time it was very well attended, and the congregation was a most important one. The exterior is not prepossessing, but the interior is cheerful and cosy.

In point of wealth and numbers, the Congregationalists or Independents occupy one of the foremost positions. They had a most humble origin, and it appears from the Church Book of the Bowdon Downs Church, that, in the year 1803, the Rev. James Turner, of Knutsford, began occasionally to pass through Bowdon in travelling to Manchester. During these journeys, states Mr. Joseph Thompson, in his contribution to "Non-Conformity in Cheshire," it occurred to him that some measures might be adopted, and ought not to be delayed, for the introduction into Altrincham or the neighbourhood of the doctrines and government of Independent Churches. The usefulness and propriety of this course appeared the more unquestionable on account of the frequency with which the members of churches in Manchester, even then, were observed to visit and reside in the district. Mr. Turner, fully possessed with his project, applied to an aged and poor widow of the name of Cox or Coe, a member of the Independent church at Gatley, but resident in Altrincham, and obtained her permission to preach at intervals in her little thatched cottage near the Market Place. The humble building has long since disappeared; but there, with very slender encouragement, this self-denying servant of the Gospel first regularly preached the truth professed by the denomination to which he belonged. It should, however, be recorded that other excellent ministers pursuing a similar "labour of love," were also received into the house by this same poor woman. These efforts of Mr. Turner were afterwards discontinued for lack of local sympathy and

V

support ; and some time appears to have elapsed before a zealous person from Manchester, named Whitworth, began to visit the district, with the like object in view, but with hardly more success : although the assistance of the Chester County Union had been enlisted for the benefit of the neighbourhood.

A few years again passed away before anything permanent or regular was attempted towards the establishment of Independency at Bowdon. But owing to the liberality of some Christian friends, the little chapel at the foot of the Downs, formerly occupied by the followers of a clergyman who had seceded from the Church of England, was purchased on the 6th May, 1839, for £465. The cost of alteration, deed of settlement, &c., raised this amount to £588. The Revs. Dr. Raffles, of Liverpool ; S. Luke, of Chester ; and J. Turner, of Knutsford, preached at the dedication of the building on July 4th, 1839. In April, 1840, the Rev. John Earnshaw became the first minister of the church,—the first Christian society consisting of ten members. We believe that his appointment was the result of the exertions of Mr. Ibbotson Walker, to whom also belongs the honour of founding and carrying on the Sunday School connected with the church. It was then held in a room in New Street, and only about 40 children attended. In 1844, the Rev. Flavel Stenner became the second minister, and the first deacons were chosen in August of that year. Mr. Stenner subsequently resigned the charge, when it devolved on the Rev. John Wilkinson, who in the May of the following year " in the youth of his days," was summoned away by death.

The increase of the population and the growing importance of the neighbourhood having rendered needful a larger and more commodious place of worship, many generous friends aided in the erection of a new church, which is the one now used by the Bowdon Downs Congregation, and which was opened in June, 1848. In 1868 it was proposed to build another chapel at an outlay of £7,000 ; but insuperable difficulties arising in the acquisition of a site, it was determined to increase the accommo-

BOWLES DOWNS CONGREGATIONAL CHURCH: INTERIOR, LOOKING EAST DOWN BAY

dation with the means then at their disposal, which was done at a cost of about £3,000. The architecture of the enlargement was Gothic, of the early perpendicular period, in conformity with the style which prevailed in the rest of the building. The internal fittings are of stained wood, the pews are open, and altogether it is an exceedingly comfortable place of worship. The pulpit, which was put in at the time of the enlargement, is most elaborately and richly carved, and the book rest is supported by the figure of an angel with outspread wings. A new organ by Jardine, of Manchester, was opened in the same year, 1868, by the late honorary organist, Mr. J. Mills. Memorial windows have been placed to the memory of Mrs. Haworth, of Ecclesfield, and a tablet also records the many virtues of Mrs. William Milne, the first deaconess of the church. Referring once more to the pastors, in April, 1849, the office was accepted by the Rev. Henry Christopherson, from Newcastle-upon-Tyne. During Mr. Christopherson's pastorate the church increased both in numbers and energy, and it was therefore with regret that the church and congregation learnt from him that he had accepted the invitation to take the oversight of New College Chapel, London. Mr. Christopherson bade farewell to his people at Christmas, 1856, In May, 1857, the Rev. H. T. Robjohns, B.A., Western College, Plymouth, accepted the pastorate. In March, 1861, Mr. Robjohns resigned his charge, proceeding to Newcastle-upon-Tyne. In the autumn of the year the choice of the church was unanimously in favour of the Rev. A. J. Morris, of Holloway ; and it determined to welcome Mr. Morris by clearing off the debt on the chapel and schools, which was accordingly done. The pastorate of Mr. Morris was, unfortunately, of brief duration. He was succeeded by the Rev. H. Griffith, a man of sound learning and erudition, who resigned in 1875, after a pastorate of nearly 11 years. The Rev. A. Mackennal, B.A., received a most unanimous call and commenced his labours the first week in February, 1877. In 1886 he was elected to the Chairmanship of the Congregational Union of England and Wales, and in the year following the degree of D.D. was conferred upon him by the Senate of Glasgow University. He is the author of various theological works, which display vivid grasp and far-reaching thought and erudition.

The day and Sunday school had been carried on for nearly a dozen years in the old chapel at the foot of the Downs, which was long felt to be most unsuitable for the purpose, the accommodation being wholly inadequate to the growth of the population, and the rooms badly ventilated, small and without class-rooms. It was therefore determined that new schools should be built. After great difficulty a site was secured in Oxford Road, Altrincham, which was then well-nigh inaccessible, there being no highway, and nothing but gardens surrounding it; and the splendid structure known as the British School in Oxford Road, was erected in 1860, at a cost of £2,600, and was opened free of debt in January, 1861. For a long time the road to it was known as British School Road. Large class-rooms have since been added, and a class for adults, quite unique in its proportions, has for many years been admirably conducted by Mr. George Wood. A tablet in the main building bears the following interesting inscription :—"To the memory of Samuel Butler, for twenty-eight years superintendent, and seven years teacher, of the Sunday school meeting here ; this tablet is erected by his fellow officers, his fellow teachers, and the scholars, all of whom honour his fidelity and love to recall his name." Connected with this church, formerly only partially, but now entirely, is the North Cheshire Rural Mission, which, as its name implies, is carried on in the country districts. It has branches at Broadheath, Baguley, Heyhead, Mobberley, Partington, &c., and does good work in places where spiritual destitution is found to prevail.

The British Schools were at first opened for preaching, but this was discontinued, when the Rev. A. Dewar opened the old chapel at the foot of the Downs. This may, strictly speaking, be called the commencement of the Altrincham Congregational Chapel. He was succeeded by the Rev. W. B. MacWilliam. The desire for a more comfortable edifice was soon felt. The old

Wesleyan Chapel in Chapel Walk, now All Saints', Regent Road, was accordingly purchased from the Wesleyan body ; and on April 10th, 1868, the Rev. C. Aylard was ordained to the pastorate. Services are still conducted in the British schools.

"Beautiful for situation" wrote the Psalmist of one of the most sacred spots on earth. "Beautiful for situation," too, are many of our own sacred places. Who can contemplate, without admiration, the beautiful setting which many a little village spire, peeping modestly out from the tufted trees, gives to the English landscape ? This may be appropriately applied to St. Margaret's. Few travellers as they are whirled through the valley on the Dunham side, in that reminder of an advanced civilization, the railway train, but turn for a moment to look at that clear cut spire, which appears to be embosomed in a forest of vegetation. Few there are, as they have passed along the Dunham Road, who have not had their progress arrested for even a brief space by one of the most lovely pictures with which nature has so lavishly blessed this beautiful land. It is one in which pastoral and sylvan scenery are intermingled in one huge panorama. Right before us, buried in the valley, is Oldfield Hall, formerly the abode of perhaps one of the oldest Altrincham families, and under whose roof more than one of the members of the noble house of Booth have breathed their last. A little to the right we try to make out the ancient hall of Riddings, with its moated grange, supposed to have existed prior to the Conquest. Further away we see the spire of St. John the Divine at Brooklands peering above the surrounding trees,—again to the left, the villas of Ashton-on-Mersey stud the ground, and the pretty church of St. Mary Magdalene is distinctly seen. Away again, and the Lancashire Hills form a massive and appropriate background. Seen on a summer's day, when the meadows are pied with daisies, and nature has put on her loveliest apparel, when the sun shines down, and by a concentration of its rays produces those beautiful tints which throw a glamour over hill and dale, it is one which a lover of the picturesque dwells upon, and in its contemplation discovers new beauties.

St. Margaret's Church is certainly the most beautiful, both as regards exterior and interior, to be found in the district. Forty years ago or more, the Earl of Stamford and Warrington was desirous of having a church erected at Dunham Massey. We believe the site originally chosen was in Racefield, but this was subsequently changed and the present position decided upon. It was contemplated at that time that the church should be built of white bricks, with ashlar dressings, but before half the length of the foundations had been put in the design was abandoned. Afterwards competitive designs were furnished by three London and three Manchester architects. Mr. William Hayley, of Manchester, proved successful.

The church which is estimated to have cost £20,000, adjoins the turnpike-road leading from Altrincham to Knutsford, and was consecrated on the 13th June, 1855, by the Lord Bishop of Chester. The style is the perpendicular, which prevailed in the fifteenth and the early part of the sixteenth century. The extreme length is 130 feet, and the width, exclusive of transepts, 60 feet, and accommodation is provided for about 700 persons. The plan is cruciform, and comprises a lofty nave lighted from clerestory windows; the north and south aisles are lighted by three-light windows, the tracery of which is of different designs; and the chancel is lighted by nine windows, varying in size and design. The exterior is of Yorkshire stone, from the neighbourhood of Sheffield, with ashlar stone dressings from Hollington, and the stone used in the interior is also from the same place. The roof of the nave is of oak open framed, with carved ribs and hammer beams, dependent from which are carved figures of angels. The spandrils are filled in with tracery. The whole of the internal fittings are of oak, and the pews have open ends. The Stamford chapel is on the south side, and it is lighted by two two-light windows, and entered by a private door. A lofty tower and spire rise at the intersection of the nave, transepts and chancel, from four moulded stone piers, to an altitude of 210 feet. The spire has enriched flying buttresses, and is surmounted by a cross.

At the east end there is a large seven-light window, with embattled transoms and bold mullions. This window, which is filled with stained glass, is 30 feet by 14 feet, and contains beautifully executed representations. In the upper division is the Saviour, in the centre of a group of which St. John the Baptist, St. Matthew, St. Mark, St. Luke, St. John the Evangelist, and St. Peter are the chief figures. In the lower division St. Paul is the centre figure, and round him are to be seen some of the principal characters of the old dispensation—Moses, David, Isaiah, Jeremiah, David, and Malachi. The west window is divided into five compartments, filled in with tracery, and on the stained glass are depicted many of the prominent female characters of both Old and New Testaments. In the upper division are figured Mary Magdalene, Mary mother of James, Mary mother of Jesus, Salome, and Elizabeth. In the lower division St. Margaret is in the centre, surrounded by Deborah, Ruth, Esther, and Dorcas. Under this window is a large doorway, with square head over a moulded arch. The spandrils are filled in with tracery, and finished with crockets, and finial. The other entrance is by means of a porch on the south side. The pulpit, reading desk, font, and reredos are of Caen stone, and the tracery and carving of all of them are finished in a most exquisite manner. The lectern is of fine proportions, standing on four lions of iron. It has a massive twisted shaft of brass with a boss of iron, illuminated with vine leaves of polished brass ; the head or desk part is of stained oak. The reredos is divided into seven parts, answering to the seven light window above, each part has an enriched canopy, and three of the centre compartments project from and rise above the others, and are supported by richly traceried buttresses, with crockets and finials, the whole being surmounted by an enriched cornice, and Tudor flower battlement. At each end of this reredos is a niche, with rich canopies, crocketed pinnacles and finials, in which are placed splendidly carved figures on pedestals. The panels of the communion table are filled in with diapered carving in relief, consisting of crosses, Tudor rose fleur-de-lys, &c. The ceilings of the chancel and the Stamford chapel are divided into panels, with

W

moulded ribs, and the tracery in the chancel is elaborately characteristic of the style, having a large boss in the centre compartment and pateræ at the intersection of the ribs. In the chancel are stained glass windows in memory of the Rev. John Kingsley, first vicar of the parish of St. Margaret's, which were placed there by the subscriptions of the congregation ; and with the surplus, augmented to the necessary amount, the architectural beauties of the chancel were enhanced by permanent decorations of a costly character. The aisles and the chancel floors are laid with polished stone and black marble diamond dots; and the floor in front of the altar is paved with encaustic tiles of a chaste design. The arrangements for lighting are novel, and have been perfected with strict regard to the requirements of the style of the church. The standards for the nave rise from the floor, with illuminated stems ; from these twisted shafts of wrought polished brass support four branches enriched with hammered foliage ; the branches again support groups of lights ; and above these round a central stem is a corona of metal work, having a circlet of stars of lights. The standards are arranged on each side of the nave, in advance of the piers, and all are visible, so that they produce a vista of light of singularly beautiful effect, in harmony with that architectural vista of nave and aisles for which the mediæval buildings are so remarkable. From the nave the eye is carried on to the chancel, in which are two standards of larger proportion and richer detail, rising from solid stone bases The shafts have interlacing fretwork, picked out with colour and the branches are entwined with leaves of the passion flower and buds formed of crystallines When lighted, each standard presents a group of 20 brilliant stars. In addition to the memorial windows already noticed, others have been put in by Mr. Sidebotham, of Bowdon, in memory of his father and mother; by the late Rev. R. Hodgson, in memory of his mother, Susan Ann Hodgson; by Charles Heaton Hinde, Esq., in gratitude to God for restoration from a serious illness ; to the memory of the late vicar, the Rev. R. Hodgson, and in memory of Mr. and Mrs. Allen, of Oldfield Hall, by members of the family.

The tower contains a peal of ten bells weighing upwards of six tons. The tenor bell weighs nearly 28 cwt., and bears the following inscription :—

> As Queen of queens, Victoria reigns ;
> I sit as Queen o'er music's strains,
> And may her subjects loyal be
> As mine ! we dwell in harmony.

The then Earl of Stamford and Warrington, patron of the living, for the purpose of endowing the church with a permanent provision, in addition to the pew rents, by an indenture dated March 30th, 1855, and made between him of the first part, Her Majesty's Commissioners for building new churches of the second part, and the Rev. George Heron, of Carrington, Samuel Holker Norris, David Reynolds Davies, Legh Richmond, of Guilsborough Park, Northamptonshire, and the Rev. John Kingsley, of Dunham, of the third part, declared his intention to provide £80 per annum, to be secured upon a competent part of the Earl's freehold estate in Cheshire ; and in satisfaction thereof, with the consent of the Commissioners, he had granted to those of the third part two several clear rent charges or annual sums of £43 15s. and £45, making together £88 15s. ; and to provide for the repairs of the church a yearly sum of £20, he had by the same indenture conveyed a clear yearly rent charge of £21 18s. 2d. to the said persons. It was directed by the Commissioners that 200 sittings in the church should continue for ever to be free sittings, subject to the appropriation of any part thereof, as the Lord Bishop, for the time being, should legally direct.

The first vicar of St. Margaret's, the Rev. John Kingsley, died on the 13th November, 1869, at the age of 60. He came to Bowdon in 1833 as curate to the Rev. W. H. G. Mann, Vicar of Bowdon, which position he held for about 20 years. On resigning, in 1854 the parishioners, as a mark of well deserved respect, presented him with the handsome sum of £1,500. The Earl of Stamford presented him with the living on the consecration of St. Margaret's, and for a period of over 14 years he

w 3

occupied this sphere. Through his efforts the schools attached to St. Margaret's were established, while he kept an immediate and vigilant supervision over the Albert Street Schools, and that at Oldfield. He was one of the leading spirits in connection with the Newtown night school, and one of his last acts was to write a form of prayer to be used in that school. His death was greatly lamented, as in the course of a long and active life he had been greatly beloved by all classes of society to whom he had endeared himself by his many good qualities. The Rev. R. Hodgson, his successor, entered upon his duties in January, 1870, and after a quarter of a century of earnest and disinterested labour he died March 14th, 1895. No one could fail to be impressed by his sincerity and singleness of purpose. There was a manliness about all he said and did which gained for him universal respect. His private hospitality was only exceeded by his open-handed charity in the poorer portions of his parish ; and in this he was ably supported by a noble band of workers. Through the liberality of Mr. J. H. Grafton the old Wesleyan Chapel in Regent Road was purchased and altered, and licensed by the Bishop of the Diocese for divine service under the name of All Saints. Services were also commenced and carried on at Dunham Woodhouses. Mr. Hodgson was succeeded in May, 1895, by the Venerable Charles Maxwell Woosnam who is M.A. of Trinity College, Dublin. He was ordained deacon in 1879 and priest in 1880. He was chaplain of the mission to seamen at Penarth, 1879-1880, and on the Tyne from 1880 to 1881, in which year he was appointed Vicar of St. Peter's, Tynemouth, which he resigned in 1888. He was Rector of Kirkby Wiske, Yorkshire, and in 1890 chaplain of the Mersey Mission to Seamen, which he resigned on his presentation to the living of St. Margaret's. He was appointed Archdeacon of Macclesfield in 1893. The Patrons are the Trustees of the Earl of Stamford and Warrington. The net income is returned at £400 per annum, and the population 3,253.

St. John's Church, which is situated in Ashley Road, was built for the working classes, and was originally styled "the

Poor Man's Church." The movement for its erection took an active form in April, 1864, when an influential committee of clergy and laity was appointed for the purpose of carrying out the object in view. The site was given by the then Earl of Stamford and Warrington, and had previously been a farmstead. The Senior Curate of the Parish Church of Bowdon, the Rev. F. Wainwright, M.A., was appointed its incumbent; and in 1865, while the church was being built, services were held in the British School, so as to collect a congregation from the district around. The school was kindly lent by the trustees, and was specially licensed by the Bishop of Chester for the purpose. Mr. Wainwright, was a scholar of Trinity College, Cambridge, B.A., 1860; M.A., 1861; Deacon, 1861; Priest, 1862. He was curate of St. Jude's, Liverpool, 1861 ; Christ Church, Everton, Liverpool, 1863 ; St. Mark's, Kirkdale, 1864 ; Bowdon 1864-1866.

The church, which was designed by Mr. Medland Taylor, of Manchester, is in the early English style of architecture. It has a broad nave of five bays, with north and south aisles, and north south transepts. The seats are of stained pitch pine, and there are 940 sittings, of which 470 in the body of the church are free. There is a large gallery over the west entrance for the accommodation of the Sunday scholars. The edifice externally is of free stone, and the spire is a very handsome one. The total cost, including the endowment, was about £7,500. The living is in the gift of the Bishop of Chester ; the gross income £500 and house, and the population is returned at 5,952. Near the church are erected National Schools, a substantial parsonage, and a parish room ; and in Islington Street, Newtown, is an infant school.

The boundaries of the parish are as follow :—Taking Bowdon Station, which is entirely within the parish, as a starting point, the boundary line travels up the middle of the Downs for some distance, when it turns down St. John's Road, and then up Delamer Road, and round by a new road into Ashley Road, thus surrounding Albert Square and Culcheth New Hall. It then follows the middle of Ashley Road right through Peel Causeway and over the railway, till it turns aside at a stile and crosses the fields into Dob Lane, which it follows up to Hale Road. Then from the top of the Hill it comes back by the way of Hale Road, till it turns to the right by a road and footpath leading to Hale Moss, opposite the end of Broomfield Lane. On the Moss there were two stones set up on purpose to mark the boundary line, which travels through the middle of the Moss along the bank of a brook which formerly ran into Moss Lane. From this last point the line goes up Denmark Street, and arrives again at the back of the station, where it began, by crossing the Goose Green Bridge. The circuit thus traced includes about 330 acres, but it has been somewhat modified by the inclusion of Broomfield Lane and Peel Causeway in the new district of St. Peter's.

St. Elizabeth's, Newtown, was erected as a chapel of ease to St. John's in 1890. The site was presented by Mr. W. J. Crossley, of Glenfield, and another generous gift of £1,000 was made by the family of the late Mr. G. Lord, of Ashton-on-Mersey, in memory of their father. The architect was Mr. John Macnamara, and the contractors Messrs. W. Lambert and Son, Hale Road, Bowdon.

An antiquated structure, nearly facing the Ashley Road, which had in the first place given the Congregationalists a local habitation, if not a name, was destined in 1867, after the removal of the Altrincham congregation, to become the temporary home of Scotch Presbyterianism, for which good cause was shown by the residence of many Presbyterian families at Bowdon. On the 25th January, 1869, the Rev. W. T. Johnson, B.A., was ordained the first minister. In the following year (1870) his congregation began to look about for a site for a new church, which they secured in Delamer Road, and which is known to old Altrinchamites as the "Radish field." The site was in every respect an eligible one; and the work of building, which was forthwith begun, was completed in 1872. The church, which is called Trinity Presbyterian Church, is an ornament to the neighbourhood, is in the Gothic style of architecture, without any of the defects which are usually associated with that style. There is a tower at the north-west corner 120 feet high. The interior has a most comfortable appearance, and is well suited to the wants of a congregation, which has assumed important dimensions in the course of a few years. The total cost of the church, with a spacious lecture hall adjoining, was about £7,000. After a pastorate of 17 years, the Rev. W. T. Johnston resigned in 1886, principally through overwork and ill-health, on which occasion his congregation evinced their regard by presenting him with an illuminated address and a purse of one hundred guineas. After a somewhat long interval he was succeeded by the Rev. R. T. Cunningham, whose shockingly sudden death at a meeting of the Presbyterian Synod in Manchester, was greatly deplored, and created a great sensation in the town and district. The present minister is the Rev. Wilson Cowie. Among the agencies connected with the church is the Victoria Street Mission, which has been productive of great good, and is in a flourishing condition.

In 1872 this old chapel was taken in hand by another religious denomination (Baptist), which was introduced by the Manchester and Salford Baptist Union. The first pastor was the Rev. H. J. Betts, and 26 persons formed the church spiritual. Its constitution is "Baptist, with open Communion," and the seats are free. In 1878, the number of members having increased to nearly 100, the foundation stones of a new chapel and schools, erected in Hale Road from the designs of Mr. William Owen, a rising young architect, were laid and carried out under his superintendence, the chief contractor being Mr. J. Pennington, of Bowdon. The building is Italian in character, and affords accommodation for nearly 500 persons.

The Roman Catholic Chapel of St. Vincent de Paul, is a small Gothic building in New Street, and will seat nearly 400 people. There are day schools in connection with it. For many years the Rev. H. Alcock laboured most assiduously, but ultimately had to retire in consequence of failing health. He was succeeded by the Rev. James O'Brien, who has laboured with much acceptance.

The only other important dissenting body is that of the Primitive Methodists, who for several years worshipped in the loft over a stable in Newtown. By the exercise of much self-denial and energy, they erected the neat little chapel in Oxford Road, which is now free from debt.

St. Peter's Church, Peel Causeway, is intended to meet the wants of a rapidly growing district, and the wisdom of the promoters in erecting an edifice of a suitable and worthy character has been fully justified. On June 16th, 1892, the church was

ST. PETER'S CHURCH, PEEL CAUSEWAY.

dedicated by Dr. Jayne, Bishop of Chester; and formally consecrated by the same prelate February 10th, 1897. The total cost was £6,155. Towards this sum Richard Hampson Joynson, Esq., J.P., and the members of his family were munificent contributors. Mr. Joynson also subscribed the sum of £40 per annum as the nucleus of an endowment. The Rev. J. R. Brunskill is the minister in charge of the parish, and its flourishing condition bears ample testimony to his assiduity and loving care.

CHAPTER XIII.

More looks into old books—Visit of strolling players—Disappearance of town documents—Appointment of town's attorney—Wages a century ago—Disturbances in Altrincham—Another Altrincham Industry—The fire engine—The old handcuffs—A jury list—The expenses of the great well—Altrincham highways indicted—Hard times; a display of public spirit—The select vestry—Extracts from the books; a stray parcel of gloves—How the town got a sun dial—Substitutes for the Militia—Disrespect for proclamations—A worthy overseer—Dread of hydrophobia, &c.

WE have looked at Altrincham in nearly all its aspects—social, historical, and romantic. We will now deal briefly with some of the more domestic phases of its existence as a country town. The general minute book available for this purpose commences in June, 1795. This appears to be the first kept by the authorities, but there is some little doubt existing owing to the fact that a company of strolling players once visited the town. They were allowed to place the boxes containing their "properties" in the little building which then served as a courthouse. When they departed they took along with them a few of the boxes containing the town accounts, to the extreme regret of those who had been entrusted with their safe keeping. That the minute book is the first may be inferred from the fact that one of the entries at the opening meeting, records "that a town's meeting be held in the Court house till further orders, at ten o'clock in the forenoon of the first Tuesday in every month, without any further or any notice." At the succeeding monthly meeting, the town resolved to indulge in the luxury of a lawyer, or rather firm of lawyers; but, it appeared afraid of showing its full blown dignity in perfection, for it states "that when an attorney is necessary to be employed by the overseer, that Messrs. Isaac and George Worthington be employed for Altrincham, when they will undertake to be so employed." There was then no resident magistrate, and the overseer had often to journey to Toft and Knutsford in order to lay informations, ask advice, and get confirmation of rates; or as they are invariably called in the books, "leys." Soon afterwards we find a prospect of employment for the Messrs. Worthington. It was "ordered that as Matthew Davies, though he receives *eight shillings* a week wages, refuses to pay one and sixpence towards his wife and child's support, that the overseer do apply to the magistrates to compel him to pay the above weekly sum, or that he be dealt with according to law." At the same meeting, it was "ordered that ten shillings be paid to Thomas Slater, for his loss of rent by the house late held by Wm. Holt standing empty." Those must indeed, have been halcyon days for the landlords, and no doubt a few in our degenerate age will, in this respect, sigh for a return of "the good old times."

Riots, as minor disturbances were termed, were not frequent, but the manner in which Saturday night was sometimes spent is illustrated by the fact that informations were ordered to be lodged before "John Leigh, Esq., of Oughtrington, against William Johnson, of Altrincham, turner, Charles Rowbottom, of Altrincham, shoemaker, William Royle, of Altrincham, gardener, Joseph Warburton, of Timperley, labourer, and John Ogden, of Bollington, wool-comber, for rioting and fighting in ye public street in Altrincham, on Saturday, the 30th day of April last, (1796) and that the constables do proceed accordingly." In the minute book the word "chairmaker" is crossed out after Johnson's name, and it may be inferred from this that chairmaking probably formed an Altrincham industry at that period. The prosecution of these men was not undertaken without due deliberation; and Mr. Leigh, of Oughtrington, advised that they be proceeded against, and the constables were directed to take steps accordingly. As a further warning, it was ordered that "advertisements be printed making public this resolution, that others may be deterred from offending in like manner." The handcuffs, however, do not appear to have been called into frequent requisition, but with a view to eventualities, the constables were instructed to have them examined "by a whitesmith, and if they can be properly repaired, to get them so repaired—if not, the constables are ordered to purchase a new pair of handcuffs." The overseers had not then an assistant who could relieve them of the drudgery of their duties, and at times much difficulty was experienced in securing a proper audit of the accounts. The salary usually allowed was £20, but in some instances as much as £25 was paid. There was a fire engine in the town in 1798, but no regular brigade of firemen. It was ordered to be worked four times a year, and five shillings was allowed each time to get men to assist in working it. At this period we come across a list (the only one given) of persons qualified to serve on juries in the township of Altrincham, October 1st, 1798, as returned by Joshua Ashcroft and Walter Watson, constables. It will form interesting matter for comparison at the present time :—

William Rigby, Esq.	Robt. Mills
John Clough	Timothy Brownell
Thomas Hancock	Thos. Royle
Peter Adshead	Wm. Howard
J. Brundrett	Samuel Howard
Wm. Pearson	Geo. Eccles
John Darbyshire	Thomas Slater
Is. Grantham	James Broom
John Atherton	Samuel Royle
Robert Twamlow	George Lupton
Samuel Haslam	Wm. Grantham
Josiah Garner	Aaron Brundrett
John Burgess	Thomas Ashley
Oswd. Leicester	John Newall
Joseph Goulden	Isaac Birch
Samuel Hardy	Michl. Lupton
Wm. Pownall	Jams. Walthew
Jos. Burgess	Frederick Boardman
John Brierley	John Holden
Willm. Ashley	James Gratrix
Jams. Brownell	Peter Bailey
Jams. Cluloe	Samuel Lucas
John Austin	David Gatley
Wm. Smith	Willm. Seddon
Vernon Poole	James Potter

For a long period subsequently there appears to have been nothing but routine business transacted at the town's meetings; but in the year 1800 the constables were ordered to "cause three painted boards to deter vagrants from harbouring in the town, to be fixed upon John Burgess's house, John Pickstone's house, and the Unicorn Stables, and that the constables do search and examine the lodging-houses, and use their best endeavours to prevent their harbouring in the town." This had only a temporary effect, and on several occasions various measures were devised for ridding the town of the vagrant nuisance, and lodging-house keepers were threatened with indictment if they offended. The deputy constables were empowered, where necessary, to relieve vagrants provided with passes, prevent them acquiring settlement, or take them before the magistrates as they might deem necessary. At a later period, watchmen paraded the streets in the day time to prevent these unwelcome strangers from coming into the town. The meetings were convened by the various officials. For instance, if the constables required any authority to take proceedings, they requested the bellman to convene a meeting, and so with the overseers. It is seldom we find the surveyors of highways doing this, but it was obvious that at times the inhabitants were required to "mend their ways." At a town's meeting held in July, 1802, it was "resolved that the surveyors be desired to purchase stones to pave the road to Ashley and the Long Lane as far as lies in Altrincham division, and that they procure a ley of sixpence in the pound to be allowed at a privy sessions, and to be assessed on ye inhabitants and owners and occupiers of land in Altrincham for the purchasing stones for such paving, and that when the said ley is expended, a further ley of threepence in the in the pound be assessed and got allowed, and that the remainder of the money wanted for the above purpose be borrowed on a note, to be signed by some of the principal inhabitants of Altrincham, which shall be repaid out of the next money raised for the repairs of the highways." It took upwards of four years to do the work, and it must have been much more expensive than at first contem-

THE OLD CHURCH, ASHTON-ON-MERSEY.

plated, several rates having to be obtained for that purpose. The accounts of the surveyor at this period contain a list of payments "respecting the great well." This was situated in Well Lane (now Victoria Street), at the corner of Springfield Road, and was a spring of running water, clear as crystal, and from this the inhabitants derived the greatest portion of their supply, although there were two or three other wells in different parts of the town. The "great well" was, however, of some importance, as the amount paid for its repairs to various parties at one time was £13 0s. 4d.

The lands of the poor house were at this time productive; and Mr. Leicester, as trustee, having a balance in his hands "of £16, or thereabouts," it was resolved that he be desired to pay the same to Mr. Robert Twemlow, the overseer, for the use of the poor of Altrincham.

In the course of the next few years the entries of disturbances in the town are more frequent, and in some cases the constables were assaulted. The offenders were invariably ordered to be indicted, after the advice of a magistrate had been sought thereon. Several cases were compromised on their paying certain amounts; entering into recognizances to keep the peace for stated periods, and signing acknowledgments to be "advertised in the public papers," the latter fact indicating that nearly ninety years ago, the press was beginning to be looked upon as a power in the land. Something out of the ordinary course of things occurred in June, 1814, when a public meeting was summoned in hot haste, with the following result :—

"Whereas, several persons made a great noise and disturbance in the town last night, and in several instances did considerable mischief, ordered that the constables do use their best exertions to discover who the parties were, and that they do prosecute them at the expense of the town in case sufficient evidence can be obtained ; and the constables are hereby authorized to give a reward of five guineas to any person or persons who will come forward to give evidence that shall lead to a conviction of the offenders—it being understood that such reward shall be in lieu of that which has been offered by Mr. Salmon and Mr. Lupton this day."

It was just possible that this was the outcome of a drunken frolic in which the participators went much further than they intended. There does not appear to be any payment of any reward made, so that the perpetrators of the mischief escaped scot free.

In 1815 a presentment was made at the Quarter Sessions on the shocking state of the roads in Altrincham A largely attended town's meeting directed the Surveyor to appear and submit to the presentment, and "that he request the attendance of two of the magistrates to view the roads and to approve of the mode to be taken for their amendment, and that Mr. Barratt, Mr. Hardey, Mr. Gratrix Mr. Hugo Worthington, and Mr. Isaac Harrop, with the surveyor, be appointed a committee to meet the magistrates and to advise on the best mode to be taken for the repair of the said roads," &c. This would seem to imply an exhaustion on the part of the town which it has not probably experienced since. Taxes of all descriptions were oppressive, as also were the rates levied for the relief of the poor. The succeeding winter was "a hard one," and a meeting was specially called in December, 1816, to consider the position of affairs. Occasionally it had been found necessary to subscribe for periods of scarcity. The Rev. Oswald Leicester, minister of St. George's Chapel, as it was then termed, presided, and the first resolution affirmed "that the pressure of the times renders it necessary that relief should be extended to the resident poor within the township of Altrincham, in addition to the usual payments from the poor rates." The second resolution gave it as the opinion of the meeting that the best mode of affording such relief would be to provide as much work as possible for such of the poor as were out of employ, "and also by purchasing provisions out of a fund to be raised by public subscription and selling the same to the aforesaid poor at a reduced price, care being taken in avoiding as much as may be those articles of food which are the dearest." Other resolutions provided for the appointment of a committee to superintend the raising and distribution of subscriptions for the employment of the poor "in opening the drains and making good the roads on Hale Moss," and in the repairing of the highways, and each individual in the town was recommended "to create as much employment for the labouring poor as possible." Four years afterwards the canal was frozen over, and on that occasion, as the poor could not pay the high price at which coals were sold which were carted from the pits, the Overseer was authorized to purchase such coals as might be necessary, and to sell them to the poor "at the price of eightpence per hundredweight, taking care that no family do have more than two hundred at one time or within the same week, unless under special circumstances." It will be seen from this that there was no lack of public spirit in the town.

Although at times the authorities having the management of affairs had to be indicted, or threatened with indictment, for not having the footpaths kept in proper repair, there are evidences all through the book of a desire for progress and improvement. Considering the difficulties under which they laboured, it is not to be wondered at that progress was slow. With a small population the burthen thrown on the few was heavy, and often the funds raised by the leys proved inadequate for attaining the object in view. The discretion allowed the officials was such as could not always admit of being wisely exercised, and for some years prior to the formation of a Select Vestry for dealing with the poor, a special committee was appointed to superintend the overseer, investigate his accounts, and to regulate the relief given to the poor. The overseers were ordered to make up their accounts quarterly and lay them before the committee, which was empowered to publish the names of all persons receiving relief in such manner as might be deemed proper. This was only the prelude to a more regularly constituted body, a Select

Vestry, alluded to in the next chapter, which was formed in 1822. Their accounts were settled at different town's meetings. The town progressed to such a degree in the course of a few years that it was enabled to engage a qualified man as surveyor, and the salary of the deputy constable was made up to £30, out of which he had to pay an assistant. The latter portion of the book is taken up almost entirely by records of the proceedings of the Select Vestry, but there are scattered up and down characteristic entries which will be read with interest :—

"7th June, 1796. Ordered that the overseer of the poor with John Burgess's assistance do immediately take an exact inventory of a parcel of gloves, &c., directed for the overseer of Altrincham, and this day produced to the meeting, and that the overseer do take care thereof until he receives further directions from a town's meeting."

"6th December, 1796. Ordered that the overseer do advertise the parcel of gloves in his hands suppos'd to be the property of Mr. Thomas Taylor, and if not owned, that he dispose of them for the town's use."

"23rd July, 1797. Ordered that Aaron Brundrett be directed to sell a quantity of gloves now in his hands, supposed to belong to Thomas Taylor, now in the poor house, and that he place the produce to the credit of ye town in his accounts."

"29th April, 1802. Ordered that James Potter having in his hands as a former constable 16s. 1d., he do pay over ye same to the overseer of the poor.—Ordered that as the late constables have applied to John Leigh Esq., respecting their accounts, that Mr. Leicester, Mr. Hardey and Mr. Burgess be requested to wait on Mr. Leigh to state what they know respecting their accounts and do get Mr. Leigh to settle the same.—Ordered that in future the constables do not collect money by a ley, but that orders be made at town's meetings upon the overseer for what money may be proper for the constables."

7th June, 1803. Resolved that the constables be directed to take the necessary steps to apprehend any person who may be guilty of tearing or pulling from the Court House any proclamations or papers affixed thereto by or by order of the constables."

"21st April, 1807. Resolved that the thanks of the meeting be given to Mr. Robert Twemlow for his essential services to the township as overseer of the poor for four years past, and that he be requested to instruct Thomas Bradbury in the said office, and that Thomas Bradbury be allowed for the ensuing year the salary of ten pounds, and that it shall depend upon his activity and good conduct in his office, whether he shall be allowed a further sum of five pounds, or not and that Mr. Twemlow is not to have any salary."

"8th June, 1813. The overseers having laid before this meeting the accounts of the expenses of providing two substitutes in the Cheshire militia in the place of Ballantine and Parker, to whose families large sums were payable weekly by this township, which expenses and the bounty paid to the substitutes amount to ninety-one pounds and eightpence, towards which Mr. Twemlow has advanced the sum of £79 2s. 8d., ordered that the overseers be allowed the said expenses in his accounts, and that he do repay to Mr. Twemlow the money advanced by him with interest thereon until the same shall be repaid."

"15th July, 1813. John Boardman having proposed to make a new sundial on the Court House upon a mahogany inchboard for two pounds ten shillings, and to be inspected when done by any competent judge, and if defective in any respect, nothing to be paid for it, ordered that John Boardman's proposal be accepted."

"31st January, 1814. It appearing that one man is wanted for this town in the Royal Congleton Regiment of Local Militia, ordered that the constable do provide a substitute, provided one can be obtained for two guineas, which the overseer is hereby directed to pay."

"1816. Agreed at a public town's meeting held this ninth day of December, 1816, in the Court House, Altrincham, . . . that such persons within the said township, who are liable to be balloted for to-morrow, to serve in the militia, and who shall subscribe ten shillings a piece, to be deposited in the hands of Mr. William Ashley, to be applied by him, with the assistance of Mr. Nathaniel Pass, in hiring substitutes for such of the said subscribers of ten shillings a piece, as may then be balloted, shall be freed from any further sums on that account; and that the surplus money, if any, wanted to hire such substitutes of ten shillings a piece shall be paid by the overseers of the poor, and be allowed by them in their accounts."

"5th February, 1822. It having been stated to this meeting that the surveyors of the highways are repairing with hard material the back lane leading from the Navigation Inn to Jeremy's o' th' Brook, ordered that the surveyors are hereby instructed not to proceed in repairing that road with hard materials."

"23rd April, 1822. It is the unanimous opinion of this meeting that it is expedient to appoint a select vestry for managing the concerns of the poor of this township, pursuant to the provisions of the 59th George the Third, chapter 12."

"18th May, 1824. At a public meeting of the inhabitants of the township of Altrincham, held in the Court House, for the purpose of considering the best means of putting a stop to the alarming increase of mad dogs in this neighbourhood, and which meeting was convened by public notices affixed upon public places within the town, and also by proclamation by the bellman . . . . resolved that in the opinion of this meeting that all dogs kept by the inhabitants of Altrincham should not be permitted to go at large, but kept confined within the buildings or yards of the owners until the first

September next, and that all dogs found at large after due notice subsequent to this day and until first September next should be destroyed."

There are two other volumes of minute books, one of which is taken up entirely by the proceedings of the Select Vestry, and the other by the operations of the inspectors under the Lighting and Watching Act, both of which will be found referred to in the next chapter.

CHAPTER XIV.

Description of Altrincham and Bowdon 60 years ago—The old Market Place ; its ancient cross, lock-ups, and star chamber—Higher Town boys v. those of Lower Town—The town field—An Altrincham Carnival—The loyalty of the town—The first Altrincham undertaker—Altrincham woolcombers and their Bishop Blaize festival—Bowdon bull baiters, and Altrincham cockfighters—Salt works at Dunham—The destruction of small birds—The churchwardens and their duties—Formation of the Altrincham Poor Law Union ; the old workhouse and its management—Cutting of the Bowdon line—Lloyd's Hospital—Introduction of coal gas into Altrincham—Formation of the Gas Company ; negotiations for the purchase of the works and their results—Altrincham and Bowdon Literary Institution ; the Altrincham and Bowdon Local Boards ; Free Library and Technical Schools—Royal Visit—Altrincham Parliamentary Division, members past and present ; the Electric Light, &c.

THIS chapter opens with a sketch of Altrincham and Bowdon half a century or so ago. The reader will therefore take a walk with us in imagination, while some of their peculiarities are described. Meeting, say, in the old Market Place, we find that it is called the Market Place still, though most of its landmarks have disappeared. In the centre formerly stood a small "public," known to posterity as the Roundabout House ; and almost under its shadow were the old lock-ups, or dungeon, through the barred windows of which the prisoners confined therein could be seen. These unfortunates were objects of great curiosity to the children, who, with bated breath and timid mien, peered in at them on their way to school ; while to their intimate friends they were the objects of much tender solicitude, as they frequently received, through the medium of pipes and straws, surreptitious supplies of beverages, which were supposed to lighten the gloom of their prison house, and raise their spirits for the hour of trial. Those more favoured by wealth and position, who might by mischance come within the clutches of the local Dogberry, could, by the judicious bestowal of a small sum, avail themselves of the privileges of the "star chamber," which was an upstairs room in an adjacent publichouse, and where they could have the creature comforts they required. Usually, the zealous constable removed the clothes of the prisoners while confined in the "star chamber;" but they in some cases have been known to effect their escape in the garb which nature provided for man in his state of innocency, to the great consternation of the not overwatchful gaoler. Near the lock-ups were the stocks, an old form of punishment which might be revived to advantage in some cases in the present day; and near this again was the ancient Market Cross, which was approached by five or six stone steps, similar to those in the other market towns of Cheshire. This cross stood for about 100 years after having been "rebuilt and made new" in 1730, by order of the Right Hon. George, Earl of Warrington, who gave five pounds towards this object. On pain of a fine of 3s. 4d., all sellers of cheese and butter were compelled to bring their produce to the Cross before selling, and no shopkeeper or forestaller was, in any instance, to buy any in his or her shop, and not at the Cross before two o'clock in the day, when the townsfolk had supplied their wants. Shopkeepers have been fined for breaches of this regulation, and others ordered to be indicted at the sessions. But roundabout house, lock-ups, stocks, and cross are all gone. The old lock-ups were succeeded by a more secure building, in George Street (now used as a meeting house) which, in its turn, gave place to the more convenient and conspicuous edifice in Dunham Road.

Church Street took its name from the fact of St. George's Church being built in the vicinity; and a little way down were the Town Fields. These fields were then more appropriately named, as they were used for a variety of purposes. Here the youthful sons of Altrincham met to settle their little differences. They were divided into two factions—Higher Town boys and

Lower Town boys—and they were animated with deadly animosity, the battles royal which often ensued being long and loudly contested. It was in the immediate neighbourhood, too, some 60 or 70 years ago, that an outburst of loyalty worthy of the good old town took place. It occurred at a time when Wellington had driven the French out of the Peninsula, and Napoleon had been overthrown by the allies at the battle of Leipsic. A town's meeting was called, and it was the unanimous opinion that a—

General rejoicing should take place in consequence of the recent glorious news and the present state of public affairs, and at the adjournment of this meeting it be considered what mode shall be adopted for that purpose, so as to give the most general joy and satisfaction.

At the adjournment it was decided that—

A subscription be opened for a bon-fire and fireworks, on the evening of Monday next, in the Bowling Green field; and that Mr. Race, Mr. Collier, Mr. Reddish, and Mr. Barratt be requested to undertake the management of them, with the assistance of the constables; and that the bon-fire be lighted at five o'clock in the evening and be extinguished at ten o'clock, and that the fireworks begin at seven o'clock.

That a public dinner be held at the Bowling Green Inn, on Monday next, at two o'clock, for which tickets shall be taken at 12s. each, on or before Saturday next, and that Mr. Race, Mr. Collier, Mr. Reddish and Mr. Barratt be requested to undertake the management of the dinner.

That a subscription be now opened for the purposes aforesaid (exclusive of the dinner), and be paid to Mr. Barrett, with whom the paper shall be left for further subscriptions.

That the Rev. Oswald Leicester be requested to take the chair at the dinner.

The town was justly entitled to celebrate this red-letter epoch in our country's history in a manner befiting the occasion. It had always done its duty loyally. So early as 1796 we find the inhabitants meeting in pursuance of an Act of Parliament for "raising a certain number of men in the several counties in England for the service of His Majesty's army and navy." Altrincham had to provide, jointly with Agden, three men; and it was decided that a general subscription should be entered into for the relief of any poor man who might be drawn in the ballot, the balance required being paid out of the town's rates. Any person not entering the subscription was not entitled to any relief. In 1803, seven men were required, "five and a half" from Altrincham and "one and a half" from Ashley. Five men were hired at a cost of £25 18s. 6d. each, and two by John Mills and John Barratt at a cost of £21 10s. each. Towards the total amount, Ashley paid £36 19s. 10½d., John Mills and John Barratt £43, and Altrincham the balance. In some towns each person had to find a substitute out of his own purse, or go to the wars himself; so that in this town a very sensible course was adopted whereby the rich came to the aid of their less favoured brethren. The lieges of Altrincham thoroughly enjoyed themselves on the occasion, the ends of several barrels being knocked in, in order that the beer might the more readily be got at, and become the means of diffusing "general joy and satisfaction." The Bowling Green Inn has long since been converted into a private dwelling.

Returning to the town proper, the visitor would have looked for Stamford Street in vain. The site was covered with gardens. A short cut into Lower Town was effected by means of a narrow roadway near, known as the "Hollow Bonk" or Bank; but the thoroughfare was by Windy harbour (afterwards called King Street, then High Street, finally Market Street), and down Shaw's Lane. In those days news had to be carried by post chaise, and it was no uncommon thing for the shafts of some rapidly driven vehicle to be sent into the door of one of the large mansions in Market Street in the attempt to get into Church Street. It was not until a fatal accident occurred that the more direct route into Dunham Road was made by Brooks' Bank. Pursuing our way through the "narrows" and down Shaw's Lane we arrive in George Street, then a cobble or kidney paved length, containing a number of thatched cottages and two or three farm houses. What is now Moss Lane was then styled Ham Lane. Lower down was Well Street, so called from a large well which was situated near the Literary Institution, and from which the inhabitants pumped a portion of their daily supply of water.

The Malt Shovels Inn was a barn, and the not very salubrious region of Police Street is still familiarly known as back o'th' barn.

Retracing our steps into George Street, we pass Beggar's Square, which consisted of one or two neat-looking white-washed cottages. A little higher up was a farm house, the occupier of which has some claim to the notice of posterity. He was named Michael Drinkwater, and may fairly be set on a pedestal of his own as the first Altrincham undertaker! He had three horses— Bobbie, Mettle, and Boxer, and he very generously gave the services, when required, of one of these valuable quadrupeds to draw the parish hearse, the only one which the town possessed— to Bowdon. "Goose green," as the name will imply, was formerly the assembling place for numerous flocks of these toothsome creatures, which were allowed to roam at large on Hale Moss, and the feeding of which formed a very profitable branch of business to several of the inhabitants.

The mention of business leads us to digress a little to describe a custom once kept up in Altrincham, but which, like many others, has long since died out. This is the festival of St. Blaise, or more properly Blasius, and it will enable us to realize to some extent the meaning of the phrase we meet with in directories that "Altrincham formerly enjoyed a considerable trade in woollen yarn." St. Blasius was a bishop of Sebaste, in Armenia, and suffered martyrdom A.D. 316. He is the patron saint of the craft of woolcombers, and his name was once considered potent in curing sore throats. There were a large number of woolcombers in Altrincham, some of the masters employing as many as 30 men, and the Bishop Blaise festival was often celebrated with great splendour. The procession was headed by a band of music, and, surrounded by guards, were a King and a Queen, Jason, and the Princess Medea, the principal figure being the Bishop himself, furnished with a pastoral crook, and attended by his chaplain. Following these were shepherds, shepherdesses, swains attired in bright green, and woolcombers wearing old-fashioned and full-flowing wigs of combed wool. At some convenient point, a piece written for the occasion was recited to the following effect :—

> Hail to the day, whose kind auspicious rays,
> Deigned first to smile on famous Bishop Blaize !
> To the great author of our combing trade
> This day's devoted, and due honours paid ;
> To him whose fame Britain's isle resounds,—
> To him whose goodness to the poor abounds.
> Long shall his name in British annals shine,
> And grateful ages offer at his shrine !
> By this, our trade, are thousands daily fed,
> By it supplied with means to earn their bread.
> In various forms our trade its works imparts ;
> In different methods and by different arts
> Prevents from starving, indigents distressed ;
> As combers, spinners, weavers and the rest.
> We boast no gems, nor costly garments vain,
> Borrowed from India or the coast of Spain ;
> Our native soil with wool our trade supplies,
> While foreign countries envy us the prize.
> No foreign broil our common good annoys,
> Our country's product all our art employs ;
> Our fleecy flocks abound in every vale,
> Our bleating lambs proclaim the joyful tale.
> So let not Spain with us attempt to vie,
> Nor India's wealth pretend to soar so high ;
> Nor Jason pride him in his Colchian spoil,
> By hardship gained and enterprising toil :
> Since Britons all with ease attain the prize,
> And every hill resounds with golden cries.
> To celebrate our founder's great renown
> Our shepherd and our shepherdess we crown ;
> For England's commerce, and for George's sway,
> Each loyal subject give a loud Huzza !

Bishop Blaise is remembered by few, and machinery has superseded hand combing, and has long had the best of the race.

Having disposed of our friends the woolcombers, we pass on, and leaving Goose Green come to the Cock Ring near to Denmark-street, where on Shrove Tuesday and at Easter the people of Altrincham "enjoyed" the game of cock fighting. Pinfold Brow is now Lloyd Street ; and Ashley Road was but a lane from which an uninterrupted view of the country to Hale

Carr could be obtained. At the foot of the Downs was an old white house surrounded by a large garden, called the Dog Kennels, where a pack of harriers was kept. By way of the Downs, where the first houses were built (near the entrance to New Street,) by Manchester merchants, who were not slow to discover the advantages of this suburban retreat, we pass Turf Lane, now St. Margaret's Road, and reach the aristocratic Firs, then familiarly known as "Burying Lane," with its projecting trees forming an umbrageous avenue on either side, through which the old church of Bowdon could be seen in the distance. Up this roadway, which a cart could scarcely pass over, once rumbled the old stage coach, the sand trickled down its sides, and the children from the town resorted thither for the purpose of gathering the blackberries, which grew in tempting profusion in the thick hedgerows. One or two of its splendid fir trees still remain, but their gradual disappearance and the more modernised style which prevails has robbed what was once a lovely picture of its arcadian simplicity.

In a field near the Firs races were held at Wakes time, in which women took an active part. A common prize was a smock or shift, and in a programme of Bowdon Wakes published in the early part of the century there occurred the following:— "The same day a race for a good holland smock by ladies of all ages, the second best to have a handsome satin ribbon. No lady will be allowed to strip any further than the smock before starting." There must surely have been a good deal of competition to have rendered such a rule necessary, to say the least of it. While cock fighting was congenial to Altrincham, bull baiting was the recognised pastime at Bowdon. A noble tree which formerly stood in front of the Griffin Inn, has at times had its branches crowded with venturesome spectators, who gazed with great delight on the scene below. There, tied to a stake, was the poor animal, and forming a circle round it were men with ferocious bull dogs, which were let loose upon it. The dog which oftenest "pinned" the bull, that is gripped it until it went down

ALTRINCHAM IN THE JUBILEE YEAR; VISIT OF THE PRINCE OF WALES.

on its knees bellowing with agony, was awarded the palm of victory—a brass collar. It was owing to the efforts of one of Bowdon's good Vicars, the Rev. Jas. T. Law, that the brutal custom was abolished.

There will be little difficulty in distinguishing Higher from Lower Bowdon; and Stamford Road is still well-known as Sandy Lane; but few will remember Heald or Yeald Common, near Heald Road, with a sheet of water in the centre, while fewer still will recognize Bowdon Moss, as being only a stone's throw of the splendid College near Langham Road, and where within a few years many specimens of bog oak have been found. These specimens are in an excellent state of preservation, and the then possessor of a quantity, (the late) Mr. Eli Morgan, of Stamford Cottage, had it made up into two neat hall chairs, which were shown at one of the exhibitions of works of art, &c., held in Altrincham. Rose Hill was then a play-ground for the Bowdon children, and Richmond Hill was unknown. Having made a fair circuit, which will enable the reader to form an idea of the rustic appearance of the place at that period, we proceed to deal with other matters associated with its rise and progress.

Salt works once existed at Dunham Massey, where there is probably one of those isolated springs of brine which are to be found in some formations in different parts of the country, and which, so far as the brine is concerned, is as strong as that at Northwich or Winsford. Those who know the dreary aspect imparted to the face of nature by the establishment of these works, leaving out of the question the damage to property by subsidence, will scarcely crave for active operations in this district.

This period, too, was the one when farmers looked upon small birds as determined enemies to their crops; and the small boys of the place received a large amount in the way of head money the constable awarding certain sums for sparrows and for eggs. Sometimes this was done by proxy, as at one of the public town's meetings,—

> It was ordered that the constables do pay out of the constable rates, such sums of money as may be paid by Mr. Leicester for sparrows killed and brought to him, and that he be allowed to pay such sums for sparrows as he may think proper and necessary.

While the small boys were busy with the birds, the churchwardens on Sundays were busy with the boys, or rather with the loiterers, who preferred the public-house to the church. These functionaries were often seen with their staves of office to issue from the sacred fold, and drive any wandering sheep in For this purpose they scrupulously searched the public-houses, and there are cynics in the present day mean enough to insinuate that this was not their only object.

The Altrincham Union for Poor Law purposes was formed in 1835. For a long time prior to this attempts had been made to deal with the constantly increasing pauperism of the country. The system of out-door relief had led to oppressive poor rates. For Altrincham, the workhouse was situated at Broadheath, having been built in 1756. This was carried on for a great number of years under the direction of trustees, although the inhabitants in public meeting appeared to influence their course of procedure to a great extent. At times there were sinister rumours as to its management, and on one occasion several gentlemen were appointed to make an investigation. They reported "that the woman who acts as governess says she is well acquainted with every article received into the house. She says all in the house have great plenty of what is good and useful, they have butchers' meat three times a week; that which was in the house was very good, and so also was the butter. The bread is very good, and the gentlemen so appointed are fully satisfied that the provisions are good and sufficient." In 1822 a Select Vestry was formed in Altrincham, and the administration of the Poor Law progressed another stage. In their first report the members express considerable satisfac-

tion that they have reduced the amount paid in relief. They indulge in a hope that a still further reduction will be made, and that the sentiments of honest independence by which the poor of this country were once characterised will gradually revive amongst them; and "that their own exertions, aided by the occasional advice and assistance of their richer neighbours" (a nice way of putting a pauperizing principle) "will always remain their surest support in the hour of distress and sickness." This pleasant piece of moonshine is concluded by an appeal to the members of the Select Vestry to attend in large numbers for the future. In the course of the following year the business of manufacturing was commenced at the workhouse at Broadheath, when five looms were started, and the net earnings which accrued in this way and the labour of one of the inmates reached the sum of £20 15s. in about five months. "In a word," continues the report (this was the second issued), "the workhouse promises under good management to be a source of profit to the township; and as none of the inmates who are capable of work are suffered to be idle, but, on the contrary, are encouraged to be industrious, the hope may be entertained, that should the number of them increase, the advantage will be augmented in the same proportion." The accounts for this period, therefore, show an indiscriminate mixture of warps and weft, of healds, and shafts and shuttles, with buttermilk, salt, smocks and frocks, and crockery; but in spite of these glowing accounts, there was, not many years afterwards, a rate of three shillings in the pound laid for Poor Law purposes, the assessment of the town at this time being £3,500. Probably the expenditure was greatly reduced in subsequent years; for in an abstract of the receipts and payments concerning the workhouse of the township of Altrincham in 1831, the expenditure for 30 weeks is given at £52 1s. 4d. Another entry shows the average number of inmates to have been 14 1-15, the cost of victualling per week 1s. 6½d, clothing 1s. 8½d.; and these, with other incidental expenses, made a total of 3s. 5½d. per head per week. For this amount, as we have already seen, the paupers were allowed the

AA

luxury of "flesh mate," as butcher's meat is spelled in the accounts, three times a week. Speaking of "flesh mate" reminds us that on one occasion the visitors appointed by the Vestry were directed to purchase a piece of beef, not exceeding 12 pounds, to be sent down to the workhouse for a feast on New Year's Day, "and that a glass of ale be allowed to such of the inmates as the governor may think fit to allow such an indulgence."

For some time, however, matters did not work smoothly in local bumbledom. The governor, notwithstanding his numerous privileges and handsome salary (£10 a year) was a man of hasty temper, as governors of the old stamp are said by tradition to have been. At one of the meetings of the select vestry, Mr. John Lupton informed his fellow members that he had been grossly insulted by the governor who had threatened to strike him! Such conduct could not of course be permitted. He was ordered to appear before them, and produced Mr. John Warren, who, he said, was fully acquainted with the circumstances. Mr. Warren, however, knew nothing of the matter, beyond that the governor was in a state of "extreme intoxication" at the time. The tables being thus unexpectedly turned, the governor admitted what was said to be correct, and added that "he did not know how the thing began or ended," and having apologized, his offence was overlooked.

But this governor was soon in greater difficulties than ever. At a meeting held on the 21st May, 1828, the overseer of the poor intimated that the governess of the workhouse had fled, "taking her clothes with her, that her husband does not know where she has gone, or whether she means to return." The vestry was very accommodating. The overseer was directed "to keep an eye to the workhouse," the governor in the meantime to go in search of his runaway spouse,—if he should feel so inclined. Whether he departed on this mission or not does not appear; but a week afterwards it is reported that the governess has not yet returned, "nor is there any probability she will return." This was more than the vestry could submit to. The governor was instantly discharged, and when appointing a successor great cautiousness was evinced, inasmuch as it was stipulated that if the new governor and governess did not come up to expectation, they would be expected to quit the house and give up the situation in a month. They gave satisfaction; for soon afterwards it was " Resolved that this meeting is of opinion that the governor of the workhouse be allowed to occupy and use one of the looms in the weaving shop for the purpose of weaving in himself, and that he be allowed to take to his own the earnings therefrom, he having requested that such liberty should be allowed to him."

We will now draw a veil over the difficulties of the Select Vestry in respect of workhouse management; and on turning to the outdoor system, we find it was not distinguished by that economy which is usually looked for. The rents of different parties were paid, and to such an extent was this carried, that on several occasions it became a question of compounding with the landlords in a body. This was not, however, confined to the town. The overseers had often to go great distances to extricate Altrincham men and women, who were unable to meet their engagements. The entries, too, are sometimes mysterious. For instance, the Government Auditor now-a-days would probably require to have the meaning of the following fully explained:—

Resolved, upon the application of (name given) that a donation of £3 be made to him to enable him to liberate himself from some difficulty under which it appears to this meeting he is at present labouring.

For some time after the formation of the Union, the meetings of the Guardians were held at Altrincham, which place was considered the most central and convenient, and from this circumstance the Union obtained its name. Difficulties, however, arose, more particularly in the acquisition of a proper site for the Union Workhouse which was ultimately built at Knutsford. Altrincham is represented by five Guardians; Bowdon and Dunham Massey by two each. In March, 1895, the name was changed from Altrincham to Bucklow. The Rural Sanitary

Authority was formed in August, 1872, and was created the Bucklow Rural District Council in 1895, Mr. Wm. Hough, J.P. being the first chairman.

In 1842, the chartists or "Levellers" paid a visit to Altrincham. In order to prevent a descent on Dunham Hall, the Earl of Stamford of that time ordered several barrels of beer, cheese, and baskets of bread, to be placed on the fringe of the Park, near the present Green Walk gate, which good things the rioters eagerly consumed. In Stamford Street, where Mr. John Siddeley now resides there was a ladies' boarding school, the mistress concealed all her valuables and the greatest part of her money, only keeping a few shillings at hand; she dressed herself in clothes which belonged to her cook, and when the rioters came to the school and demanded money &c., she gave them the trifle she had by her, and pleaded that she had a very hard mistress, who gave her but scanty wages, and so escaped any further loss, the servants and several of the boarders had to turn out their pockets and contents of their boxes.

In July, 1845, the Act for making the Manchester, South Junction, and Altrincham Railway was passed. It authorized the raising of £400,000 (£133,333 by loans) for a length of nine miles thirty chains. By this Act the Manchester, Sheffield, and Lincolnshire Railway Company were authorised to subscribe £175,000, and subsequently the same Company, in conjunction with the London and North-Western Railway Company, purchased the Earl of Ellesmere's original share in the South Junction and Altrincham line—the Earl undertaking to stop the plying of the "swift" passenger boat on the Bridgewater Canal, when the railway was opened. Hitherto this packet boat had formed the only means of "swift"—as it was certainly thought then—communication with Manchester, and judging from the remarks made at that time concerning the canal, which was described as "black and filthy," winding like some huge snake amongst the meadows, emitting an exceedingly offensive and noisome stench, the formation of the new line would no doubt be hailed with joy and gladness. The railway is divided into two portions, the South Junction line and the Altrincham line. The first-named is one and three quarter miles in length, commencing at London-road Station, curving from west to east along the south side of the town, and connects every railway, having its terminus in Manchester, the one with the other. Ground for the construction of both lines was broken near Knott Mill, about six months after the passing of the Act, but for a period of a year and a half the works were paralysed, chiefly owing to want of funds, the commercial crisis, and the state of the money market. The line was, however, opened on July 20th, 1849, for both goods and passenger traffic. The Altrincham line proper, with which we are more immediately concerned, commences in Castle Field, about 200 or 300 yards from the Knott Mill Station. Here it diverges from the South Junction line, passing through Castle Field close to the canal, and goes under the Altrincham turnpike-road to Old Trafford by a slightly curved tunnel, the only one on the line of 1,144 yards in length. After leaving Old Trafford, which is just two miles from Oxford Road, the lines pursues a straight and nearly level course until Edge Lane, or what is now better known as Stretford Station, is reached. Hence the line is carried through the level vale of the Mersey; and Sale, Brooklands and Timperley Stations appear in succession. At that time Altrincham, just eight miles distant from Oxford Road, was the terminal station of the line. It was afterwards carried on to near the foot of the Downs, and although the station is called Bowdon Station, it is really in the Township of Altrincham, and nearly one mile distant from Bowdon Church. The first train from Altrincham left the station at eight o'clock, July 20th, 1849, with 65 passengers, and notwithstanding a delay of several minutes at Stretford, reached Oxford Road Station before nine o'clock! The next train, which was the express, left Altrincham at 8-40, contained 15 passengers, all first-class, and accomplished the eight miles in 18 minutes. The next train, at nine a.m., reached Oxford Road within the half-hour with 40 passengers.

This was all done in face of the formidable competition of a number of omnibusses. Since then, considerable modifications have been made; and the Bowdon line, as it is now familiarly called, ranks as one of the best managed in the kingdom. The present Altrincham and Bowdon Station was opened in April, 1881.

Prominent among the charities of the town, and probably the most beneficial to the inhabitants, although not the most ancient, is Lloyd's Fever Hospital. The poor and afflicted we have with us always, and there is a large amount of human suffering which has to be dealt with promptly, or the common weal might suffer. Mr. Edward Jeremiah Lloyd, of Oldfield Hall, was a practical philanthropist. He left by will a certain sum for the purpose of erecting and endowing a hospital for the reception and benefit of the poor inhabitants of Altrincham and Bowdon afflicted with fever or other diseases of an infectious or contagious nature. This hospital was erected on a site on Hale Moss given by the Earl of Stamford and Warrington, the total cost being £600. The land and buildings were vested in 12 trustees, of which the Earl of Stamford, for the time being, is one, new trustees being appointed as occasion requires. After doing excellent work for a long period, it was in 1878 handed over to the Altrincham Local Board for a term of 21 years, at a rent of £50 a year. The trustees bound themselves to contribute a sum not exceeding one-half the clear income of the said charity in aid of the funds of the hospital, this, however, being conditional on the hospital being carried on by the Local Board to their satisfaction. The residue of the income was to be applied, under conditions, in aid of the funds of any well-established Infirmary, Hospital, or Institution, including the Altrincham Provident Dispensary, treating cases of accident, or receiving convalescent patients.

The Altrincham Provident Dispensary, of which notice is taken in the preceding paragraph, is a valuable auxiliary to the Fever Hospital. It was erected out of funds accruing from the Altrincham Workhouse Charity. This charity arose out of an indenture of grant dated 22nd December, 1755, between the Right Honourable George, Earl of Warrington, on the one part, and various residents of the town on the other part, which recites that a certain piece of ground (being part of the waste in Altrincham) called Broadheath, belonging to the said Earl of Warrington, as Lord of the Manor of Altrincham, and containing 4½ acres of land, Cheshire measure, or 8½ acres, statute measure, had, with the consent of the said Earl, been enclosed, in order that a workhouse for the said borough or manor might be built on part thereof, by voluntary contributions or otherwise, the residue of the said ground being improved for the benefit of the said poor. The Earl consented to vest this land in certain parties for ever, paying a yearly rent of 5s., upon trust; the workhouse or poorhouse as soon as built to be used by the overseers of the poor, for the poor of the town of Altrincham. In 1831 these premises became by deed vested in John Mort, Edward Jeremiah Lloyd, Isaac Harrop, Hugo Worthington, Charles Poole, John Barratt, and John Mort, junior; and a portion of the land, about two acres in extent, was sold to the Warrington and Stockport Railway Co. for £2,243 10s. 10d, which was invested under an order in Chancery in the purchase of £2,343 2s. 8d. Three per cent. Consuls. A building had been constructed on the land, and was for a long period used as a workhouse for the poor of Altrincham, and the rents and profits of the residue of the waste ground were applied in accordance with the trust. The premises were subsequently converted into cottages, and occupied by the workmen employed by the Bridgewater Trustees. Great public apathy existed in reference to this Charity and its application, but in 1858 a committee of the Altrincham Ratepayers' Association, of which Mr. Thomas Partington was the honorary secretary, addressed certain communications to the overseers, and after a long correspondence, in which the assistance of the Charity Commissioners was invoked, in July, 1860, a scheme was drawn up for the application of the income, or a sufficient part thereof, to the establishment and maintenance of baths and washhouses;

the remainder of the annual income not required for these purposes to be given for the benefit of *deserving resident* poor of the parish. The Vice-Chancellor approved of the establishment of baths and washhouses; but no such buildings were erected, owing to legal difficulties arising, which need not be discussed here. Most of the Trustees having in the meantime retired or died, new trustees were appointed, who set to work with determination, and the result was the erection of the Provident Dispensary as being most likely to be of the greatest use to the poorer inhabitants of the township. The foundation stone of the new building was laid in September, 1869; in a cavity being deposited a document, of which the following is a copy :—

The corner stone of this Dispensary and Hospital, erected by the Trustees of the Altrincham Workhouse Charity, under the sanction of the High Court of Chancery, was laid by Henry Hall, Esquire, the agent of the Right Honourable the Earl of Stamford and Warrington, the Lord of the Manor of Altrincham, on Tuesday the 28th day of September, A.D., 1869, in the year of the Mayoralty of James Southern, Esquire; trustees, Samuel Barratt, (chairman), Joseph Gaskarth, John Davenport, Matthew Fowden, William Greenwood, John Astle Kelsall, William Hill Parkes, John Balshaw, John Shelmerdine Mort, ; treasurer, Thomas Riley Knight; secretary, Charles Heaton Hinde; law clerks, Nicholls, Sudlow and Hinde; architect, Peter Pons; chief contractor, John Douglas; sub-contractors, Humphrey Davies, brickwork, Isaac Drinkwater, stonework, and Charles Walton, plumbing, glazing, &c.

The institution has its main front to Bowdon Road or Market Street, and has a most imposing appearance.

The yearly allowance of £5 from Dame Elizabeth Booth's charity has been already noticed. There are two or three other bread charities in the district: John Barratt, Esquire, left, by will, £200 to be invested, and the dividend to be given in bread to such of the poor people of Altrincham as attended Divine service at St. George's Church; and William Chapman, of Hale, in 1714, charged an estate in Hale with a yearly rent charge of £2, payable to the churchwardens at Christmas, to be laid out in the purchase of bread for the poor of Bowdon parish, for ever, respect being had to the poor of Hale especially, to be given to the poor every Sunday for ever. Robert Twemlow, of Altrincham, in

1826, left £100 to the Vicar and churchwardens in rather a different way. He directed that the interest should be "laid out in the purchase of threepenny loaves, to be made of sound household flour, and to be distributed on each Sacrament Sunday." The sum of £267, left by George Norman (£40), Edward Leigh, Esq. (£100), Mrs. Mary Booth (£5), River Bellfontaine (£11), Joseph Walton (£40), the Earl of Stamford (£52 10s.), and others (£19), was invested in Three per Cents., and the annual income is expended in the purchase of bread and distributed weekly, on every Sunday, among the poor of the parish of Bowdon, by the churchwardens for the time being. Mrs. Holland also gave a certain sum for bread to be distributed amongst the poor attending St. George's Church. Cooper's charity arises out of a house and land at Partington, given in 1807, the clear rent being distributed, on every Christmas Day, yearly amongst such of the poor householders or inhabitants of Altrincham, 50 years old and upwards, as the Vicar of Bowdon, the Minister of St. George's, the warden or wardens of the said chapel, and the owner of Délahey's farm in Timperley for the time being, should appoint. Each poor person was not to have more than 40s. and not less than 20s., and it is generally distributed in money to the recipients. The Earl of Warrington left in 1754 the sum of £5,000, the annual proceeds to be yearly for ever applied in placing out poor children, in the parish of Bowdon, apprentices, or for sending them to school, or for the clothing of them, or for the clothing or other relief of aged or infirm poor inhabitants of the said parish. The application is restricted to these charitable purposes only, particular regard being had to the township of Dunham, and to such chiefly as do not receive relief from the overseers of the poor. The sum of £5,610 2s. belonging to this charity has for a long period been invested in the Three per Cent. Reduced Bank Annuities, and the interest received is distributed by such Trustees as the possessor of Dunham Massey from time to time appoints. In the years 1813 and 1816, Sarah and Elizabeth Cooke, of Altrincham, by will, gave £200 to the officiating clergyman and wardens of St. George's, and to the Vicar and churchwardens of Bowdon, to be invested, and the dividends applied half to the poor, and half to the education of poor children in the Sunday Schools upon a Sunday. If the Sunday Schools in Bowdon or Altrincham are discontinued, then the whole goes to the poor. The sum of £2 per annum, left by the Rev. John Ashton, of Calton Green, Staffordshire, in 1722, is payable to and is distributed by the overseers of the poor of Altrincham amongst the poorest inhabitants of that township. A like rent charge of £2 per annum is paid in aid as a subscription by the overseers to Bowdon Parish schools for the teaching of so many poor children, inhabitants of Altrincham, as the Vicar of Bowdon shall think fit. A rather peculiar charity is that by which the interest on the sum of £110 is applied as follows :—£1 10s. to the Sunday School at Altrincham ; £1 to the Sunday School at Carrington ; £1 to be distributed in religious books in Carrington and Partington ; and the remainder in Bibles and Common Prayer Books to be given among the poor of Bowdon parish as the owner of Dunham Massey may think proper, pursuant to the will of George Cooke, dated 9th November, 1790.

An important epoch in the town's history was the introduction of coal gas, in the year 1844, by Mr. George Massey, the then landlord of the Unicorn Hotel, who put down a small works near the present bowling green. It must not be inferred, however, that there had been no previous attempt at lighting the town. In 1832 the Lighting and Watching Act was adopted, and what has been derisively called the "Charlie" system came into vogue. There had been watchmen before, no doubt, as there had been great men before Agamemnon ; but henceforth they were to be invested with more official dignity. They were to be provided with large "blue coats, with red collars;" they were to carry "lanthorns," and were ordered to call the hours of the night when on duty. A public subscription set up oil lamps, and watch boxes, in the latter of which it is no fiction to state—for the minutes oft record it—the watchmen enjoyed many a comfortable sleep. At times the calling of the hours was voted a nuisance. It appears to have been finally dispensed with in 1852, the watch boxes having been removed four years previously. The first public gas lamp was put up outside the Unicorn Hotel; and Mr. William Walton, then a town's constable, but for many years the respected station master at Bowdon old station, lighted it amid the most intense excitement on the part of the townspeople. The superiority of the new light being made manifest, measures were taken for supplying gas on a more extended scale; and in March, 1846, the Altrincham Gas Co. was registered with a capital of £4,000, in 800 shares of £5 each. This Company purchased the existing establishment; but as it was totally inadequate to their requirements, the Directors chose the present site on Hale Moss, then nearly half a mile from the nearest inhabited part of the town, as being the least objectionable. The new works were opened on the 29th May, 1847; and the price of gas at that time was ten shillings per thousand feet. Three years afterwards it was reduced to 8s. 4d., which was said by the Local Government Inspector, at an enquiry concerning a Local Board, to be much above the average charge for gas in other towns; and his report embodied a suggestion that the Local Board, when formed, should treat for the purchase of the Gas Works, in order that they might be managed for the benefit of the ratepayers generally. Efforts were made from time to time with this object in view; but in each instance have they proved futile. In 1871 there appeared to be some probability of a successful issue, the price named being £57,000; but at a town's meeting held in July, 1871, a resolution was passed by a large majority that no further action be taken. In 1872, several interviews took place between the Local Board and the Gas Company's directors, and an offer was made to them of £52,000 or £13 per share for 4,000 shares; the directors offering to sell at £55,000. They had, in the first instance, named £60,000 as the sum, but subsequently they reduced this to £54,000. The difference of £2,000 was the rock upon which the affair collapsed. Firmness to their limits was maintained by both parties; and ultimately the Company intimated that they did not consider themselves bound by their offer, having left it open for a certain time for the Local Board's acceptance or rejection. The Company obtained an Act of Incorporation, which received the Royal assent June 3rd, 1872. By this Act they are placed under certain restrictions in regard to the supply of gas to the inhabitants of the district; they are amongst other things bound to keep up the quality to a certain illuminating power, and the maximum price is fixed by the Act, as is also the maximum amount of dividend to be paid. In 1893 the Gas Company were once more approached on the subject of the purchase of the undertaking by the then Local Board. After protracted negotiations an understanding was arrived at between the Directors of the Company and the Board whereby the works, plant, and other rights, privileges, &c., should be transferred to the township of Altrincham for a sum of £162,500. The proposal, however, was unanimously rejected at a public meeting of ratepayers.

The Altrincham and Bowdon Literary Institution has the honour of a mention in the last edition of Ormerod's Cheshire, of which it is in every respect deserving. It was established in the year 1847 in most humble premises at the top of Victoria Street. The promoters intended by "means of a well-selected Library, a Reading or News-room, Lectures and Evening Classes, to supply, to the young men of the neighbourhood, opportunities of mental cultivation and improvement, at a cheap rate, at the same time that it affords to the adult inhabitants a rational and agreeable mode of spending their leisure hours." It was well supported, and was so successful that in 1852 the present institution was erected by subscription, at a cost, including fittings, of about £800. There was then a large news-room, and three good class-rooms, land adjoining being left for the future growth of the institution; this was taken up by the splendid lecture hall, which was opened in November, 1866, at a cost of £800. Its management was vested in a Board of Trustees and Directors, a certain

ALTRINCHAM FREE LIBRARY AND TECHNICAL SCHOOL.

number of the latter retiring annually, whose election was in the hands of the members. The Lecture Hall was destroyed by fire in November, 1878, and was rebuilt on an enlarged basis.

The time rapidly approached, however, when Altrincham was to give an opinion on the Free Libraries' question. In September, 1889, a poll of the inhabitants was taken, with the following result :—For the adoption of the Act, 1,159 ; against, 421 ; giving a majority of 738 in favour of the adoption of the Act. In 1892, after protracted negotiations between the Altrincham Local Board and the Directors of the Literary Institution, the buildings, with Library and various classes, were transferred to the town. Saturday, October 1st, witnessed the important ceremony of opening the Free Library. Temporary premises were found in the Building Society's rooms (now Oddfellows' Hall), Market Street, where news-rooms were provided, and the Library of about 5,000 volumes housed. A donation of £300 was made by the Trustees of the Mayor's Land Charity—£100 for the purchase of books, and £200 for current expenses. A number of gentlemen were entertained in the evening at the Town Hall, by Mr. John Newton, the chairman of the Free Libraries' and Technical Instruction Committee. The Local Board also adopted the Technical Instruction Act, and thereupon the Cheshire County County Council contributed the sum of £496 to the Building Fund of the Technical School, George Street. Meantime building operations in connection with the enlargement of the Lecture Hall and Technical School were vigorously carried on, the sum of £4,000 being borrowed by the Local Board for Free Library and Technical Instruction purposes. This amount was largely supplemented by private donations. The nucleus of the new buildings was in the old Literary Institute, and additional land having been purchased, they were erected from designs of Mr. Frank Popplewell, architect, of Manchester. The large hall will now seat 700 persons, and its capacity and convenience have already been well tested. Indeed what has now been carried out is almost entirely on the lines suggested after the building was burnt down 13 or 14 years ago, but which want of funds then prevented. The library has space for 12,000 volumes. The elevation in George Street has been extended to about three times its original length, but its appearance would be decidedly enhanced were it placed on rising ground, instead of having its first storey practically buried. The new gable, however, rises prominently above the other parts, with corbelled out pinnacles on each side, and a large window with pointed head, which is certainly a redeeming feature and decidedly handsome. The surplus land on the west and south sides has been tastefully planted by Messrs. W. Clibran and Son, of Oldfield Nurseries. In the Technical School are lofty and spacious rooms for the art classes, as also for other departments for cooking, laundry, dressmaking, shorthand, &c. The principal contractors were Messrs. Wm. Lambert and Son, Hale Road, Altrincham; and the sub-contractors:— Mr. R. Campbell, joiner; Mr. J. H. Holt, mason; Messrs. H. and J. Drinkwater, plasterers; Mr. Joseph Gallimore, painter; Mr. Thomas Vernon, smith; and Mr. James Smith, Mill Street, heating apparatus. The plumbing work has been carried out by Messrs. Josiah Drinkwater and Sons.

With an increasing population the adoption of the provisions of the Public Health Act of 1848 was rendered absolutely necessary. A Government Inquiry held in 1850 disclosed the fact that the sanitary condition of the town was exceedingly defective— typhus fever, dysentery, and other complaints of the bowels prevailing more or less every year; and that the death rate was exceedingly high—$29\frac{1}{2}$ per thousand per annum of the population. The geographical position and contour of the town were favourable to the highest degree of longevity attainable; but natural advantages were counteracted by the want of an efficient system of drainage and complete sanitary regulation. The want of a proper water supply also contributed to it. A Local Board was formed consisting of nine members, which held its first meeting on the 4th April, 1851. Loans were subsequently obtained for drainage purposes, and a complete system of sewerage laid down. The sewage

Tulip Hill
(NOW DISMANTLED)

is disposed of by irrigation at the Sinderland farm, at a cost of about 5½d. per head of the population. In some towns it is or has been as high as 5s. per head. There is no doubt that the plan is admirably adapted for such places as Altrincham. In 1890 the Altrincham Local Board acquired Woodcote Farm, at a cost of £11,000, to be repaid, principal and interest, in 50 years. With the water supply the Board did not deal so successfully, but private enterprise stepped in to fill the gap. The North Cheshire Water Company, which was formed in 1857, and incorporated in 1864, conferred upon the district the priceless boon of a supply of pure water from the reservoirs of the Manchester Corporation. In 1878 the Board purchased the market tolls from the Earl of Stamford and Warrington for the sum of £1,000 ; and in the latter part of the same year the erection of a new Market House in Market Street was commenced, the sum of £4,500 being borrowed to cover the cost of the tolls, building, and other charges incidental thereto. The building was erected from designs by Maxwell Roscoe, Esq., Mr. M. Stone being the contractor. The Local Board ceased to exist in 1894, and became merged in the Altrincham Urban District Council. Information as to loans, &c., will be found in the Appendix.

In February, 1864, the Bowdon Local Board held its first meeting. Its principal work has been the sewering of the township, which was executed under the superintendence of John Newton, Esq., C.E., at a cost of £2,493 16s. 3d. In December, 1865, the lighting by public gas lamps was carried out. Since then the same gentleman has laid down a system of sewage disposal by irrigation, which has been highly successful.

In 1886 the preparations for celebrating the Jubilee of Queen Victoria were begun, the ancient Court Leet and the Altrincham Local Board co-operating most harmoniously to make the affair a complete success. The year 1887 will stand out prominently in the annals of the good old town in having been honoured with a visit from Royalty in the persons of T.R.H. the Prince and Princess of Wales, who were guests of Lord Egerton of Tatton, at Tatton Park, on the occasion of the opening of the Jubilee Exhibition at Old Trafford, on the 4th of May in that year. Triumphal arches of mediæval design were erected in Dunham Road and Station Road, and the town was gay with flags and bunting. On arriving at the railway station (Altrincham and Bowdon), the Mayor, Mr. Joseph Gaskarth, was presented to the Prince, and a beautiful bouquet was presented to the Princess by Miss Katherine Cocks, daughter of the late Mr. Robert Cocks, agent to the Dunham estate. Beautifully bound copies of the programme of the day's festivities were presented to the Prince and Princess. They were printed in gold, bound in light leather, lined with white silk, the production of Mr. S. Butler, of George Street, and highly creditable to Altrincham enterprise. Afterwards the Band of the Third Cheshire Volunteers headed a procession of school children to Dunham Park, where refreshments were served and games indulged in. The celebration of Jubilee Day was fixed for Tuesday, June 21st, on which occasion the arrangements were carried out by the Local Board, of which Mr John Newton was chairman. The day was observed as a general holiday, and a special thanksgiving service was held in St. George's Church, where an appropriate sermon was preached by the Vicar, the Rev. George London. In the afternoon a grand procession was formed in the new Market Place, embracing members of the Local Board, the Fire Brigade, the Sunday scholars about 4,000 in number, and the various Friendly Societies in the town and district. A special medal was struck and presented to each scholar, and special badges were provided for the committee and stewards, of which there was a large number. The old people of the age of the Queen (68) were entertained to a substantial repast in the Market Hall, by Alderman Griffin, J.P., Mayor; sports were held in Dunham Park, and the day's proceedings were brought to a close by a display of fireworks.

The Altrincham Parliamentary Division of Cheshire was formerly included in the northern part of the county; in 1868 it formed a portion of the Mid-Cheshire Division, which then

SIR WM. C. BROOKS.
THE LATE MR. JOHN BROOKS.   MR. CONINGSBY DISRAELI.

PAST AND PRESENT MEMBERS
FOR THE ALTRINCHAM PARLIAMENTARY DIVISION.

covered a wide area, extending to Runcorn in the west, Northwich in the south, Sale on the north, and Congleton on the east. At the general election of 1885, which took place on the formation of the Altrincham Parliamentary Division, Mr. John Brooks was selected as the Conservative candidate, and Mr. Isaac Saunders Leadam as the Liberal. The contest was lengthened and severe, and on both sides exceptional ability was displayed. In the aggregate Mr. Brooks polled 4,798 votes, as against 4,046 by his opponent, a majority of 752 for Mr. Brooks. On that cold March day when news arrived of the untimely death of Mr. John Brooks, the eyes of the party naturally turned to his uncle, Sir William, who had most enthusiastically supported his nephew, and he was induced to come forward. He was returned by a majority of 583, and at the general election in July, 1886, he was returned unopposed. Sir William retired in 1892, and for the third time, and last, Mr. Leadam came forward in the Liberal interest. On this occasion he was opposed by Mr. Coningsby Ralph Disraeli, only son of Mr. Ralph Disraeli, Clerk of Parliament, and nephew of the Right Hon. Benjamin Disraeli, Earl of Beaconsfield. He was born in 1867, and was educated at Charterhouse and at Oxford. Again Mr. Leadam was defeated, this time by a majority of 798. In July, 1895, at the general election, Mr. Disraeli was returned by a still greater majority, the largest ever known in the history of the division, over Mr. A. M. Latham. Mr. Disraeli married, March 2nd, 1897, Marion Grace, only daughter of Mr. Edward Silva, of Testcombe, Chilbolton, Hants. Records of the voting will be found in the Appendix.

The introduction of the electric light into Altrincham may be briefly stated. In the beginning of 1894 a private company was formed under the style of "The Altrincham Electric Supply," and received Parliamentary powers for supplying electricity throughout Altrincham and surrounding places. A large and fully equipped works and generating station was erected on land adjoining the Bridgewater Canal at Broadheath, and the supply was started in the last months of 1894. A year's running proved the popularity of the supply and the enterprise of the inhabitants.

During that period more than 14 miles of mains were laid and an equivalent of 10,000 eight-candle power lamps connected. Among the more important installations may be mentioned the Downs Congregational Chapel, St. John's Church, the Altrincham Conservative Club, and St. Margaret's Institute, as well as a great many of the largest houses in the district. The company is now extending its mains under the powers of a new Act into the districts of Ashton-on-Mersey and Timperley, which will also be fed from the Broadheath centre. On other pages will be found illustrations showing the Electricity Generating Station and also the interior of the Congregational Chapel as lit by the electric light. It is worthy of note as indicating the increased enterprise in the district that the blocks from which these views are taken have been made in Messrs. Walker and Co.'s Electric Light Studio, the Downs, Bowdon, by means of one of the most recent of the now very popular "process" methods. The sole contractors for all the work done for the Altrincham Electric Supply have been the Manchester Edison Swan Co. The buildings at Broadheath were erected by Mr. James Hamilton, contractor, of Altrincham.

For many years, up to 1880, Hale Moss was in a condition which constituted a grave danger to the public health. Owing to efforts put forth in various quarters, the Earl of Stamford and Warrington presented a site for a public park covering about 16 acres of the best part of the Moss, and this was converted by the Altrincham Local Board into a park and recreation ground, with large cricket field, football ground, tennis courts, bowling greens, ornamental lakes, &c. The grounds were laid out from a very tasteful design of the late Mr. John Shaw, F.R.H.S., who was a past master in the art of landscape gardening ; and the work of laying out and planting was executed by his son, Mr. John Shaw. The opening in 1880 was attended with considerable rejoicing, and in the evening a dinner was given at the Town Hall by Joseph Gaskarth, Esq., the then chairman of the Local Board, to which the principal inhabitants were invited. Stamford Park is greatly resorted to by the inhabitants, by whom it is highly appreciated, and in summer, when the flowers are in bloom and the trees in foliage, presents a picture of great beauty. At the time of writing these lines, negotiations are in progress between the Altrincham Urban Council, the Bucklow Rural District Council, and the Trustees of the Earl of Stamford and Warrington for acquiring certain portions of the Moss still unoccupied, and from the manner in which they have been carried out up to the present, there is every reason to think they will be crowned with success.

Although the question of additional burial accommodation, in view of the rapidly diminishing area at Bowdon, had been frequently referred to at public meetings, the first practical step in this district was taken at a meeting held in July, 1890, in Altrincham, when a resolution was passed requesting the Local Board to take the necessary steps to provide a cemetery. A committee was appointed, and ultimately a suitable site of about ten acres, situate in Hale Road, in the Township of Hale, was selected. The decision was fiercely contested by the Township of Hale, but the Local Government Board decided in favour of the Altrincham authority by sanction to the loan as given in the Appendix to this work. The grounds have been laid out in the most approved style, and a handsome mortuary chapel erected from the designs of Mr. William Owen, A.R.I.B.A., Hale and Manchester. The cemetery was formally dedicated to the public use in 1893, a gold key of handsome design being presented to Alderman William Griffin, J.P., the chairman of the Cemetery Committee on the occasion.

As these pages go to press, preparations are being made in Altrincham and district for providing a permanent memorial of the Diamond reign of Her Majesty, Queen Victoria. At a public meeting held on March 10th, 1897, it was resolved that such memorial shall take the form of public baths, and thus meet a want which has been long felt. The question of the incorporation of the town was also incidentally mooted, but as this is forming the subject of inquiry by a Committee of the Urban District Council, it is one which will have to be considered and decided upon at some future period.

CHAPTER XV.

What Sale was—A glance at the past—The Masseys of Sale—A gracious permission to marry from the Pope—Lord Strange on the march to Manchester—Some looks into old township books—The official mole catcher—Sale Vineyards—Constables' Staves—The poor law and its administration—Troublous times—A lady's interest in township matters—A local Hampden—Sale township schools, &c.

A HUGE moor, in summer yellow with broom flowers, and in winter black with the blackness of desolation, such were the characteristics of Sale within living memory. Out of this it may appear difficult to extract an interesting story, such as we might do had we picturesque hills and lovely valleys in which, nestled in verdant foliage, were some ivy-covered ruins where the lordly baron once presided and held his little court of acknowledged sovereignty. We have no rocky ravines to explore or roaring waterfalls to listen to; yet we could learn had we time, that, as the records of a misty past are brought into the light of our high civilization, Sale has a history—one in which Roman, Dane, Saxon, Norman play their several parts. Here we have Cross Street which the Roman legions made not merely for an age, but as if for eternity. Who knows but that in the terrible time when the fierce Norseman swept over the country, he did not leave as a remembrance a bloodstained path to be known in after ages as Dane Road. And when the Norman came and the once fiery Saxon succumbed to his disciplined onslaught, who knows but that Sale may have been the scene of many a stubborn fight ere the broad acres and manors of the adjoining country changed hands and right gave place to might.

The whirligig of time whirls us on, and we read of the exploits of a **Massey of Sale at Poictiers**, and of rewards at the hands of England's most potent Prince, who won for it never ending glory at Agincourt. It will be our pleasant task to set forth a little that to the writer invests even this once barren moor with a glamour of romance, and which may lead more than one of its inhabitants to turn aside from the cares of business and to seek relief in the relaxation which a perusal of this chapter may afford.

The derivation of the word Sale is involved in so much obscurity, and authorities differing, like doctors are said to do, no good purpose would be served here by any lengthy dissertation on the origin of names in general, or Sale in particular. It is enough for our purpose that Sale has been known by its present name for upwards of 200 or 300 years, and we may therefore safely take it on trust that it was so known for centuries previously, although the fact that Sale is not mentioned in Doomsday Book shows it to have been then of little importance. The first authentic light is shed on its past history by that father of Cheshire history, Sir Peter Leycester. He tells us, although Sale is not mentioned in the Doomsday Book, that it was a fee of the ancient barony of Halton. The events of that period seem to point to the fact that at the Conquest the township of Sale formed a portion of the vast possessions of Hamon of Dunham Massey, a powerful baron who resided in his castle there. It was from his second son, who had issue two sons, one of whom was named Robert, that the Masseys of Sale sprung in the time of Richard I. or King John, A.D. 1189-1199.

In the year 1216, Robert Massey is traced by Leycester to have held the land of Sale, and in 1367 another Robert, who had been guilty of outlawry, was pardoned on account of his services with Edward, Prince of Wales. The men of Cheshire were distinguished for their bravery in these campaigns, and the same Robert, who found his former services so useful at a pinch had, for his gallantry under the Black Prince at Poictiers, been created bailiff of the Hundred of Bucklow, an office of much importance and emolument. The lawlessness which prevailed at the period, and the value of "a previous good character," are also illustrated by the fact that Richard Massey, having caused the death of

William del Hull, was only pardoned by Richard II. on the prayer of John, Duke of Castile and Duke of Lancaster, the famous pretender to the Crown of Spain at that time. In the year 1411, a pardon or permission to marry was given to Robert, son and heir of Roger le Massey, of Sale, and Margaret, daughter of "the noble man, George de Caryngton, Knight, of the Diocese of Lichfield," by Thomas, Bishop of Durham, under the letters "of happy memorial of Lord Alexander the sixth, Pope, his true Leaden Bull, with . . . . . . after the Roman Court bulled sound and whole and free from all voice and sinister suspect," &c. The marriage portion of the lady was to be £40. In 1556, Hamlette Massey, of Sale, made a will, copied amongst those published by the Chetham Society, in which, having ordered that his body be buried in the "Channcell of Asheton in Mersey Bank Parysh Church," he bequeaths to his bastard sons, Henry, Edward, William, and Thomas, certain cattle, horses, wheat and rye, silver spoons, and to Elizabeth Maseye, "my bastard dau'r, one curtall whyte nagge, a black cowe, a bay weninge colt, and one silver spone." The Masseys of Sale took a somewhat prominent part in the thrilling events which marked the fourteenth century, and probably in consequence of the rapid increase of the family, a rather unkindly cynic was induced to write that in Cheshire

Masseys were as plentiful as asses, and Davenports as dogs' tails.

In the reign of Richard II., as was in many instances the case in other townships, the eldest son would assume the name of Sale as a surname, and that of Massey would become subsidiary. A member of the Holt family from Lancashire, having married a daughter and heiress of Thomas Sale, a portion of the land of Sale came into possession of the Holts. A partition seems to have taken place, and a little over 200 years ago there were amongst other owners of land in Sale, Lord Delamer of Dunham, Geoffrey Cartwright, William Williamson, Richard Wrenshaw or Renshaw, Sir Edward Moseley, Mr. Gerard, of Riddings, Edward Legh, of Baggilegh, and Robert Tatton, of Wythenshawe,

ASHTON-ON-MERSEY FORD, SEPTEMBER 23rd, 1642.
LORD STRANGE'S FORCES CROSSING TO BESIEGE MANCHESTER.

held certain lands in lease from Mr. Massey. The Massey family at Sale appears to have become extinct in 1746, and the Massey share of the property passed by marriage to the Nobles and Mainwarings, and the Moores. These shares were afterwards purchased by the Egertons of Tatton, and the whole of the land in the township now divided and sub-divided to an extent that to give all the names would exhaust more space than we can well afford.

We now come to a period more recent, and one which we venture to think will present, therefore, more features of interest to the general reader. The township books of Sale, which give us a fair idea of the manners and customs of the inhabitants prior to the time of which we have already spoken, commence in the year 1805. The first meeting mentioned therein, over which "C. White" presided, has reference to the repair of the causeways in Deane Lane, and the providing of a new well in lieu of the old one destroyed; Mr. Mort, probably of Altrincham, furnishing the township with a quantity of excellent gravel. In 1806, it was ordered that the valuation for the township, which would be produced by the Commissioners for the purpose of dividing and enclosing the waste lands, was ordered to be the only assessment by which the rate for the poors "lay," church lay, constable lay, and highway lay, should in future be made after such valuation by the said Commissioners was finally arranged and settled. Then comes an entry of an important matter which at sundry times and in divers manners exercised the powers that were at Sale. A special meeting, notice of which had been given at the Parish Church two successive Sundays, was held June 30th, 1806, when it was unanimously agreed that the sum of £8 per year should be given for mole catching, the time to extend over seven years. At the side of the book is written "I, Edward Morris, do agree to catch moles in the township of Sale for the term and on the conditions above named, as witness my hand." This was somewhat paradoxical, as Edward could not write, and made the orthodox mark instead. Sale then possessed machinery for thief catching as well. All necessary expenses incurred by the society for prosecuting felons were ordered to be paid by the constable out of his general receipts. No property on which the assessment had not been made under the bond was to be protected, and at the same time the new enclosures made on Sale Moor were to be assessed according to the risk of each lot. Many of these were distinguished by such names as Adam's Vineyard, Vodry's Vineyard, &c. Subject to the approbation of the magistrates, Ashton Kelsall was appointed assistant surveyor at a salary of twelve guineas per annum, from which it may be inferred that Sale was beginning to assume important proportions, and to recognise its responsibilities. This even extended to maintaining the prestige of the constable in a becoming manner, a public meeting being held soon after at which "it was agreed that a constable's staff should be immediately ordered for the said township similar to the Ashton constable's staff". One can imagine these two important personages heading the processions, with their staves of office shining with the effulgence of gilding and ebony, and being as requisite for the proper carrying out of business as the Mace is in the House of Commons. What unsophisticated youngster, whose ancestors have probably served the honourable office, has not gazed on this emblem of departed authority with reverential awe, as it has hung from its place on the wall, a much valued heirloom in the family! The modern disciples of Sir Robert Peel have very effectually superseded the ancient Dogberry, who, in nine cases out of ten, was as great terror to evil doers as his modern prototype.

In proof of this, the author ventures to relate an anecdote which he heard narrated by an old inhabitant of Altrincham. A brutal outrage had been committed on a Staffordshire man, who had been left for dead. At this time Ashton wakes were in full swing. Acting, not exactly on "information received," but from his own conviction that a certain Weston was the chief actor, the the Altrincham constable, well remembered as " Natty " Pass, proceeded to Ashton. He watched the bull baits which took place amid the shouts of the crowd, and afterwards entered a public-house, which was occupied by a disorderly rabble, gathered from all parts of the country. He was a man of portly form, but he had a pistol ready for use in case of emergency. Seizing Weston he informed him that he was his prisoner. The very suddenness of the act seemed to paralyse the onlookers, and before they could recover from their surprise, he had his man outside and carefully manacled. On the way he made a confession of the crime, and was removed to Staffordshire to be tried. He was in all probability leniently dealt with for those times, as our informant suggestively said, "he knew he was neither hanged nor transported." This little incident, while imparting flavour to Ashton wakes, at the same time records the bravery of an old-fashioned constable.

At this period the value of small birds to the farmer was either not known or appreciated. The unfortunate moles were doomed to pressing attention on the part of the duly appointed official. It now came the turn of the poor sparrows. A penny a head was given for old sparrows, a halfpenny for young ones, a halfpenny per egg for each sparrow egg up "to the number of five or under per nest, provided also that the old hen be brought along with them." In November, 1808, the greatest consternation was caused by a great robbery of potatoes, and a reward of five guineas was offered for "the discovery, apprehending, and convicting of persons or person concerned in the said felony." To meet the expenses of this a rate of threepence in the pound was ordered to be levied.

The evils of the poor law system began to manifest themselves. Sale does not, however, appear to have indulged in the luxury of of a workhouse for some years subsequent, and its administration of the poor law was as loose as that which prevailed at Altrincham. It must have steeped the population in pauperism, as the system of "piecing-out," now utterly condemned, prevailed to an alarming extent. The sum of three shillings was given to one Scipio Leigh as "occasional relief," while the sum of £2 was allowed to Thomas

Hamnett towards his rent. These entries are very numerous. That Sale felt the "hard times" which were now prevailing, owing to continued wars abroad and the unsettled state of home industries, is apparent from the fact that in 1812 a meeting of inhabitants was held. The notice stated that it was called for the purpose of taking into consideration the best method of affording relief to the honest, industrious poor of the township. It was resolved that a subscription be entered into for purchasing potatoes, and that every encouragement should be given to the cultivation of this now indispensable esculent. The meeting sympathized, or, as it is put, "feels" for the sufferings of the poor, and wished to afford them all proper relief. It, however, highly disapproved of asking charity by going from house to house in numbers, and that all persons doing so, "or using any expressions tending to inflame or make uneasy the minds of their neighbours," would be excluded from any benefit in the subscription, in the distribution of which regard would be had to the character of the applicants. The meeting particularly recommended to the publicans in the neighbourhood to allow no improper tippling in their houses, but to shut them up at ten o'clock in the evening, and "to discourage all conversation tending to inflame the public mind, and as it is suspected that evil-disposed persons are travelling about the country to excite a spirit of discontent and uneasiness, they are requested to be particularly watchful of all strangers who may enter their houses."

This entry refers to the times of our grandfathers. Thousands living can remember them, and will be able to account for the extraordinary precautions which are indicated above. There were serious riots in many counties in England. The Luddites, or "levellers," made a house to house visitation, and it was woe unto the householder who did not comply with their demands. In Sale, which had then a population under 1,000, it will be readily inferred that a great deal of the resolution passed at this meeting was directed at the Luddites. There would, no doubt, be many unwelcome visitors from Manchester, and, as incendiarism was very rife, it would require all the watchfulness of Boniface, coupled with the efforts of the constables to quiet the alarm which would be naturally felt by the better-off classes. Greater stringency was manifested in prosecuting felons, and Sale became a branch association, on the recommendation of the magistrates, "for the protection of property and the preservation of the peace." One of the rules provided for the calling of the members together and the raising of an alarm as soon as possible, the constable being provided with a rattle for that purpose. It was recommended that every "considerable" farm house should have one where no constable resided. At the same time, the principal inlets to the township—the public roads and the canal banks—were to be "considered as constant objects of attention." At one of the meetings held at this period, the name of a lady appears as having been present—Sarah Hulme. She signed her name, the handwriting being very neat, and it is all the more worthy of record as being the first and last occasion on which the signature of a lady is to be found in this book.

Another proof of the growing importance of Sale is to be noted in the fact that in March, 1813, it was deemed beneficial to elect a standing officer to conduct the whole of the offices of the township, vested interests being considered, Mr. J. Heap, the village schoolmaster, continuing "to be secretary to the town." Peter Whitehead was the standing officer appointed at a salary of £40 and reasonable expenses for journeys.

We have already referred to numerous entries of the amounts granted in the way of relief to the poor. Some of them which we now drop across are very interesting. Applications were founded on various pretexts. Most are for sickness, but one good lady is stated to be "big with child;" John Cotterill wanted a new spade; William Royle obtained 10s. as relief, his wife being "at lying-in;" a violin was ordered to be purchased for a lame boy, evidently for the purpose of enabling him to earn his living; a person had £1 5s. allowed him for his wife's coffin; Barbary Hulme wanted, save the mark, two shifts, and while we would reluctantly draw the line at these sacred articles of ladies' wearing apparel, truth compels us to add that Sarah Leigh was ordered to be supplied with a "petty coat" towards winter. Peter Culcheth applied for a loom, which shows, in conjunction with other similar entries, that weaving was a means of livelihood to many of the inhabitants. In 1815 it was agreed that a workhouse should be built for the township as soon as convenient.

That in some cases the inhabitants helped themselves is illustrated by what may be termed a peculiar entry :—On Thursday, 28th day of August, 1817, Thomas Leigh saw Margaret Cotterill getting potatoes in John Cookson's field, near the road, about ten o'clock, or between ten and eleven o'clock at night. He says he saw her getting potatoes and putting them in her pocket and run into the wheat, and he ran after her, and took hold of her, and called her Peg, and she said 'What?' He said, 'How can thou foreshame to pull up the man's stuff?' She said 'Do not tell.' He did not say whether he would or would not. He felt at her pockets and was certain they were potatoes. He saw her go out of the field with them, and she said she only wanted a mess." (Breakfast or dinner). There were many others of a questionable character resident in Sale at this time. The cause had already begun to show the effect. Another minute states that the poor houses " having long been inhabited by persons who neglect their work and their families, and are frequently seen going up and down in pursuit of game, and complaints having been very justly made by Mr. Moore and neighbouring gentlemen, that the said poor houses shall be appropriated, it be and hereby is requested that the trustees of the said premises take measures to remove the said families from the said premises." A meeting subsequently declared that the wanton and malicious damage done to the young timber trees belonging to the Earl of Stamford and Warrington, and to the young fruit trees belonging to Mr. Heald and John Moore, Esquire, was a disgrace to the township and that no pains or expense be spared to bring the offenders to speedy justice. We must hope that for the credit of the township this disgrace was wiped out.

As time sped on, the absurdity of this method of administering relief became apparent. The overseers had a lively time of it in visiting various parts of the country and arranging for the payments of the rents of persons who claimed Sale as their birthplace. Extraordinary apathy was manifested by the ratepayers. Two meetings were called on this subject. At the first no ratepayer attended, and at the second only two. A postponement took place, and a sufficient number having been got together, it was decided that the payment of rents should be discontinued. In 1821, the growing importance of this matter was more fully recognised by the appointment of a select vestry for the management of the poor. Under the auspices of this body it was decided to draw up a case in order to ascertain what powers the landowners of Sale had to enclose waste lands adjoining their premises, and also as to the right of landowners with respect to the herbage of such lands, the advice of Messrs. Nicholls and Worthington, of Altrincham, to be taken on the subject. Notice of this meeting was duly " cried " two Sundays in the church.

Meanwhile other matters of interest to the well-being of the township received due consideration. A village Hampden, or at any rate a gentleman having at heart the interests of the place, arose in the year 1826. His name was John Hulbert : he was mainly instrumental in obtaining the assessment of such portion of the Bridgewater Canal as passed through the township. The trustees of the Duke objected to pay, and persons were appointed by the overseers to watch the canal in order to ascertain what would be the amount received in the way of tolls and the profits therefrom. Arbitration was proposed by the trustees, but as the inhabitants thought that this was only introductory to expensive proceedings in the Court of King's Bench, they stoutly resisted it, unless some proposal were made by which their rights should be respected. Litigation dragged its slow length along for two years, but right prevailed, and the inhabitants were victorious. The chief actor in the drama, Mr. Hulbert, the then assistant overseer, received his reward. A committee was appointed who collected £10, which was expended on a silver cup, suitably inscribed, and presented to him at a public dinner at the Bull's Head, as some remuneration to him for his laudable and indefatigable exertions in obtaining a confirmation of the assessment in question.

At a meeting of the inhabitants of the township of Sale and such inhabitants of the township of Ashton-on-Mersey as contributed to the building of the new school in Sale, held in the said school this 31st December, 1810, pursuant to public notice given, the following resolutions were proposed by Charles White, Esquire, the chairman, and unanimously passed :—

(1) That the new school in Sale, together with such land, buildings, or interests as do now belong or may hereafter become attached to the said school, shall be properly secured and vested in trustees, to be nominated and appointed at this meeting.

(2) That the Rector and Churchwardens of the parish of Ashton-upon-Mersey for the time being, Charles White, Esquire, John White, Esquire, Joseph Atkinson, Esquire, John Moore, Esquire, Rev. Robert Harrop, Isaac Harrop, Peter Heywood, William Leobridge, Joseph Clarke, John Smith, John Whitelegg, Robert Newton, be, and are hereby appointed Trustees of the said school and its appurtenances, and that Messrs. Worthington, Harrop and Worthington, Solicitors in Altrincham, be and are hereby instructed to draw a deed proper for this purpose, and for conveying and securing to the trustees, if necessary, the usual authority to execute and continue the trust.

At the same time Mr. Heap was unanimously elected to fill the office of schoolmaster for one year on trial, in place of the late Mr. Holt. In 1811 it was considered desirable that a proper residence should be provided for the schoolmaster. A few further facts about the school and its origin may be interesting. The school was really a small thatched cottage situate in Springfield, then waste. This was followed by a mixed school two storeys in height, and, be it noted, fronted a country lane now scarcely recognisable in School Road.

The great impetus given to building in Sale by the opening of the Manchester, South Junction and Altrincham Railway, and the increased population thus formed, again rendered the school too small ; and we find in 1854, when Mr. James Warren was schoolmaster, it was reported to be "very defective." It had a flagged floor, very much out of repair, with only one common fire-grate in a room 33 feet long by 19 feet 6 inches wide ; it was cold and comfortless for scholars in winter, and the school fittings were in bad condition. To remedy these defects a wooden floor was substituted, a stove introduced, and other improvements made internally ; and thus it continued till 1861, when it was found necessary to erect an infants' school, 38 feet by 20 feet, and schoolmistress' residence to relieve the mixed school, which under the teaching of Mr. Henry Dixon, Mr. Warren's successor, had become too crowded. The infants' school thus erected was soon filled to overflowing—Mrs. Cartledge being the schoolmistress—and in 1874 an additional room, 27 feet by 20 feet was added to it.

Still short of accommodation in the mixed school, the schoolmaster's house (which for some years had been used as the Local Board offices) was in 1876 absorbed by the mixed school and used as class rooms ; but even with this addition, under the teaching of Mr. Adam Watson, the present master, the building was filled with children, and the results obtained at the annual examinations, as certified by the Government Inspectors, extremely creditable to him, considering the difficulty he laboured under in having the children crowded together in rooms ill adapted for teaching, and on different floors.

The present buildings have an imposing frontage of one storey to School Road, and are entered through a large Gothic archway surmounted by an open belfry, with a public clock. This archway divides the mixed from the infants' school. The mixed school on the right has separate entrance porches for boys and girls, with convenient and well-fitted lavatories, cloak-room, &c., between. The principal room is in form of the letter L, 96 feet long and 20 feet wide inside, class-room 16 feet by 20 feet, each open to the ridge, and with an average height of 18 feet. The large room is divided by three moveable curtains into four divisions or class-rooms, and heated by three open fires, whilst the ventilation has been carefully attended to. Advantage has been taken of the inclination of the site to get a covered play-ground under this part of the building. The infants' school consists of the room built in 1861, 38 feet by 20 feet, a large room 42 feet 6 inches by 20 feet, and class-room 21 feet 10 inches by 14 feet 7 inches. There is also a room 22 feet by 14 feet 6 inches, with entrances from Springfield Road and the school play-ground, fitted up as a Board-room for the trustees to hold their stated meetings in.

The schools accommodate 550 children. The architect for the new buildings was Mr. A. G. McBeath, Sale; the contractors, Messrs. Luke Winstanley & Son, Sale; mason work, Mr. Thomas Kirkley; plaster work, Mr. Alfred Garner, Sale; plumber and painter's work, Messrs. Robert Collier and Co., Sale.

At the beginning of the century, and for some years afterwards, Sale moor was used as an exercising ground for the troops in garrison at Manchester, and a grand review was held there, which was attended in vast numbers by the people. Old Sale Hall was an ancient seat of the Masseys, and passed to Mr. Moore, and afterwards by purchase to the late James Worthington, Esq., J.P. There is another seat on the Western side of the township called Sale Hall, and formerly the residence of Dr. White, whose services to the township are perpetuated in numerous ways.

The volunteer movement in Sale seems to have dated from the early part of the century. In June, 1804, the first muster roll appears to have been drawn up. Capt. John Moore, junr., a name well known in Sale annals, is the first on the list, and

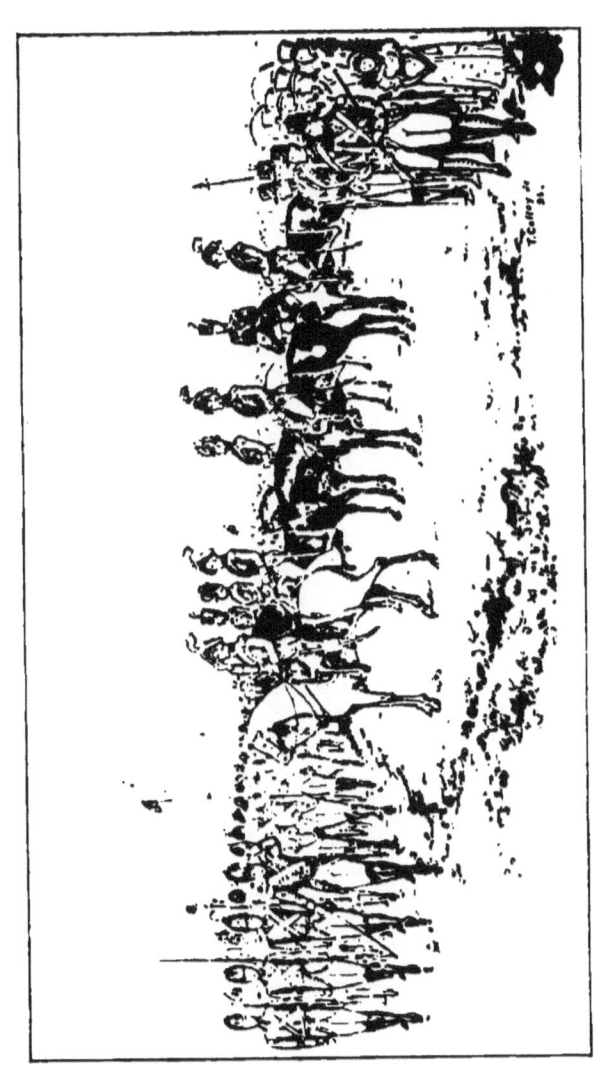

REVIEW OF THE MANCHESTER AND SALFORD VOLUNTEERS ON SALE MOOR, APRIL 12TH, 1804, BY PRINCE WILLIAM OF GLOUCESTER.

the other principal officers were Lieut. Robert Say, Lieut. Robert Williamson, Ensign Wm. Leebridge, and Surgeon Charles Poole, of Altrincham. There are 128 names in all. On the 9th April, 1804, the "Ashton-on-Mersey-cum-Sale volunteers" were inspected by Lieut.-Col. Cuyler, who expressed his approbation of the improved discipline of the company, and on the 12th of the same month they had the honour of assisting the 5th dragoons in keeping the ground at Sale Moor during the review of 6,000 volunteers, on which occasion Prince William Frederick of Gloucester was present. At this review the grand stand, erected half way down what is known as Hope Road, fell, by which many people were seriously injured, one fatally. In 1808, the company was disbanded, Napolean's projected invasion of England having been abandoned. In discontinuing their services, Lord Castlereagh, in a communication to the Earl of Stamford and Warrington, Lord Lieutenant, says, "Your Lordship will be pleased to assure them that His Majesty will never cease to entertain a just sense of the zeal and public spirit which incited them to come forward in defence of their country, and it is only for giving speedy effect to the views of the Legislature in the important object of establishing a local militia, that His Majesty is now induced to dispense with their further services." On Sunday May 26th, 1811, when their colours were deposited in Sale and Ashton-on-Mersey Parish Church, a sermon was preached by the Rev. Frances Gardner, curate, from Jer. iv, 6, "Set up a standard towards Zion," which was printed, at the request of those present, by Haufan and Davies, &, Hanging Ditch, Manchester. It is pleasurable to record that the patriotic spirit has not died out. In 1859, when rumours of invasion were spread through the country, Sale responded as of old. The name of Capt. A. Watkin will be long remembered, and it will be seen that he did his duty well. Captain A. E. Marsland, Captain Scott, and others, will also be long thought of in maintaining the efficiency of one of the finest companies in the Third Cheshire Battalion Volunteer Rifles.

Sale Burial Board was formed in 1862, and the Cemetery in Marslands Road, consisting of about six acres, was opened. The Board solved the religious difficulty very efficiently by providing an edifice divided into chapels which could be made use of by various denominations. One half of the cemetery was consecrated according to the rites of the Church of England. Although originally intended to meet the increasing requirements of the inhabitants of Sale, the cemetery attracted persons from Manchester and district. The surplus profits were devoted in relief of the poors rate, and in this way the sum of nearly £15,000 has been realised. The management of the cemetery is now merged in the Sale Urban District Council. An additional plot of six acres has been added, but although a portion has been consecrated it has only been used to a limited extent.

CHAPTER XVI.

Ashton-on-Mersey and its parish—Some notices of old Vicars—Restoration of St. Martin's—The beginnings of modern nonconformity—Old Cross Street Chapel; Wesleyanism; Congregationalism, &c.—St. Anne's; St. John's, Brooklands; St. Paul's; St. Mary's—Sale Local Board—Progress of Sale—Sanitary arrangements, etc.

THE parish of Ashton-on-Mersey was not an extensive one, and at an early period appears to have received spiritual oversight from Bowdon, as, indeed, a certain portion of the township is still included in that ancient parish. Ash-town is the town of the sacred tree, and mear's-ee or eye (according to Dr. Ismel Renshaw) appropriate to the condition of the river Mersey before it was banked in to its proper channel. About A.D. 1,300 its first parish church was built and dedicated to St. Martin. Ashton-on-Mersey, in 1402, was held as to one half by Sir George Carrington. In 1666 the greater portion of Ashton-on-Mersey belonged to the Breretons of Honford or Handford, and Lord Delamer, of Dunham Massey, held about an eighth part. Afterwards it descended by purchase and otherwise in 1749 to the Earl of Stamford, and was sold by the seventh Earl to the late Samuel Brooks, Esq., who devised it to his son, Sir William, who holds a court annually, as already noted, as Lord of the Manor. The old church was anciently valued at £13 4s. 7d., and there was once a chantry chapel here dedicated to the Virgin. The ancient edifice had not many claims to architectural features, and was exceedingly plain in its proportions. The interior, owing to the arrangement of the pews, was very inconvenient and uncomfortable, and in the aisles at one time was placed a continuous bench for the Sunday Scholars, which had to be stepped over by each worshipper who entered the pews. The church now consists of chancel, with organ chamber, nave, baptistry, vestries, and a tower containing one bell and a peal of

13 Harrington tubular bells. In 1884 and 1885, the interior was refurnished and refitted with open oak benches, the framing of the old pews being converted into panelling for the chancel walls. In 1887, through the liberality of Sir William Cunliffe Brooks, Bart., the vestries, tower, and handsome lych gate were erected, the work being carried out from the designs and under the superintendence of Mr. F. H. Oldham, F.R.I.B.A., of Manchester, and Mr. Truefitt, of London. There is a lengthy list of rectors, curates

LYCH GATE, ASHTON-ON-MERSEY.

and other ministers commencing in A.D. 1305 with Willielmus de Sala, who was succeeded in 1307 by Robertus Ashton, rector in 1331, and with whose name is linked that of Thomas de Ashton. In 1350 Robert Ashton was rector, and he was succeeded in 1362 by Jordan de Hulme. He was succeeded by Johannes de Massey two years later, and there is also a mention of Matheo de Sale, clerico, as having been witness to a Congleton charter dated July 3rd, 1381, although Johannes de Massey is named as rector in several deeds, notably 1382, 1389, and 1401. In 1409, the names of Nicholas de Wynbelegh or Wynkylegh and Roger de Kingesley appear, followed a year later by Ricardus Twemlowe. Then in quick succession we have Dns Walto Seymor (1412), Robertus Lyster (1413), Wms. Bagelegh (1419), H. Downham or Doneham (1428), Ric Dokedale or Dugdale (1435), Ranulphus de Ashton (1457), who endowed a charity in the parish church with land in Sale, on which a barn was built. In April, 1505, John Honford presented, and in 1522 Hugh Tippinge was rector, and he had a dispute with Mr. Massey in respect of the tithe of a corn mill at Ashton-on-Mersey, which was settled by arbitration. In 1567, John Robinson, clerk, is named in the will of Thomas Vawdrey in that year, although Ric. Shelmerdyne is returned as rector in 1567. The oldest presentation, now at the Diocesan Registry, for this parish is that of Thomas Richardson, in 1582, followed by those of George Tipping, in 1613, and Daniel Baker, M.A., in 1620, whose tragic death on April 1st, 1632, is recorded by Hollingworth as follows:—"Anno 1632, Daniel Baker, M.A., rector of Assheton on Mercy-bank and fellow of the Colledge, having on Good Friday (as it is called) administered the Lord's supper, and being, as it is feared, somewhat over-charged with drinke, in Salford, was found dead in the morning in the water under Salford Bridge; whether he fell downe of himself, being a tall man, and the battlements then but low, or whether hee was cast downe and put over the bridge, it is not certainly known to this day. This death of his, as also Dr. Buttes, the Vice-Chancellor of Cambridge, hanging himself on Easter day after and some other ministers and professors coming that year to an untimely end, as allso the above mentioned difference between the ministers, seemed to the Papists . . . . signal evidences of God's anger and wrath, and presages of the ruine of the Reformed Religion."

Ralph Stirrup, M.A., was represented in 1632, and it was during the incumbency of this gentleman—so Dr. Israel Renshaw informs us—was begun in 1636, the parish Register containing Christenings, Weddings, and Burials, within our parish of Ashton super ripand Mersey, A.D., 1636. Mr. Stirrup died in 1639, and was succeeded in 1640 by Richard Heyricke, B.D., Fellow of

All Souls' College, Oxford, who was also a warden of Manchester Parish Church, at a stipend of £70. During the period of the interregnum he complied with the requirements of Parliament, and was appointed preacher to the town at a stipend of £100, when the office of Warden was abolished. At the Restoration he was reappointed warden by Charles II. The next presentation to the living was by Sir William Brereton, and the parish Register states that Mr. Jonnsonnsonne (Mr. Johnson's son) was "chosen minister of the Word of God at Ashton sup Mersey, the 1st of June, 1642, free selected by all the people of the parish of Ashton, and not by virtue of any prelate or other absurd usurpation, and was possessed by the right worshipful and truly honoured Sir William Brereton, patrone of the same, and for hee preached the 1st day of June being the fast day, in the year of our Lord one thousand six hundred and forty two." Although according to some authorities, Mr. John Ford was ejected for nonconformity the parish Register records "John Ford, minister of the Gospell and pastor of Ashton, was buried 16th Oct., 1661." It is difficult to reconcile this with the fact that Mr. Ford died before he was ejected. Is it possible that Calamy, a great authority on this subject, may have been misinformed? It may be that the man ejected was Mr. Ford's son, as he could not have been ejected after his death. On Nov. 6th, 1661, Henry Hesketh became rector on the presentation of Sir Thomas Brereton, and in 1663 was succeeded by Hugh Hobson, who signed a declaration in the parish register respecting the use of the Book of Common Prayer, and the unlawfulness of taking up arms against the King. In 1679, Robert Brown, M.A., chaplain of Manchester College, was presented by Richard Massey, Esq., of Sale, and in 1706, Thomas Ellison, who was also rector of Pulford, was appointed. It was during his incumbency that the church was rebuilt. In 1717, the Rev. Massey Malyn, LL.D., of Sale, was presented, who is described on a marble tablet, erected by his sorrowing widow, as the most excellent rector of this church, who suddenly, though not immaturely, snatched away, rendered his spirit again to God, on the 31st day of the month of October, in the year of Salvation 1729, in the year of his age 42. The Rev. Thomas Whittaker, M.A., who succeeded him on the presentation of the Bishop, was rector upwards of 37 years, and died on the 29th June, 1767, in his 77th year. Three curates meantime ministered in the parish, and in 1767, the Rev. John Green, LL.B., was appointed, during whose incumbency Mrs. Hannah Smith bequeathed a sum of £20, the interest to be applied to the poor. In 1774, Richard Popplewell Johnson became rector, and he died in 1835, at the age of 86 years, having had charge of the spiritual concerns of the parish for the long term of 61 years. In the same year he was succeeded by the Rev. Charles Backhouse Sowerby, M.A., who resigned and was succeeded by the Rev. Joseph Ray, M.A. The present Vicar is the Rev. Abraham Mendel Hertzberg, who studied at St. Aidan's Theological College, and was ordained Deacon in 1888, and priest 1889. He was curate of Hilgay, Norfolk, 1888, Vicar of N. Petherton, Somerset, 1890, and rector of Ashton-on-Mersey (St. Martin's), 1894, of which living he is also patron. The income is made up of a tithe rent charge of £700, averaging £519, with 27 acres of glebe, value £105; fees, £20; Queen Anne's bounty, £5; gross income, £649; nett, £535 and house; population 3,700.

Sale, until very modern times, does not attract much attention from a nonconformist point of view. We hear of Ashton-on-Mersey, and also of Cross Street, and we read that in the then Frodsham Deanery, in 1662, Mr. Ford, of Ashton-on-Mersey, was ejected from his living for nonconformity. So it is stated by some authorities, but it is just possible that the Mr. Ford referred to was a son of the rector who died in 1661. In 1647, the famous Adam Martindale, a former Vicar of Rostherne, had been invited to become the minister, and in 1662, he stated he had been asked to minister at Ashton, at double the salary his people paid him. From a list of dissenting chapels and ministers in Cheshire, compiled between 1715 and 1729, we find that at Cross Street "on ye fund books, Ashton-on-Mersey," one Michael Fletcher was the preacher, and that out of a total congregation of 322, which included five gentlemen, 30 were voters for the County. This is without doubt the "Presbyterian meeting house," now merged in the Sale Unitarian Sunday School, which is referred to by Bishop Gastrell, in his *Notitia Cestriensis*, as being "a place to which great numbers resort, anno 1716." The Rev. Robert Harrop, whose name appears in the Sale township books, preached at this chapel for 37 years, and retired "with the undivided respect and affection of his flock." The old chapel at Sale, the exact age of which appears to be uncertain, was vacated on the opening of the chapel in Atkinson Road. Of its late ministers, the late Rev. J. McConochie is perhaps the best known for his scholarly attainments and breadth of thought. This chapel was burned down December 20th, 1896, and damage done to the extent of £3,000.

It was at Cross Street, too, that independency or congregationalism was cradled, to develope into the powerful organization it has since become. In the year 1800 services were held in a cottage there, and three years after a chapel was built, which will be recognized as the Sale Institute, capable of holding about 400 hearers, and in 1805 a church consisting of 12 members. After many vicissitudes the chapel was closed for about two months. It was then that at the request of the Trustees the (late) Rev. E. Morris, of Stretford, undertook the pastorate, and in October, 1842, a second church, consisting of 11 members, was formed. The substantial growth which followed, consequent on the rapid increase of the township, required the erection of another chapel, which is built on a site in Montague Road, presented by the late Mr. Samuel Brooks, and opened in 1852. It is in the early English style, faced with stone. There are Sunday Schools adjoining and all the equipments for a thriving congregation. The Rev. E. Morris was succeeded by the Rev. Adam Scott, now of Southport, the present minister being the Rev. T. Hallett-Williams. The Ashton-on-Mersey Congregational Church is situate in Cross Street, and contains a stained glass window, designed by Sir E. Burne Jones to the memory of Mrs. Catherine Johnson.

ST. ANNE'S CHURCH, SALE.

Wesleyanism, at an early date, began to be a power for good, and Wesley Chapel, School Road, and the handsome Trinity Chapel in Northenden Road are substantial evidences of the feeling existing. What may be regarded as off-shoots, although really older than what may be regarded as the parent churches are Barker's Lane, Ashton-on-Mersey, the Egerton Street Mission School, and flourishing branches at Partington and Sinderland. The growth of Scotch Presbyterianism is shown in the handsome structure in Northenden Road, erected in 1874, at a cost of £9,000, with manse. The first minister was the Rev. J. Thoburn McGaw, B.A., D.D., who was succeeded by the Rev. W. A. Sim. St. Joseph's Catholic Chapel in Hope Road is a neat edifice in the French gothic style, and for many years past the Rev. Canon Crawley has laboured with much patience and self denial. The Primitive Methodist Chapel is situate in Northenden Road. St. Anne's Church, the first in the township of Sale, was erected on a site given by the late Samuel Brooks, Esq. It is a building of stone in the early English style, consisting of chancel, nave of four bays, aisles, north and west porches, and a north west embattled tower, with pinnacles and octagonal spire. To meet the growing wants of the congregation it was enlarged in 1864, just ten years after it was opened, and again in 1887, furnishing sittings for 900 people. The first vicar was the Rev. J. Johnson Cort, M.A., late Fellow of St. John's College, Cambridge. The interior is adorned with a new reredos and communion table, the gift of John Kendall, Esq., to the memory of his wife, and a brass tablet let in the wall states that "in loving memory of Eliza Jane Kendall, this sanctuary was beautified and reredos erected, 1893."

The new three manual organ, 40 stops, by Harrison and Harrison, is considered the finest organ in the parish.

In the Chancel is a marble tablet inserted in wall, to—

"The Rev. Jonathan Johnson Cort, M.A., Fellow of St. John's College, Cambridge, Vicar of Sale. This monument was erected by the congregation. Born January 26th, 1827; died October 10th, 1884."

Another marble tablet in the Chancel certifies—

"In loving memory of George Vardon Ryder. Born 4th March, 1803; died 22nd June, 1888." "Sarah Starkey, his wife. Born 2nd March, 1804; died 26th March, 1889."

In the Transept is a stained-glass window—

"In loving remembrance of the late Thomas Byron Hollinworth. This memorial is dedicated. Died August 8th, 1867; age 34." Subject: Christ blessing little children, and in Temple.

Another stained-glass window—

"In affectionate remembrance of Williami Wilson. This window is erected by his widow and children. Died April 1st, 1875; age 58 years." Subject: The Epiphany.

A stained-glass window—

"To the memory of William Joynson, of Ashfield. Died December 27th, 1882." Subject: The Transfiguration.

In the aisle is a stained window—

"In memory of Mrs. Cort, wife of the late Vicar of Sale. Erected by members of congregation." Subject: Dorcas, St. Anne and B.V. Mary, St. Elizabeth.

Marble tablets—

"To the memory of Marion, the devoted wife of Charles Samuel Evans. This tablet was erected by her husband."

To "John Wallace Murray, of Fraserburgh, and afterwards of this parish, who died at sea, on his way to Melbourne for the benefit of his health, October 28th, 1868, aged 30 years."

To "Charles Samuel Evans. Born September 27th, 1791; died September 6th, 1857." A three-light stained-glass window to "Elizabeth Hayes, died July 4th, 1888, aged 49 years." Subject: Faith, Hope, Charity. Stained-glass window to "Phœbe Nancy Hayes, died September 24th, 1882, aged 17 years." Subject: Martha and Mary.

"In loving memory of our dear parents, John Henry Waltham, born March 29th, 1824, died March 21st, 1893; also Elizabeth, his wife, born May 19th, 1824, died June 10th, 1894, who were for nearly 40 years members of this congregation."

A large east window was erected by J. J. Occleston in 1863. Subject: The Ascension.

The Rev. John Patchett Cort, the present vicar, is the only son of the Rev. J. C. Cort, the first vicar of the parish. He is a graduate of St. John's College, Cambridge, where he took the degree of B.A. in 1879, in which year he was ordained Deacon, taking priest's orders in 1880. He was curate of St. Philemon's, Sheffield, in 1879, and curate of St. Anne's, under his late father from 1881 to 1884, when he succeeded him as vicar. He was made an honorary B.A. of Owen's College, Manchester, in 1882. The living is in the hands of Trustees. The amount of the income from the endowment is £40; rents, £350; fees, £44; gross income, £434; net, £300; with a population of 5,956.

The Church of St. John the Divine, in Brookland's Road, was erected in 1867. It is built of freestone in the Gothic style, consisting of chancel, nave, transepts, north west porch, and a turret on the western gable containing one bell. There are 500 sittings. In the west end is a memorial window to the memory of the late John Brooks, Esq., M.P. There is a large Parish room in Marsland's Road, and a National School on Baguley Moor connected with the parish, which is ecclesiastically in the township of Baguley. The first perpetual curate of St. John's was the Rev. Thomas Brooke, and was afterwards first vicar.

The Rev. Hugh Bethell Jones, who succeeded the late Rev. Thomas Brooke, the first vicar, is a graduate of Trinity College, Dublin, and took his B.A. degree in 1861, and M.A., 1875; University College, Durham, *ad eundum*, B.A., L.Th. He was ordained deacon in 1863, priest in 1867, and B.D. in 1895. His first curacy was Whalley Range, Manchester, from 1863 to 1867, when he was appointed Vicar of Christ Church, Appleton-le-Moors, and from 1870 to 1876 he held the important curacy of St. Clement's, Chorlton-cum-Hardy, which he vacated on his preferment to the vicarage of St. John the Divine, Brooklands, or Baguley. He is the author of "*Preces Liturgicæ*, Lectures on the morning and evening prayer," (1873), "Some thoughts on the Establishment of the Church of England," (1880), etc. The patrons of the living are Sir William Cunliffe Brooks, Bart., and Thomas Brooks, Esq. The gross income is £300, and the population 627.

The growth of population on the westerly side of the Bridgewater Canal, necessitated the formation of a new ecclesiastical district, and in 1883, the fine church dedicated to St. Paul was erected. It is in early English style from designs of Mr. H. R. Price, of Manchester, and contains 750 sittings, 250 of which are free. The first vicar was the late Rev. T. A. Livesey, whose learning and piety are remembered and appreciated by many of the early worshippers at this church. He died after a too brief ministry in 1887. Near the church is a Sunday School and parish room.

The Rev. William Edward Chadwick, the present vicar, is a scholar and exhibitioner of Jesus College, Cambridge, where he graduated B.A. (Ægrot. Math. Tripos), and M.A. in 1881. He was ordained deacon the same year, and was curate of Holy Trinity, Coventry, 1881, and took priest's orders in 1882. He was curate of All Saint's, Bradford, Yorks., from 1884 to 1887 when he was appointed Vicar of St. Paul's, Sale. The living is in the hands of Trustees; gross income, £450, with house; and population of parish, 3,126.

The growing requirements of the parish of Ashton-on-Mersey rendered necessary the erection of a Chapel-of-ease, which was dedicated to St. Mary Magdalene, and opened in March, 1874. The site was given by Sir William Cunliffe Brooks, Bart, who also contributed liberally to the cost of the building—about £9,000 – raised by subscriptions. The parish was formed in 1894. The architecture of St. Mary's is of the early decorated period, and was erected from designs of Messrs. Wilson and Oldham. The building consists of nave, with north and south transepts. The pulpit is in Caen stone, with marble steps, and illuminated texts adorn the walls. The ceiling is of dark wood, moulded and panelled, and with bosses relieved by black and gold. The tower and spire are on the south side of the chancel at the junction of the transept with the nave.

On the division of the ancient parish of Ashton-on-Mersey, in 1894, the Rev. Christie Chetwynd Atkinson, who had held the

ST. MARY'S CHURCH, ASHTON-ON MERSEY.

senior curacy under the Rev. Joseph Ray, a former rector, since 1882, was appointed by the Trustees the first vicar of S. Mary Magdalene. He is a M.A. of Keble College, Oxford, where he took a fourth class in the Theological School in 1878. He was ordained Deacon in 1879, and Priest in 1880. He was assistant master of All Saints' School, Bloxham, and curate of Hempton, Oxon, 1879 to 1880, assistant master of St. Paul's, Stony Stratford, 1880 to 1882, when he was appointed to the curacy of Ashton-on-Mersey. The gross income of the living is returned at £265 per annum, and nett, £90, with an estimated population of 3,108. Already schools and a parish room are built to meet the increasing educational and social wants of the parish.

If the saying be true that happy is the country, and let us in the present instance add township, that has no history, then Sale may be regarded as being exceptionally favoured in this respect. There is very little to be said as to the proceedings of its Local Board from its formation in 1867, which is specially striking, and it is chiefly remarkable for the business-like way in which its members set about bring the affairs of the township up to date in the matter of sanitary and general administration. Wm. Joynson, Esq., J.P., whose venerable appearance and sound good sense inspired universal respect, was unanimously elected Chairman and under his able direction the proceedings of the Board were distinguished by smoothness and harmony. Under the superintendence of Mr. A. G. McBeath, the surveyor and engineer to the the Board, a complete and efficient system of drainage was laid down, and the roads of the township greatly extended and improved. This policy, the Sale Urban District Council, on succeeding to the inheritance left by the defunct Board, in 1894, has continued, and in accordance with the requirements of the Mersey and Irwell Joint Committee, a scheme for the purification of the Sale Sewage, has been laid down near Dane Road, where about two million gallons per day is dealt with in order that a satisfactory effluent may be passed into the river Mersey. The works have been constructed from plans of Mr. McBeath.

Particulars of the increase of the township will be found in the appendix, but it should be added that the Free Library and Technical classes in Tatton Road are in a flourishing condition, and a School of Art adjoining is now completed.

The total amount borrowed by the Sale Local Board and Sale Urban District Council up to and including July, 1895, for works of sewage and public improvements amounted to £45,385, of which at the end of March, 1896, the sum of £23,219 9s. 4d. had been repaid, leaving a balance of £22,165 10s. 8d., extending over a period of 30 years, at the low rate of three and a half to four and a half per cent. interest. Excluding Bowdon, which has a remarkably low district rate, Sale compares most favourably with surroundings authorities, having a comparatively low district rate, while its death rate, considering the rapidity of increase of population is next to Bowdon, as low as can be found in any similar area and number. In 1895, the township was divided for electoral purposes into five wards, viz.: North, South, East, West, and Central, each with three members.

CHAPTER XVII.

Wythenshawe Hall and the Tattons—Carrington Moss, with an account of Carrington fight, a memorable local event—Manchester Ship Canal—A Bishop from Carrington—Baguley Hall and the Leghs— Ruddings Hall—The Gerrards and the Vaudreys—Edleston's Lepidoptera of the Bollin Valley; ornithology, etc.—Ashley Hall, a notable meeting; a little-known tragedy—The murder at the Bleeding Wolf, etc.

THE name and family of Tatton of Wythenshawe have been identified with this district for many centuries. Mr. Earwaker, the historian of East Cheshire, points out that records relating to Wythenshawe are extant for quite 550 years, and it is noteworthy as one of the few estates which have been handed down in the same family from one generation to another since the middle of the 14th century. In all probability the descendants of Hamo de Masey, or Massy, of Dunham, very soon obtained possession of the land at Wythenshawe, as there was a branch of the Mascies there about 1275.

Robert de Tatton, of whom mention is first made, owned land in Northenden in 1297, and his grandson marrying a daughter of William Mascy, brought Wythenshawe into the Tatton family in 1370. Robert and William seem to have been for generations favourite family names. There is one Nicholas, who was Baron of the Exchequer of Chester in 1451, but down to the year 1700 Robert is either succeeded by William, or William by Robert. In 1747, William Tatton, of Wythenshawe, Esquire, married for his second wife, Hester, eldest daughter of John Egerton, Esquire, of Tatton Park. She was sister and sole heiress of Samuel Egerton, Esquire. The result of this marriage was to cause the Tattons of Wythenshawe to assume, by royal license, the name and arms of Egerton of Tatton, which was done by William (Tatton) Egerton, Esq., of Tatton Park and Wythenshawe, who was M.P. for Cheshire at the time of his death in 1806. By his first marriage with Frances Maria, eldest daughter of the Rev. John Fountayne, Dean of York, he had two sons and one daughter, who retained the old name of Tatton; those by his second wife, Mary, second daughter of Richard Wilbraham Bootle, Esq., of Rode, preserving the name of Egerton. Their eldest son, Wilbraham Egerton, Esq., of Tatton Park, was the father of the late Lord Egerton, of Tatton. Their second son, Thomas William, resumed by royal license, dated 9th January, 1806, the name and arms of Tatton, on succeeding to the Wythenshawe estates. He was High Sheriff of Cheshire in 1809. By his marriage with Emma, daughter of the Honourable John Grey, a younger son of Harry Grey, fourth Earl of Stamford and Warrington, he was brought into still greater contact with our own district. He was succeeded by his eldest and only son—there being eight daughters—Thomas William Tatton, the late worthy and beloved possessor of the estate of Wythenshawe. He was born on the 2nd June, 1816, and was married January 25th, 1843, to Harriet Susan, eldest daughter of Robert Towneley Parker, Esq., of Cuerdon, Lancashire. She died in London, February 20th, 1873. Their eldest son, Thomas Egerton Tatton, Esq., born May 31st, 1846, is married to Essex Mary, second daughter of Col. The Hon. T. G. Cholmondeley, of Abbott's Moss, near Northwich. He has two brothers, Robert Grey Tatton and Reginald Arthur Tatton, and one sister, Mary Emily. The late possessor of Wythenshawe was well known and highly respected throughout the county. Amongst those with whom he was brought into immediate contact, not only in the family circle, but amongst his tenantry, he was justly beloved. Courteous in his bearing and kindly in his manner, the merest stranger received a patient hearing at his hands. He qualified as a Magistrate for the County on the 17th October, 1842, and in 1848 was High Sheriff of Cheshire. In his magisterial capacity he was Chairman of the Altrincham Petty Sessional Division. In all matters relating to the social, moral, and physical well-being of the people, he took the deepest interest. When the fear of an invasion on the part of our French neighbours—a fear happily found to have little or no real foundation—caused a national call to arms to resound through the land, Mr. Tatton practically recognised his duty as a patriot, and took a prominent part in the formation of the Volunteer force in this district. He was for many years the respected Colonel of the 3rd Battalion C.R.V., which had its headquarters at Altrincham, and his resignation was greatly deplored. His latest act of any great public importance, was the laying of the foundation stone of the Church of St. Wilfrid, at Northenden, on the 11th April, 1874. In this work he took the deepest interest, and in addition to restoring the north and south chapels at his own cost, he gave £750 towards the subscription for re-building the main body of this venerable fabric. In politics he was a Conservative, but in the moderateness of his views he was a pattern worthy of imitation by the members of any political party. Indeed we may apply to him most truthfully, the lines of Pope, which have already been applied to another member of the family :

> A fair example of unblemished worth,
> Of modest wisdom and pacifick truth ;
> Compos'd in suff'rings, and in joy sedate,
> Good without noise, without pretension, great !

Wythenshawe Hall, which next claims attention, stands about two and a half miles from Sale. Originally, the structure was in the black and white style of Cheshire, and surrounded by a fortified wall and moat. It has numerous gables, which lend to it an air of great picturesqueness, and at various periods it has been the subject of many alterations and additions. As will have been already seen, the family has been singularly fortunate in retaining possession of the ancestral home. Webb, in his Itinerary (1614), states that "Wythenshawe, or Withanshaw, is a goodly Lordship and stately house, the mansion of Tattons, men of great worship and dignity. A race of them for a descent or two, through the variable inconstancy of all mortall happinesse, much eclipsed.

And the heir of that house, though a gentleman of rare sufficiency and parts, answerable every way to the great worth of his ancestors, yet by troubles and encumbrances, whereunto greatest estates are oft subject, obscured : that he never yet shined in his own sphear ; and the chiefest hope now of raising the house remains in the Grandchild of his own loyns, a towardly child in minority." It will be thus seen that the family has passed through many vicissitudes.

Although Robert Tatton was married in 1628-9 to Anne, daughter of William Brereton, Esq., of Ashley, a near relative of Brereton, one of the leaders on the Parliamentary side in the Civil War, this did not prevent him from warmly espousing the cause of King Charles. He suffered greatly in consequence, and Mr. Earwaker in his "East Cheshire," states there is preserved at Wythenshawe an "Inventory of all the Goods and Cattels of Robert Tatton, of Withenshaw, Esq., viewed and praysed the 2 June 19, Charles I., 1643," the total value being set down at £1,649 2s. 8d. Soon afterwards Wythenshawe was besieged by the Parliamentarian forces under Col. Duckenfield, and for a year and a half it was defended by the owner. Amongst the defenders were—Edward Legh, cf Baguley, Esquire, Mr. Richard Vawdrey, Mr. John Bretland and his man. Out of Baguley, William Hamnett, Robert Chapman and Nicholas his brother, Thomas Hill. Also Robert Deane of Altrincham, Hugh Newton, Richard Grantham, of Hale, Robert his sonne, and George Delahey of Timperley. Mr. Thomas Gerrard of the Riddings, and Mr. William Davenport of Baguley, are also mentioned. The house was taken on Sunday, February 25th, 1643-4, two pieces of heavy ordnance which were sent for from Manchester being brought against it. Had it not been for this, the besiegers might have had to beat a retreat. During this memorable and trying time, one of the maid-servants is credited with a most daring act. Captain Adams was so bold that he ventured to sit on the outer wall. Being seen by the domestic in this exposed position, she asked for and was furnished with a musket, and so true was her

WYTHENSHAWE HALL.

aim, that the officer was shot dead. However questionable this may be, there is no doubt Captain Adams met his death there. Six skeletons were found in the last century lying close together in the garden. They are supposed to have been the soldiers who fell under the fire of the garrison, and were buried as they lay. For his " Delinquencie," he had his estates sequestered by Parliament, and although it was stated that he had been "damnified since theise troubles by the losse of his goodes, rentes, waste of his houses and tymber," £2,500, and in other ways probably £2,000 more, the resolution of a committee convened by the Parliament, inflicted a fine of £804 10s. 0d. This was subsequently reduced to £707 13s. 4d., a fine heavy enough in all conscience to appal the stoutest heart. It is satisfactory to note that Mr. Tatton lived to see the Restoration of Charles II. "He died," says Mr. Earwaker, "August 19th, and was buried at Northenden, August 24th, 1669; and it is somewhat strange that amongst the numerous monumental tablets to the various members of the Tatton family in Northenden Church, there is nothing to commemorate the life and character of one who suffered so much for his loyalty to his sovereign, at a time, and in a part of the country where loyalty was a crime and treason a virtue to be highly rewarded." However much we may question the accuracy of this sweeping statement, viewed in the light which history has unfolded, all will concur in the opinion that there is no record of the kind indicated to teach us a lesson of at least consistency and perseverance.

Numerous articles were removed from Wythenshawe after the siege, amongst them two bells, which appear to have confounded historians somewhat. By one it is stated that the old house bell was carried off, but afterwards restored by Charles II., with a small silver snuff-box, having the donor's initials and medallion upon it, as a mark of his esteem. Another has it that this bell remained with Col. Duckenfield's successors until the 20th October, 1807, when Sir Henry Duckenfield, their then representative, "gracefully restored this prize of war to the then representative of Withenshaw Hall, in which house it now hangs ; and so a trophy snatched in a time of civil war was restored in a time of domestic peace, after a lapse of more than a century and a half." The inscription on this bell is

'Gloria in Excelsis Deo.'
MDCXLI.".

Mr. Earwaker states, however, that the chapel bell, which is evidently the one here referred to, after having been preserved at Duckenfield Lodge for over 200 years, was recently presented by Mr. Astley to Mr. Tatton, and is now at Wythenshawe. Cromwell stayed at Wythenshawe Hall, and the room he slept in is still called "Oliver Cromwell's room." The bed which is dated 1619 is of elegantly carved wood, the furniture and mirrors matching it and of the same age. " All's well that ends well."

A vigorous stride across the country brings us to Carrington Moss, and it is very amusing to read in this connection the quaintly droll description given by Mr. Leo H. Grindon, in that notable and delightful work, "Manchester Walks and Wild Flowers." He says, "Should any of our unknown companions in these rambles be vegetarians, they will please here take notice that Carrington Moss in the summer time is a scene of ravenous slaughter, such as cannot but be exceedingly painful and shocking to them. It will appear the more repulsive from the high character for innocence ordinarily borne by the destroyers, who are the last beings in the world we should expect to find indulging in personal cruelty, much less acting the part of perfidious sirens. Having given this warning, our friends will of course have only themselves to blame should they persist in following us to the spectacle we are about to describe ; and now it only remains to say that the perpetrators of the deeds alluded to are *plants*." Then we are treated to a description of the Sarracenias, and the Droseraceæ or Sundews ; the pea green Sphagnum, in the little marshes ; the Lancashire Asphodel, which grows very profusely ; the Rhyncospora Alba, the Cranberry, the Andromeda, and the

Cotton Sedge, all in great abundance, with luxuriant grasses peculiar to moorlands, and the finest specimens of purple heather to be seen within so short a distance from Manchester. Owing to its acquirement by the Manchester Corporation, the Moss is being rapidly brought into cultivation, and while the advance of population has its drawbacks, yet the borders of the Moss and the lanes approaching it are prolific in curious plants. "July," says Mr. Grindon, "is the best time. Then the foxgloves lift their magnificent crimson spires, and the purple tufted vetch trails its light foliage and delicate clusters beneath the woodbines ; and the tall bright lotus in coronets of gold, and the meadow sweet, smelling like hawthorn, make the lady fern look its greenest, while in the fields alongside stands, in all its pride of yellow and violet, the great parti-coloured dead nettle, which here grows in luxuriant perfection. All the lanes leading to Carrington Moss are remarkably rich in wild flowers and ferns, the latter including the Royal fern or Osmunda, and in early summer show great plenty of the white lychnis, called, from not opening its petals till evening, "the vespertina." The pink-eyed lychnis, or "Brid e'en," or Bird's eye of our country friends, is always open. There is also abundance of blackberries, wild raspberries, &c., and nature's gifts are everywhere found in great profusion and beauty.

Carrington Fight, or "feight," as it is termed by the natives, occupies a relative position in the annals of this primitive village, that the battle of Agincourt does to those of England. It was formerly held up to strangers as an overwhelming proof of the victoriously pugnacious propensities of their ancestors, and at the wakes and other festive gatherings, its recitation, generally by one of the " rude forefathers of the hamlet," was a feature in the proceedings. It is moreover a reminder of those little neighbourly battles which took place something like half-a-century ago, when it was regarded as a privilege for the boys of one village to give those of another place a thrashing—if they could. It was a period, too, when strength amongst the lower orders was a synonym for brutality, and when there were no neighbours handy a little battle was occasionally fought between themselves for the mastery. Carrington fight is, in the flowing cups of the Carringtonites still both freshly and freely remembered. It has been worked into verse by a local "poet," and from this fact and the implements used, it may be inferred that the conflict was of a more than usually sanguinary character. Pikels, axes, sticks, stones, and similar things were brought into requisition, but singular to relate, no lives were lost, probably owing to the opponents of the Carrington men thinking discretion the better part of valour, and disappearing with marvellous celerity. There are no fewer than 18 verses in this extraordinary "poem." The first is inviting in its character:—

> Good people, pay attention to what I'm going to lay down,
> It is of a dreadful battle that was fought in Carrington town ;
> The Flixton men they did come here, thinking to have some fun,
> But as soon as Carrington lads stept up, they showed how things were done.
>
> CHORUS.
> We're all true-hearted lads, my boys,
> We all fought in one mind,
> We made Packer with his pikel run
> And leave his troop behind.

The gentleman alluded to as Packer was evidently a celebrity who was engaged in the packing of wool, the combing of which was a pursuit in the Flixton district, and was not probably his real name. The second verse describes the circumstances under which the encounter takes place. It was on Soft Tuesday (Shrove Tuesday ?) and at the local races the Flixton men showed their vexation that their favourites did not win. A sufficient *casus belli* is found in their determination to take "that hat off Smith," when he went to "the Bell" for refreshments. The Partington men shouted for fair play, but

> "As soon as the Carrington lads went in
> They made them cut away."

In the fourth verse the battle rages. Five of the Flixton men flew away like lightning, and by the time the fifth verse is reached the reverse has become a rout, and the others ignominiously effect a retreat by the back door of the "Bell" down to the river side. Those who have read the Greek poets are only too familiar with the hairbreadth escapes they make their heroes run on many occasions. It is thus with our local Homer :—

> It was at Parson's Sale second fight began,
> These Flixton men came shouting, thinking we were gone,
> "Come out, ye Carrington rebels, we know you've had enough,"
> As soon as Carrington lads stepped up, into th' Windy Mill they flew.

What they did when they got inside the Windmill Inn is vividly depicted—

> Now when they geet in th' Windy Mill, thro' windows they did peep,
> They said to one another, "Lads, up th' chimney let us creep;"
> The landlord sat in his arm-chair, and cocking up his face,
> He shouted to the landlady, "They're hiding in th' clock case!"

Some disappear in various directions. One old blacksmith from Flixton, more terror-stricken than the rest, runs into the furnace hole. When he gets home his face is covered with soot, and he describes to his wife his actions and feelings very truthfully. Another battle is imminent. The "Carrington lads," armed with "axes, swords, and bills," again go forward to meet the Flixton men with "loud huzzas."

> The Flixton men they did run off, feer't lest they all geet killed,
> One of them shouted out, "I see the savage men,
> I wish I could get Flixton, for I'd ne'er come here again."

In this encounter four of the defeated party were so badly wounded that they had to be removed to the Manchester Infirmary, where one of them regrets his visit.

> One said unto the doctor, "My wounds are very sore,
> I'll ne'er go ower Carrington bridge a feightin' any more."

A magisterial investigation followed, in which we are told "two 'tornies" and two justices were engaged for two days at the Blue Bell, with what result deponent sayeth not.

That magnificent feat of engineering skill, the Manchester Ship Canal, enters the Altrincham Union at Partington, passing through Carrington, Warburton, and Thelwall, &c., on the way to Eastham. It is not necessary here to go over the vicissitudes of this undertaking. For some years it was in abeyance, and although Lord Egerton of Tatton was appointed Chairman of the Directors of the Ship Canal Co. in February, 1887, it was not until November of the same year that the first sod was cut. The contract with the late Mr. T. A. Walker, was £5,750,000, but his demise caused the work to be taken in hand by the Ship Canal Co., with the result that when the Canal was opened in January, 1894, the total cost amounted to nearly £15,000,000, of which the Manchester Corporation provided close upon £5,000,000. The formal opening by Her Majesty the Queen, did not take place until May, the occasion being marked by great rejoicings and a most loyal and enthusiastic welcome. The Canal, which is about $35\frac{1}{2}$ miles in length, has been excavated throughout to a depth of 26 feet, which is the depth of the large docks at Manchester, the smaller docks being 20 feet.

The bottom width at the full depth of 26 feet is 120 feet, with the following exceptions :—

(a) At the curve at the Weaver Outfall, the width at the full depth is 140 feet, and at the bend at Runcorn, approaching the Runcorn Railway Bridge, it is 150 feet.

(b) For a distance of about $2\frac{1}{2}$ miles, between Latchford Locks Partington Coal Basin, the bottom width is at present only 80 to 90 feet, and large vessels are not allowed to pass each other on that portion of the Canal.

(c) From Barton Aqueduct to the Manchester Docks the bottom width is 170 feet.

For purposes of comparison it may be stated that the Suez Canal had, until recently (when widening operations were begun), only a bottom width of 72 feet, except at the passing places. The tidal portion of the Ship Canal from Eastham to Latchford Locks (21 miles) is maintained at a level of 9 feet 6 inches above mean tide level. When the tide rises above this level it flows in and out of the Canal over three tidal weirs and three sets of sluices. The fixed bridges across the Canal are 75 feet above the normal water level, but as the headway is necessarily a few feet less when high tides or floods occur, to avoid detention masts should clear the bridges at 70 feet above the water level. The locks and swing bridges are all connected by telephone with each other and with the Dock Office at Manchester. The Manchester Docks are equipped with transit sheds of new design, hydraulic and steam cranes, and other appliances for giving quick despatch in loading and discharging. The railways of the Company convey traffic direct between the various loading and discharging berths at the docks and along the Canal, and are connected with all the railway systems of the country. The Canal and docks are in direct communication with the whole of the barge canals of the district. The chief engineer was Mr. (now Sir) E. Leader Williams, a resident for many years past at Altrincham, and formerly the principal engineer to the Weaver Trust and the Bridgewater Canal undertakings, the last named now merged in the Ship Canal Company.

John Rider, Bishop of Killaloe, Ireland, was born at Carrington in 1562. He was a graduate of Jesus College, Oxford, and after passing through many successful preferments, was made Bishop of Killaloe in 1612. He was the author of several political and controversial tracts, of a Dictionary (English-Latin and Latin-English), printed at Oxford in 1689. His career is fully dealt with in Athena Oxoniensis (*Bliss*).

Within a few square miles of Altrincham we have the remains of halls and other residences, now mostly converted into farmhouses, indicating the existence of families, some of whom have in a certain degree left their mark on the history of this country. For instance, the family of Brereton, so far as this district is concerned, has faded from popular memory. It was as ancient and honourable as any in the county, and we will briefly sketch its descent, and the manner of settlement of one of its branches at Ashley. For this purpose, let us look a little way over the hill tops of time. The Breretons, like many others, took the names of the townships or places in which they lived, and they were settled in the township of Brereton about the time of the Conquest. In 1632, they claimed a moiety of the Barony of Malpas by descent, and their branches spread over the county, their connections by marriage being the Leghs of Booths, Meres of Mere, the Dones, and Leghs of High Legh, &c. In the reign of Henry VIII., Richard Brereton, of Lea Hall, Middlewich, younger son of Sir William Brereton, married Thomasin, daughter and heiress of George Ashley, Esq., of Ashley. The estate continued vested in the Breretons till the middle of the seventeenth century, when it was left by Thomas Brereton to be divided amongst his three sisters who had married into the Tatton, Barlow, and Ashton families.

Baguley, or, as it is anciently spelled, Baggiley, was held along with Sinderland at the coming of the Normans by Edward and Suga, Udeman and Pat, who are described as "gentlemen," and later the township gave its name to the family of Baggiley, who were seated here as early as the 18th of Henry III. (1234), and in one charter it was granted to one John Baggiley the payment of 12d. for all services, saving to Wm. Baggiley, John's third best pig when the pig could find mast for itself. Afterwards, the Leghs, one of whom wrote several historical poems, entitled "Scottish Fielde," in the reign of Henry VII., held the township for a long period, until the line terminated in Edward Legh in 1688. After passing through the hands of several owners, the township is practically owned by the Tattons of Wythenshawe. Of great interest to antiquarians, as well as excursionists, is Baguley Old Hall, with its ancient oak wood work. Only one large apartment of the old hall remains, the greater portion of the structure having at some remote period been destroyed by fire. Here is still to be seen the effigy of Sir William de Baggiley, formerly in Bowdon Parish Church. The tumulus on Baguley Moor was opened many years ago, and from the remains is supposed to have been the site of an old windmill.

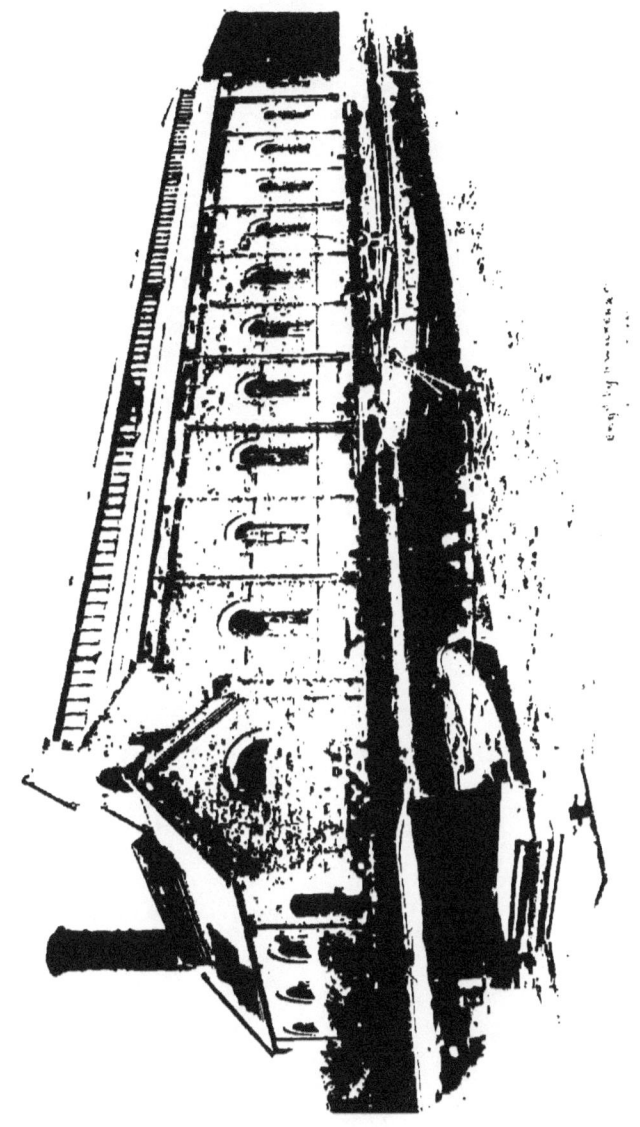

The Manor of Timperley was held at a very early period by a family assuming the local name, and amongst the charterers is Thomas Gerard, of Riddings, gent., Riddings Hall, having been purchased from the Vaudreys. Bank Hill (Bank Hall) and Riddings were both seats of the branches of the Vaudreys, of Bowdon, and in 1567 Robert Vaudrey, of Riddings, made a lengthy will, in which he wills that his "bodie be chested decentlye, brought home and buryed at the Parishe Churche of Bowdon, in the Chappell, and placed where my parents do lye." "Item to sixe of the poorest men of my ten'ntes wth-in the parishe of Bowdon, vj. white gownes, desirynge they'm heartfullye to praye for me, and to go afore my corps to the churche and buryall of the same. And to other vj. of the poorest of my ten'ntes wth-in the parishes of Northerden and Ashton-upon-M'see banck other vj. gownes of blacke cotton, desyrynge and hertfullye prayinge theym likewise to praye for me in comynge next after my corps to the Churche and buryall. . . . . The testator also disposes of his property and manors in Bowdon, Bollington, Hale, Ashley, Chester, &c., and to Margaret V. (Vaudrey, his daughter) at suche tyme as she shall leave her dishonest and uncleane lyvynge for and durynge all such tyme after as she shall lyve honestlye V^{li} by yeare." There are bequests to his relatives and to poor kinsfolk friends, poor "maydes," poor men, poor children, and to the curates and clerks on certain feast days. He had a large number of God-children, to every one of whom he left iiij^{d} "by estymation xxiiij^{li} viij^{s}." "I do bequeath and forgyve my disobedyent sonne Thom's all such and those sum'es of moneye wch he hath wrongfullye receyved (embezzlement was not unknown in these times) and taken from me, and also the sum'e of C^{li} xvijsiiij^{d} wch he alsoe is indebted to me or such p'te thereof as shall remayne vulgived me at the tyme of my decease accordynge as by a bill of his hand appeareth willynge and com'andyne and upone my blessynge chargynge and requyrynge hym to use sobrietie, and to leave all evell and drynkynge companye and for to say o'r Lordes praier with such other praiers and thankes gevynge to God as he shall gyve his grace and put hym in mynd daylye uppon his knees everye mornynge humblye besekyne hym to have m'cye uppon all his creatures, and to gyve hym grace to lyve honestlye and iustlye in the world uppon my blessynge, also willynge hym to say the Articles of o'r fayth, the Crede, once everye week, and to be lovynge, kynde, and helpynge to his mother, brethren, and sister, exortynge her to repent her evell lyfe, and to lyve honestlye from henceforth, and also to be kynde and helpynge in his powre to all his poore cousens and friendes and to all the ten'ntes of the landes wch God hath lent me and I have left hym, and to take nothynge of theym nor of any of theym but only their due rente ande servyce, inasmuche as God hath sent hym the landes without labor, and they must labor and paye for theym, and to be satisfied wth the same wch is much better than was left me, and wuld have byn better to hym if he wuld have byn counselled or advysed by me or have shewed hym selfe obedient or lovynge toward me, for although I wuld not yet I rather desire to have hym dye affore me than to lyve to do hurt after me, wch God forbid, and uppon my blessynge I warn the said Thom's from, requryeynge hym to love areade and to serve God, to frequent to charitie, &c." For this he forgives him his "mysbehayvyor and tresspesses done to me, and gyve the my blessynge, besekynge God to do the same, &c." There are other legacies of personal effects, including more than "one bowe and a shoff of arrowes," and to Cousin William Barneston's two boys "iijsiiij^d to buy theym bookes." "To my sister Brock vj' viij^d and a lambe." He appointed Ales, his wife, during her widowhood only, his sons, John and Richard Vaudrey, and the Rev. John Robinson, his executors. Wm. Arderne, of Timperley, gent., is supposed to have been Mayor of Altrincham in 1560, but in the list of Mayors the name is given as Ardron. Alexander Vaudrey is said to have been Mayor in 1616, and George Vaudrey, also of Timperley, Mayor in 1636. The land in this and other surrounding townships came by heirship and otherwise to the Earl of Stamford, who in or about 1857 sold his possessions in Baguley, Timperley, Hale, Ashton-on-Mersey, Carrington, Partington, Sale (that portion known as Brooklands), to the late Mr. Samuel Brooks, banker, of Manchester. How this large property was developed is well known. The large water drain, considered at the time of its construction a perfect triumph, extended from Hale to the river Mersey, a distance of over three miles, and was made at a cost of £12,000. Mr. Brooks, as lord of the Manor of Ashton-on-Mersey, revived the ancient court leet, and his views and ideas have been well carried out by his son, Sir William Cunliffe Brooks, Bart.

Bank Hall, Hale, another residence of the Vaudreys is supposed to have been a monastic institution, but there is no historical evidence, and tradition is only supported by the yew trees planted in the neighbourhood of the house. The "Oaklands" at Timperley, formerly the residence of the late Mr. George Falkner, the head of the famous Manchester printers, is the scene of "Sybilla," a short but interesting story by Mrs. G. Linnæus Banks. Christ Church, Timperley, has little pretension to architectural beauty. It was opened in 1849, the Rev. Edward Dowling, M.A., being appointed incumbent. He was succeeded by the Rev. S. Wilkinson, the present vicar.

Quoting from Mr. Grindon's delightful "Country Rambles," we find that on the Cotterill side of Mobberley the country resembles that in the vicinity of Castle Mill, consisting of gentle slopes and promontories, often wooded, and at every turn presenting some new and agreeable feature. The little dells and and cloughs, each with its little rill of clear water scampering away to the Bollin, are delicious. The botany of Cotterill is also reproduced in its best features ; mosses of the choicest kind grow on every bank—Hypna, with large green feathery branches, like ferns in minature ; Jungermannias also ; and the noblest plants of the hart's-tongue fern that occur in the district. One of the dells positively overflows with it, excepting that is, where the ground is not pre-occupied by the prickly shield fern. All the Spring flowers open here with the first steps of the renewed season. Mr. Grindon says the interest of the Bollin Valley is quite as great to the entomologist as to the botanist. The late Mr. Edleston, whose magnificent collection was then well known, states that the meadows near the river Bollin from Bank Hall to Castle Mill produce more diurnal Lepidoptera than any other locality in the Manchester district, the following butterflies being a select list :—Gonepteryx Rhamni, brimstone ; Pieris Brassicoe, large white ; Pieris Rapæ, small white ; Pieris Napi, green veined white ; Anthocaris Cardamines, orange tip ; Hipparchia Janira, meadow brown ; Hipparchia Jithonus, large Heath ; Hipperchia Hyperanthus, wood Ringlet ; Cœnonympha Pamphilus, small heath ; Cynthia Cardui, painted lady ; Vanessa Atalanta, Red Admiral ; Vanessa Io, Peacock ; Vanessa Uturicœ, small Tortoise shell ; Melitœa Artemis, greasy fritillary ; Chrysophanus Phlocas, small copper ; Polyommatus Alexis, common blue ; Thanaos Tages, dingy skipper; Pamphila Sylvanus, large skipper. Moths : Procris Statices, green forester ; Anthrocera Trifollii, five spot Burnet; Anthrocera Filipendulæ, six spot Burnet ; Sesia Bombyliformis, narrow bordered bee hawk ; Heliodes Arbuti, small yellow underwing ; Euclidia Mi, Mother Shipton ; Euclidia Glyphica, Burnet.

Mr. T. A. Coward has supplied me with the following information :—The vertebrate fauna of the district includes a larger number of species than might be expected from the proximity to the large manufacturing towns, and in spite of the rapid growth of the population, there are still a great variety of animals and birds thriving within a few miles of Bowdon and Sale. The extensive park land of Dunham, the water-meadows of the Mersey and Bollin, and the numerous coverts devoted to the preservation of game, afford shelter or suitable feeding grounds for many of our most interesting species. Five bats have been identified in the district, the old timber in Dunham Park, Tatton, and elsewhere, supplying their diurnal and winter resting places. The long-eared bat, pipestrelle and noctule or great bat are the commonest, and may be observed in many suitable localities any fine summer evening. The whiskered bat is not uncommon, and Daubenton's bat skims over the surface of the water on all the larger pools and the straight reaches of the Bollin. All the Insectivora included by Bell in his British Quadrupeds occur: the hedgehog, mole, and the three shrews—a skull of the lesser shrew, one of the smallest and rarest British mammals, having been obtained from an owl pellet picked up in Dunham Park. Squirrels may often be seen when the trees are bare of leaves, and the dormouse has been reported from the Tatton estate. Field, bank, and water voles are abundant, the last, locally known as the water-rat, must not be confounded with the brown or common rat, which often frequents the banks of streams and ponds, and lives a semi-aquatic life. The common, and long-tailed field mouse are both too plentiful.

Hares and rabbits are partially preserved, but the former are not as plentiful as they were a few years ago. An extensive domesticated herd of fallow deer exists in Dunham Park. Of the Carnivora, we find foxes preserved for sporting purposes, and we have seen them within a very short distance of houses both in Bowdon and Sale. The polecat or fonmart is practically extinct, one of the latest records is of one killed near the shooting grounds about six years ago. Incessant persecution has failed to make much impression on the numbers of weasels and stoats, though it has told upon the otters, which are only rarely seen now. A short time since one was killed in Dunham village, and their footmarks may still occasionally be seen on the mud of the Bollin and Birkin.

About seventy-eight species of birds breed in the district, and many others visit us regularly every winter; the autumn migrants from the far north filling the gaps left by those that only spend the summer with us, and also increasing the numbers of the resident species. Besides these, there are a large number of birds that do not remain with us, but may be occasionally seen as they stop to rest on the migration, or are storm-driven from their usual haunts, and which may be termed accidental visitors.

The song thrush and blackbird are particularly abundant, and breed freely with us; the missel thrush is not as common as it was a few years since, but its nest in the fork of a tree may still often be found. The fieldfare and redwing come to us in autumn, and though the latter is notoriously shy, in hard winters we have seen it feeding on the holly berries on Bowdon Downs. The wheatear is only an accidental visitor on migration, breeding on the higher land, in East Cheshire and the Peak. The whinchat and stonechat visit us, the former breeding occasionally. The smart redstart is evidently increasing in numbers and familiarity, and we have known it successfully rear its brood within a few yards of the gates of Dunham Park. The cheerful song of the robin is familiar to all, for he sings when all the other birds are silent. The whitethroat is far more abundant than its smaller relation, the lesser whitethroat, which occasionally nests in the district. The songs of the blackcap and garden warbler are about the prettiest of our summer chorus. The goldcrest sometimes breeds with us: Mr. Grindon says in the yews in Dunham Park, but it is far commoner in flocks in winter, when the over-sea migrants have arrived. The chiffchaff, willowwren, and woodwren come to breed, and their pretty songs are most welcome heralds of spring. The sedge warbler breeds among the rank herbage of almost every pond, skulking in the undergrowth, and singing a song which is a curious mixture of beautiful notes and harsh grating sounds. From his habit of singing at night, he has been mistaken for the nightingale, a bird which to our knowledge has never visited Bowdon. In 1863 one created quite a sensation at Wilmslow, and last year we had the good fortune to hear one at Romiley; but the reported visit of one of these wonderful songsters to a plantation near Sale Station some years ago requires confirmation. Suspended to the tall reeds round Rostherne Mere, the beautiful deep nest of the reed warbler may be found, and in secluded spots we may have the good fortune to hear the long trill of the grasshopper warbler, though this bird is only a very rare breeder with us. The long-tailed tit sometimes builds its beautiful round nest of moss and lichen in the plantations, but is commoner in flocks in winter. The great, marsh, cole, and blue tits are resident with us, and in the spring the notes of these birds are the commonest sounds in Dunham Park. The wren builds its cosy nest under the banks of the rivers, or among the roots of fallen trees; and behind loose bark we may sometimes find the home of the tree creeper, that sombre-tinted little bird that runs up the boles of trees like a mouse, as it searches the crevices for insects. Only two wagtails breed with us, the pied and yellow, but the grey wagtail frequently comes down from its breeding grounds on the hills to visit our streams in winter. The meadow pipit is perhaps the commonest bird in the water meadows of the Bollin and Mersey, and in the park land its place is taken by the tree pipit, who frequently becomes the foster parent of the cuckoo, a bird especially abundant in Dunham. The spotted flycatcher is a common spring migrant, often building in creepers on houses, but the pied flycatcher is only known as an accidental visitor on its migration north, to its breeding haunts in the Lake District and Scotland. The swallow, house martin, and sand martin are most abundant, the last bird digging its holes in gravel pits and the sandy banks of the rivers. The monotonous note of the greenfinch is familiar to all, and its rarer relation, the hawfinch, is a resident with us, though it is so exceedingly shy that it is seldom seen except when it visits the market gardens in search of food. The goldfinch does not breed with us, but is occasionally seen in winter, sometimes in company with linnets, which, also owing to the lack of suitable places, do not nest in the immediate neighbourhood. The lesser redpole or jitty, as it is locally called, is an occasional breeder. In hard winters siskins visit us in flocks, and the same remark applies to the snow bunting. The house sparrow is everywhere, and the tree sparrow nests in a few suitable spots. The mountain linnet or twite formerly bred on Carrington Moss, but probably now does not visit the district. The bullfinch is by no means rare, in fact the fruit growers complain that it is far too common.

The wheezy notes of the corn bunting may be heard in Sale meadows, but it is very local, and cannot be called a common bird. The yellow-ammer is the most familiar member of this family, and the black headed or reed bunting is to be seen near most of the ponds. Starlings or shepsters are increasing in numbers almost everywhere, and this district is not an exception. After the breeding seasons, the birds gather in flocks, and roost together in some covert or reed bed; up to a few years ago a plantation in Ashton was monopolised by these birds, and countless thousands used to arrive about dusk, gathering together from all the country round, and from an ornithologist's point of view it was one of the most interesting spots in the district. The bright plumaged jay inhabits the preserved land, and its noisy scream is a familiar sound in Dunham Park. Magpies are rare near Bowdon, but exceedingly plentiful about Sale and Northenden, and when the trees are bare in winter, the huge domed nests are most conspicuous objects. The old timber in the park supplies plentiful nesting holes for jackdaws. Some years ago a pair commenced to nest in the spire of the Bowdon Presbyterian Church, and have occupied it annually ever since, and now a branch colony has been started in St. John's (Altrincham) Church spire, and we hope the cheerful birds may long be left in possession. Large rookeries have existed for years at Oldfield and Ashley, and lately smaller branch rookeries have been started in many places, such as the Higher Downs, and Hope Road, Sale; and we welcome these respectable birds wherever they will build. The carrion crow, that bugbear of the game preserver, builds when not molested in one or two localities. Skylarks breed plentifully, and in winter consort in large flocks, feeding in the fields. The swift is another of our birds that has increased within late years. It returns to its haunts with great regularity every spring, and announces its arrival by flying backwards and forwards with its curious but not unwelcome scream. One of our most noteworthy spring migrants is the goatsucker or nightjar. For years two or three pairs have inhabited Dunham Park, and on spring evenings the churring notes may be heard; and the two eggs laid on the bare ground have several times been found. The green woodpecker formerly nested in the Park, and is still an occasional visitor a little further afield. The starlings occupy most of the holes that the greater spotted woodpeckers made. Kingfishers are common in winter, and still breed where not disturbed. Four owls occur, the barn, tawny, long eared, and short eared owl, the first three breeding, the last only as a winter visitor, although it formerly nested on the mosses. The barn or white owl breeds in the roofs of one or two houses in Bowdon; and often cause alarm by appearing in unexpected places. One made its appearance during service in St. John's Church, Altrincham; and a couple were captured in the clock tower of the Town Hall in the Old Market Place, after terrifying the man who had gone up to clean the clock. The sparrow-hawk and kestrel represent the resident hawks, but as breeding birds are far from common now, though both have nested near Dunham within the last few years. Some of the rarer raptorial birds have been killed in the neighbourhood, among them the noble osprey was obtained at Rostherne many years ago, and quite recently two were observed for several days capturing fish in the mere.

Many years ago a heronry existed in Dunham Park, but now the bird is only seen as a visitor, the nearest existing heronry being at Tabley. In the early morning herons still visit the old man pool in Dunham Park, and we have often seen them flying over Bowdon. Large numbers of ducks and geese pass over Bowdon on migration, but the mallard is the only breeding species, nesting in the Park and in preserved plantations.

Wigeon, pochard, teal, and tufted duck, come in large flocks to Rostherne Mere in the winter. The last named bird may possibly remain to breed, though we have no certain evidence, but as the tufted duck is extending its breeding range all over England, it is possible that in a few years it may be numbered amongst our residents.

Woodpigeons or ringdoves abound especially in the neighbourhood of Wythenshawe and Sale, and cause great annoyance to the farmers in winter. The stock dove breeds in several places, and the rare little turtle dove probably nests in secluded spots, as we have heard of several in the spring, and obtained a specimen in full breeding plumage from Dunham Park. Before Carrington was drained red grouse were abundant, but now we doubt if more than one or two pairs are left.

Pheasants and partridges are strictly preserved. The visits of the quail are erratic, and for many years none are to be seen but in quail years it has been observed in fair numbers, and has nested within a few miles of Bowdon. The grating notes of the corncrake sound in our fields every summer, and the bird has been obtained in the winter at Sale. The water rail has been seen on several occasions, and may possibly breed, but its habits are so retiring that it easily escapes notice. Waterhens and coots are plentiful, the former breeding in the smaller ponds, and the latter in large numbers at Rostherne, Mobberley, and other large waters. The great crested or tippet grebe is one of our most interesting birds, many pairs breeding on Rostherne Mere, where their wet floating nests are attached to the tall reeds. The dabchick or little grebe breeds there, as well as on some of the smaller ponds. Lapwings inhabit the fallows, and when they congregate in large flocks in winter, golden plover may often be seen in their company. Woodcock come as winter visitors, and the common snipe, though more frequent in winter, breeds in a few marshy spots. The sandpiper frequents the Bollin in summer, and breeds on the shores of Rostherne Mere. The curlew formerly bred on Carrington Moss. Storm driven or wandering gulls and terns, such as herring gulls, blackheads, and lesser black backed gulls, and common and arctic terns, may often be seen on the meres, or in the meadows when the water is out; and two of the skuas have been obtained in the neighbourhood. It is a noteworthy fact that since the opening of the Ship Canal, large numbers of blackheaded gulls follow the line of the water, and afford "sport" to the local pothunters.

The common frog and toad, and two newts, the crested and great warty newt, represent the amphibians. When Carrington Moss was in its original state, viviparous lizards and vipers were fairly abundant, and some years ago a ring snake was captured near Peel Causeway, but the district is now almost, if not entirely, destitute of true reptiles. Most of the coarse fish are to be captured in the numerous ponds and streams, such as pike, roach, dace, and eels, and we hope now that active steps are being taken to prevent the sewage of the manufacturing towns from entering the streams, we may soon welcome back to the waters of the Bollin trout and grayling, which have been almost banished to the clearer waters of the Birkin and smaller streams.

The romantic village of Rostherne also claims attention. At the time of the Doomsday survey this manor belonged to Gilbert Venables, baron of Kinderton, and was held under that barony at a very early period by the family of Rostherne, which ended in two female heiresses in the reign of Henry II. In 1320 the Venables' share was conveyed by William Venables to the ancestor of Leighs of Booths, and Peter Leigh sold it to Wilbraham Egerton, Esq., grandfather of the present Lord Egerton of Tatton, who, as the descendant of the Masseys of Tatton, now owns the entire township. The church, dedicated to St. Mary, was carefully restored under the direction of Lord Egerton of Tatton, and the interesting features of the ancient edifice have been retained. The memorials are not only numerous but interesting. There are several monuments to the memory of members of the Egerton family, amongst the most noteworthy being a fine production by Westmacott to the memory of Charlotte Lucy Beatrix Egerton, who died suddenly November 10th, 1845, in her 21st year. It represents the recumbent figure of the young lady as she was found on the morning of her death ; over the body, in a stooping posture, is the representation of an angel with expanded wings, with the inscription underneath :— "Weep not, she is not dead, but sleepeth." There are also memorials to the Masseys, the Daniels, and the Leghs. It was currently believed by that somewhat mythical personage, "the oldest inhabitant," that Rostherne Mere has no bottom, and the old superstition was that it had underground communication with the Atlantic Ocean. The legend of the mermaid of Rostherne Mere is derived from this idea. This lake, "Rood's Tarn, (Roderstorne), or the Lake of the Holy Cross, points to a long antiquity for Rostherne Church. It is supposed that the tower was completed and the bells hung in the belfry. An evil spirit, however, seems to have possessed one of these bells, which rolled down the bank into the Mere, and it sank to sleep —

> Where mortal fingers ne'er dared to creep,
> For ever — evermore.

ROSTHERNE CHURCH.

On Easter morn the mermaid appears on the floating bell, and sings her song. Then —

> The song dies out, and the waves roll on,
> The sunbeams rest where the metal shone,
> The bell has sunk with a sad refrain,
> The Naiad bindeth her locks again;
> With a mocking laugh she bids adieu,
> Then dives, mayhap, to the deeper blue;
> For a purple mist enshrouds her fate,
> And the mere rolls drear and desolate.

Thus sings John L. Owen in his "Lyrics from a Country Lane," and they are much more harmonious and to the point than a "morning," quoted by an elderly and worthy dame about its peal of bells, as follows :—

     Higher Peover pans,
     And Lower Peover kettles,
     And Knutsford sweet roses,
     And Rostherne great drones.

Hale Barns, in the township of Hale, derived its name at a comparatively recent date from the tithe barns which existed in the district for many years, one of which stood until after 1848 just behind the Mission Church. The smithy and wheelwrights' shops were built about 1883 upon the sites of the old thatched ones. In the immediate neighbourhood is "vallum field," which is supposed to have been the site of a Roman camp or township. In support of this view we may quote from Watkin's "Roman Cheshire" (pp. 306-7), the author of which bestowed much care and research on his subject. "It is probable," he writes, "there has been a Roman villa at a place called 'Wall Field,' at Hale Barns, near Bowdon. This wall field lies on the western slope of a ridge of land which runs between two small streams and points to Bowdon. The soil from the eastern or upper part of the field seems to have been in a great degree removed to the western side, which is all "made ground" for the purpose of producing a level surface. The western side still rises for a length of about two hundred yards, about six feet higher than the field immediately beyond. There is a large ditch, now filled up to a great extent, at the boundary between them, and this, which runs in a straight line, is exactly parallel to the elevated field above it, the surface of the latter, as before said, being level and forming a sort of terrace. In the ground to the east of wall field stands a house, purchased some years since by the late Dr. Leigh, Medical Officer of Health for Manchester, with the ground around it. This is on the summit of the ridge. Dr. Leigh informed me in 1880 that in the previous year in taking down a portion of the house, which is an old half-timbered one, the foundations of the walls were found to be formed of red tiles, about two inches thick and seven and a half inches square. Many

ALTRINCHAM CEMETERY CHAPEL, HALE.

hundreds of these were found, and he considered them Roman. In digging up the old courtyard to extend the garden, a small piece of 'Samian' ware, embossed with vine leaves was also found; so that with this evidence before us, there seems from the construction of the ground, the etymology, the remains found (scanty though they may be) a *primâ facie* case that a Roman villa may have existed on the ground. I must own, however, that I have seen none of the bricks named, which are small in size, though we have undoubted instances occurring on Roman sites, and it is also well known that bricks of this size and shape were made in the middle ages. We must take the evidence for what it is worth." Precisely. And the writer of these lines is prepared to offer confirmation of the highest character. He was informed by the late Mr. Titus Hibbert-Ware, to whom reference is made later in this chapter, that in his father's days there were in this field distinct marks of the existence of a Roman camp, the vallum being exceedingly well defined and distinctly Roman in appearance and character.

Nearly opposite the smithy is the old cottage, where the late Mr. John Clarke, who was stricken with physical deformity, kept school on old fashioned lines. He did not spare the rod, and thereby spoil the child, and it is subject of local comment that many of his quondam pupils are now substantial farmers, who have also in course of time risen to the dignity of parish councillors. The "manor house," now the residence of H. Sowler, Esq., has been built to harmonise with the old Cheshire "Magpie" style of farmhouse, which has been amalgamated with it. A little further on southwards, at an ivy-covered house, Dr. Hibbert-Ware, the learned author of the foundation of the Manchester Collegiate School, lived for many years until his death in 1848. His son, Mr. Titus Hibbert-Ware, barrister-at-law, resided in Stamford Road, Bowdon, and with his gifted wife, was the instrument of great good. He was the means of mediating amongst neighbours, and many sought his advice on legal matters. This was given with a kindly disinterestedness which was highly appreciated. Mrs. Hibbert-Ware is a novelist of high merit, and her numerous works have been well received. Her review of the life and times of "Beau Nash," under the title of the "King of Bath," was very painstaking and natural, and there are other works from her pen which have found a place in contemporary literature. Amongst her local works we have "The Bleeding Wolf," a tale of old Bowdon Parish, wherein is related the murder about Christmas time of a Scotch traveller or packman in the neighbourhood of that now locally well-known "public."

There are many traditions connected with Ashley Hall, more or less reliable, the narration of some of which would cause our readers to grin "like a Cheshire cat chewing gravel." According to Axon, this phrase takes its origin from the unsuccessful efforts of some wandering showman whose lions were humorously suggestive of the domestic species, to encourage them into activity by a surreptitious long pole. The crest of the Egertons of Tatton, "the ruddy lion ramped in gold," as the poet hath it, when over the door of a village public, as at Ringway, is better known as the "Romping Kitlin," or "'th Romper," just on the same principle that the Legh Arms, at Cross Town, Knutsford, is known as "'th Sword and Serpent," or vulgarly, "Snig and Skewer."

Ashley or Asseley Hall was the ancient seat of the Brereton family. One tradition affirms it to have been built by King John for a hunting seat. However that may be, it is a place of great antiquity. Remains of furnaces, &c., and iron occurring in nodules, which have been found, show that iron smelting was carried on here by the Romans. Mary Queen of Scots is stated to have stayed a night when on her way to Beeston Castle. Like many other ancient mansions it is fairly encompassed with tragedy and tradition, the spectre of the "White Lady," and a blood stained handkerchief retaining their hold on popular imagination until a comparatively recent period. It has no doubt many secret rooms, and it is even now thought by many that a subterranean passage communicated with Bowdon Church, whereby the inmates of the Hall might attend divine service in troublous times, when, to have gone by road would have been a source of danger. A most notable event, and one which has historical basis, took place at Ashley Hall in 1715. George I. had only the year before ascended the English throne, and party feeling ran high. Many of the Cheshire Squires were descendants of Cavaliers, while on the other hand there were many powerful Whig families who were strongly favourable to the House of Hanover. Risings had taken place in the North, and James III. had been proclaimed, and his army had marched to Preston. Under the circumstances Squire Asheton, to whom the Ashley estate had descended, invited fourteen fellow squires to a conference, which took place one autumn afternoon at Ashley Hall. They were equally divided. Seven were for mounting the "white cockade," while seven were for joining the Royal forces then at Manchester. Squire Asheton, with true Cheshire caution, and a keen perception of the trend of events, gave his casting vote in favour of the reigning house. Subsequent events showed that his prescience was justified, and to celebrate this notable meeting those present had their portraits executed in oil and presented to Squire Asheton. These portraits, by an unknown artist, hung at Ashley Hall until 1879, when they were removed to Tatton. About 1730 Ashley was the seat of Sir William Meredith, and in 1841, it was the residence of Mr. Hill, Q.C., whose father, Captain Hill, fought at Waterloo, and who is immortalised as Captain Brown in Mrs. Gaskell's "Cranford."

Later on the hall and land passed into the possession of Asheton Smith, Esquire, reputed the finest horseman of his age, who sold it to the late Wilbraham Egerton, Esquire. The hall and farm were afterwards let to tenants, the late Mr. William Whittingham being the first ; he was succeeded by his son, who was a quartermaster in the Tatton troop of yeomanry, and very popular. He left about 1879 and has since lived in retirement near Sandbach. The present tenant, Mr. Charles Sherwin, is well known as a Judge at Agricultural Shows, and in his hands the farm has been brought into a highly prosperous condition, and is a model of what good farming should be. He also holds the rank of quarter-master of "A" squadron in the Cheshire yeomanry, and has also filled various public offices in connection with the township most creditably. The schools at Ashley were built about 1850 by the first Lord Egerton of Tatton, and the new church, which is a remarkably neat and well designed edifice, is also due to the munificence of the Tatton family, by whom it was erected in 1879. The designs were drawn and the work superintended by the Hon. Wilbraham Egerton, M.P. (now Lord Egerton of Tatton). The present Vicar is the Rev. Geoffrey Birtwell, whose unostentatious and self-denying labours are warmly appreciated by his parishioners.

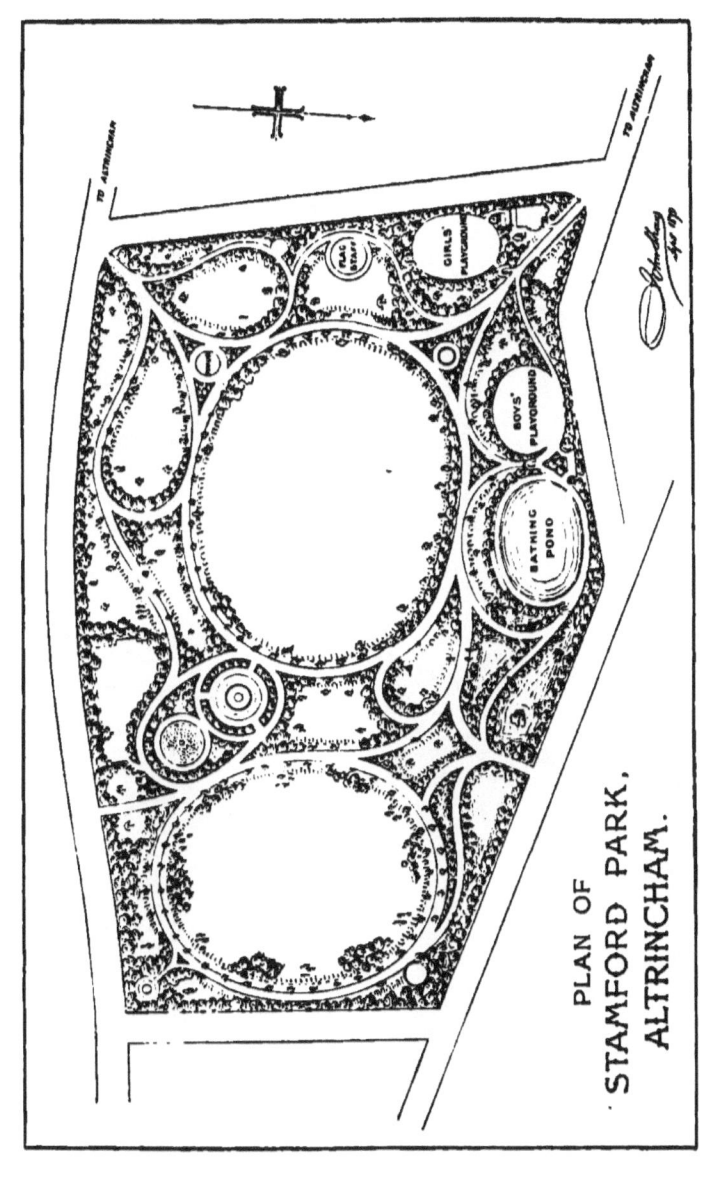

APPENDIX.

First Cheshire County Council—Bucklow Union and Rural District Council—Magistrates for Altrincham Division—Altrincham Local Board ; list of members and contested elections, etc.—List of Towns and Villages in the neighbourhood, with population, acreage, rateable value, distances from Chester, Altrincham, etc.—Sale Local Board—Altrincham, Bowdon, and Sale Urban District Councils, etc.— Election Records — Altrincham Parliamentary Division, etc.

Names and Addresses of the County Aldermen.

NAME.	ADDRESS.
ARMITAGE, WILLIAM	Townfield House, Altrincham
BATES, RALPH	Acres Bank, Stalybridge
BEDELL, ALEXANDER	Remenham, Wilmslow, Cheshire
BEELEY, THOMAS	Pole Bank Hall, Hyde
COLLIER, THOMAS	Ashfield, Alderley Edge, Cheshire
GREENALL, EDWARD	Grappenhall Hall, Warrington
HEWITT, DAVID BASIL	Winnington House, Northwich
HODGKINSON, SAMUEL	Woodville, Marple
KAY, CHRISTOPHER	Davenham Hall, Northwich
NEILD, HENRY	The Limes, Higher Whitley, via Northwich
ORTON, ROBERT OLIVER	Bank House, Tattenhall, Chester
RIGBY, THOMAS	Sutton Weaver, via Warrington
SMITH, JAMES	Dalmorton House, New Brighton, Cheshire
SYKES, THOMAS HARDCASTLE	Cringle House, Cheadle, Cheshire
TOLLEMACHE, THE HON. WILBRAHAM FREDERIC	Tilstone Lodge, Tarporley
TOMKINSON, JAMES	Willington Hall, Tarporley
VERDIN, JOSEPH	The Brockhurst, Northwich
WEBB, FRANCIS WILLIAM	Crewe
WESTMINSTER, THE DUKE OF, K.G.	Eaton Hall, Chester

COUNTY COUNCILLORS.

NAME.	ADDRESS.	DIVISION.
ANTROBUS, JOHN COUTTS	Eaton Hall, near Congleton	Congleton
ASHTON, WILLIAM MARK	Heyscroft, Didsbury, Manchester	Newton Ward, Hyde
ASHWORTH, JOHN	Lakes Villas, Dukinfield	Dukinfield West
ATKINSON, JAMES	Mirion House, Crewe	East Ward, Crewe
BARLOW, JOHN EMMOTT	Torkington Lodge, near Stockport	Bramhall
BATE, ROGER	Ash Hill, Tarporley	Tarporley
BECKETT, JOSEPH	Belvidere, Wirswall, near Whitchurch	Audlem
BRATT, HENRY	The Poplars, Winnington, near Northwich	Witton
BROCKLEHURST, WILLIAM BROCKLEHURST	Butley Hall, near Macclesfield	Division 4, Macclesfield
BROWNSON, GEORGE	Gower Hey, Hyde	Werneth Ward, Hyde
CHEETHAM, JOHN FREDERICK	Eastwood, Stalybridge	Division 3, Stalybridge
COOKE, GEORGE	Clayley Hall, Handley, near Chester	Tattenhall
CREW, THOMAS	Park Villa, Macclesfield	Division 3, Macclesfield
DAVIES, CHARLES BRERETON	Eardswick Hall, Minshull Vernon, near Middlewich	Church Coppenhall
DAVIES, JAMES	Hollinfare, near Warrington	Bowdon
DIXON, GEORGE	Astle Hall, Chelford, Cheshire	Alderley
DYSON, ARTHUR KAYE	Lee House, Sale	Sale
DYSON, JAMES	Gatley Hill, Cheadle, Cheshire	Cheadle

COUNTY COUNCILLORS.—Continued.

NAME.	ADDRESS.	DIVISION.
EARP, WILLIAM RICHARD	The Tannery, Preston Brook, Cheshire	Daresbury
EDDOWES, STANTON	Brookfield House, West Kirby, Cheshire	West Kirby
EDWARDS, JOHN	Haslington Hall, near Crewe	Willaston
EGERTON OF TATTON, WILBRAHAM BARON	Tatton Park, Knutsford	Knutsford
EVANS, JOHN JAMES	Brackenwood, Higher Bebington, Birkenhead	Bebington
FENTEM, MARK	Beechwood, Stalybridge	Division 2, Stalybridge
FODEN, EDWIN	Elworth House, Bradwall, near Sandbach	Sandbach
FRANCE-HAYHURST, COLONEL CHARLES HOSKEN	Bostock Hall, Middlewich	Davenham and Church Hulme
GRAHAM, D.	The Lydiate, Willaston, near Chester	Neston
GRAVESON, MICHAEL TYSON	Hill Side, Rowson Street, New Brighton	Liscard
GREEN, PETER	Silver Hill, Hyde	Godley Ward, Hyde
GREG, EDWARD HYDE	Quarry Bank, Handforth, Cheshire	Wilmslow
GREG, FRANCIS	Turner Heath, Bollington, near Macclesfield	Bollington
HAZLEHURST, CHARLES WHITEWAY	Runcorn	Runcorn, North
HIRST, JOSHUA	Oaklands, Godley, Hyde	Mottram-in-Longdendale

MM

COUNTY COUNCILLORS.—*Continued.*

NAME.	ADDRESS.	DIVISION.
HODGSON, WILLIAM	Helmsville, Crewe...	West Ward, Crewe
HOPWOOD, ROBERT	Brooklands, Stalybridge	Division 1, Stalybridge
HORNBY, ALBERT NEILSON	Parkfield, Nantwich	Nantwich
JOYCE, JOHN	Sea Bank House, Liscard	Seacombe
KILLICK, THOMAS WILLIAM	Gracemount, Altrincham	Altrincham
LEIGH, JAMES	Manor House, Brinnington, near Stockport	Bredbury
LEWIS, JOSEPH SLATER...	Stechford, near Birmingham	Frodsham
LISTER, CHARLES	Agden Hall, near Lymm, Cheshire	Lymm
MILNER, EDWARD	Hartford Manor, Northwich	Northwich
MOSS, EDWARD HOWARD	Ravenscroft Hall, near Middlewich	Middlewich
NEEDHAM, JAMES	Roe Wood House, Higher Hurdsfield, near Macclesfield	Division 2, Macclesfield
NEVILL, CHARLES HENRY	Bramall Hall, near Stockport	Marple
PARKER, THOMAS	Churton Hall, near Chester	Malpas
PARR, JOSEPH CHARLTON	Grappenhall Heyes, near Warrington	Appleton
SMALE, JOHN	The Brooklands, Macclesfield	Division 1, Macclesfield
SMITH, JOSEPH WILLIAM	Ivy House, Weaverham, Cheshire	Weaverham
SPEAKMAN, PHILIP	The Mount Higher Runcorn, Runcorn	Runcorn South

APPENDIX.

COUNTY COUNCILLORS.—*Continued.*

NAME.	ADDRESS.	DIVISION.
TATTON, THOMAS EGERTON	Wythenshawe, Northenden, near Manchester	Timperley
THOMPSON, JOHN	Netherleigh House, Chester	Chester Castle
THORNYCROFT, CHARLES EDWARD	Thornycroft Hall, Chelford, Cheshire	Sutton
TURNER, WILLIAM	Over Hall, Winsford, Cheshire	Winsford
WELCH, CHARLES	The Royal Hotel, Nantwich Road, Crewe	South Ward, Crewe
WILBRAHAM, GENERAL SIR RICHARD, K.C.B.	Rode Hall, near Stoke-on-Trent	Astbury
WRIGLEY, EMOR GREEN	Victoria House, off Yew Tree Lane, Dukinfield	Dukinfield East

GUARDIANS OF THE BUCKLOW UNION.

Altrincham :
   North Ward... FULLERTON, HUGH, Westwood
   South Ward ... ARMITAGE, MRS. KATHERINES., Townfield House
   East Ward ... O'BRIEN, JAMES, 77, New Street
   West Ward ... GRIFFITHS, ALFRED, Normans Place
   Central Ward.. MEADOWS, HENRY, Barrington Road
Ashley .... SHERWIN, CHARLES, Ashley Hall
Ashton-on-Mersey HALL, WILLIAM, Hawthorn Villa
   ATKINSON, CHRISTIE C., Fairfield House
Aston-by-Budw'th HORNBY, RICHARD, Aston Park
Baguley .... ROGERSON, T., Ashfield Road, Altrincham
Bollin'tn & Agden DAVIES, WILLIAM, Bollington
Bollin Fee......... NORBURY, WILLIAM, Rotherwood
   PRINCE, CHARLES H., The Moss, Moss Brow
Bowdon............ HALL, JAMES, The Vale
   STEVENS, HENRY, Stamford Road

APPENDIX.

GUARDIANS OF THE BUCKLOW UNION.—*Continued.*

Carrington	WALKDEN, WILLIAM, Carrington
Dunham Massey	HIGHAM, ALFRED M., Dunham Massey
	GIBB, JAMES, Dunham Massey
Hale	RIDGWAY, GEO. E., Ashley.
	HIGNETT, REV. CANON, Vicarage, Ringway
High Legh	CROSS JOHN EDWARD, High Legh
Knutsford	HOUGH, JAMES, King Street, Knutsford
	GARSTANG, DR. T. W. H.
Lymm	SMITH, J. R., Birch Brook Lodge, Heatley
	MERCER, WILLIAM, Newfield View
Marthall	STANIER CHARLES, Marthall
Mere	HOUGH, WILLIAM, J.P., Mere
Millington	WALKDEN, THOMAS, Millington
Mobberley	LEYCESTER, E. G., Mobberley Old Hall
Northenden	BAKER, REV. E. J., The Rectory, Northenden
Northen Etchells	SIMPSON, J., Northen Etchells
Ollerton & Toft	WILKINSON, WILLIAM, Moss Farm, Toft
Partington	OCKLESTON, THOMAS S., Partington
Peover Inferior & Peover Superior	KINSEY, JOHN, Peover Superior
Pickmere	MORETON JOHN, Pickmere
Plumley & Tabley Inferior	HALL, H., Tabley Lawn, Tabley Inferior
Rostherne & Tatt'n	SMITH, JOHN T., Tatton Dale
Sale	ATKINSON, MISS JANE, The Laurels
	BURGESS, HENRY, 153, Marsland Road
	CORT, JOHN P., The Vicarage
	LAWSON, WM. E., 81, Chapel Road
	TAYLOR, WILLIAM, 6, Irlam Road
Styal	GREG, ROBERT A., Quarry Bank, Styal
Tabley Superior & Bexton	BEECH, W., New Road End, Tabley Superior
Timperley	BELL, WM., Addison Villa, Timperley
	ASHTON, ROBERT, Charlecote, Timperley
Warburton	DAVIES, PETER, Moss Lane, Warburton
Wilmslow	CLARE, GEORGE, Alderley Road
	DALE, JOHN GOODIER, Morley
	JESSOP, DAVID, Grove Street

APPENDIX. 299

BUCKLOW RURAL DISTRICT COUNCIL.
**Population 20,382. Area 56,199 Acres.
Rateable Value £192,452.
Mileage of District Highways, 248 miles, 5 furlongs, 92 yards.**

Townships.	Names of Representatives.
Ashley	SHERWIN CHARLES, Ashley Hall
Aston-by-Budw'th	HORNBY RICHARD, Aston Park
Baguley	ROGERSON, T., Ashfield Road, Altrincham
Bollingt'n&Agden	DAVIES, WILLIAM, Bollington
Carrington	WALKDEN, WILLIAM, Carrington
Dunham Massey	HIGHAM, ALFRED M., Dunham Massey
	GIBB, JAMES, Dunham Massey
Hale	RIDGWAY, GEORGE E., Ashley Heath, Hale
	HIGNETT, REV. HARRY A., Vicarage, Ringway
High Legh	CROSS, JOHN EDWARD, Metton, High Legh
Marthall	STANIER, CHARLES, Marthall
Mere	HOUGH, WILLIAM, J.P., Mere
Millington	WALKDEN, THOMAS, Millington
Mobberley	LEYCESTER, E. G., J.P., Mobberley Old Hall
Northenden	BAKER, REV. E. J., The Rectory, Northenden
Northen Etchells	SIMPSON, JAMES, Northen Etchells
Ollerton & Toft	WILKINSON WILLIAM, Moss Farm, Toft
Partington	OCKLESTON, THOMAS S., Partington
Peover Inferior & Peover Superior	KINSEY, JOHN, Peover Superior
Pickmere	MORETON, JOHN, Pickmere
Plumley & Tabley Inferior	HALL, H. TABLEY LAWN, Tabley Inferior
Rostherne&Tatton	SMITH, JOHN T., Tatton Dale
Styal	GREG, ROBERT A., Quarry Bank, Styal
Tabley Superior & Bexton	BEECH, W., New Road End, Tabley Superior
Timperley	BELL, WILLIAM, Addison Villa, Timperley
	ASHTON, ROBERT, Timperley
Warburton	DAVIES, PETER, Moss Lane, Warburton

CHAIRMEN OF THE ALTRINCHAM UNION SINCE ITS FORMATION.

1836-37	EARL OF STAMFORD AND WARRINGTON
1838-40	WILBRAHAM EGERTON, ESQ.
1840-43	REV. ROBERT CLOWES
1843-59	JOSEPH SWINBURNE, ESQ.
1859-64	ROBERT ARMSTRONG, ESQ.
1864-67	W. T. POWNALL, ESQ.
1867-69	CHARLES BALSHAW, ESQ.
1869-76	REV. THOMAS BRIERLEY
1876-87	JOHN AMBLER, ESQ.
1887-93	JOHN GOODIER DALE
1893-94	WILLIAM HOUGH, ESQ.
1895	REV. CANON HIGNETT

CHAIRMEN OF THE ALTRINCHAM RURAL SANITARY AUTHORITY.
(Now Rural District Council).

Date of First Meeting, 23rd August, 1872.

1872-76	REV. THOMAS BRIERLEY
1876-83	NICHOLAS KILVERT, ESQ.
1883-84	WILLIAM FAIR, ESQ.
1884-85	CHARLES HOLT, ESQ.
1885-87	JOHN GOODIER DALE, ESQ.
1887-88	CHARLES HOLT, ESQ., AND JOHN GOODIER DALE, ESQ.
1888-93	WILLIAM HOUGH, ESQ.
1893-94	T. W. H. GARSTANG, ESQ.
1894	T. W. H. GARSTANG, ESQ., AND REV. CANON HIGNETT
1895-96	WILLIAM HOUGH, ESQ., J.P.

ACTING MAGISTRATES FOR THE ALTRINCHAM PETTY SESSIONAL DIVISION.

	When Qualified.
BAZLEY, SIR THOMAS SEBASTIAN, Hatherop Castle, Gloucestershire...	14th Aug., 1860
ALLEN, BULKELEY, ESQ., West Lynn, Altrincham	19th Oct., 1885
ARMITAGE, GEO. FAULKNER, Stamford, ,,	20th Jan., 1894
BELLHOUSE, WALTER, Mynshall Mills, Manchester	7th April, 1879
BOWEN, GEORGE, George Street, Altrincham......	1st Jan., 1897
BRABAZON, WM. PHILIP, Brook House, Lymm...	1st Jan., 1890
CROSFIELD, ERNEST MORLAND, Lymm	7th April, 1896
CAWLEY, HUGH, Arden House, Ashley............	2nd Jan., 1893
CLEGG, NEVILLE, Oldfield Brow, Altrincham ...	2nd April, 1894
DEWHURST, G. LITTLETON, Beechwood, Lymm...	7th April, 1896
*DYSON, ARTHUR KAYE, Lee House, Sale	1st Jan., 1890
GADDUM, H. T., Green Walk, Bowdon	21st Nov., 1882
GILL, R. P., Woodheys Hall, Ashton-on-Mersey..	7th April, 1879
HAWORTH, ABRAHAM, Green Walk, Bowdon	15th Oct., 1883
HAWORTH, JESSE, Green Walk, Bowdon	15th Oct., 1883
HOGG, ADAM, Silverlands, Bowdon	15th Oct., 1883
JOYNSON, ED. WALTER, Ashfield, Sale	4th Aug., 1881
JONES-PARRY, ADMIRAL JOHN, Thelwall Hall, near Warrington	14th Oct., 1895
JOYNSON, RICHARD HAMPSON, Park Rd., Bowdon	6th Jan., 1875
KILLICK, THOS. W., Gracemount, Altrincham ...	30th Dec., 1889
KENDALL, JOHN, Moorlands, Sale	7th April, 1896
LEGH, H. M. CORNWALL, High Legh..............	19th Oct., 1877
MILLS, A. W., Green Walk, Bowdon..............	4th Aug., 1881
MOTHERSILL, C., Alton House, Buxton	15th Oct., 1883
NEILD, ALFRED, East Downs Road, Bowdon......	20th Nov., 1883
NORRIS, T. POTTER, Eagle Brow House, Lymm	16 h Feb., 1875
PLATT, JOHN, The Oaklands, Timperley	4th Jan., 1888
POLLITT, WILLIAM, Fernlea, Bowdon	7th April, 1896
PLATT-HIGGINS, FRED (M.P.), Bowdon	17th Oct., 1892

* Died October 19th, 1896.

ACTING MAGISTRATES FOR THE ALTRINCHAM PETTY SESSIONAL DIVISION.—*Continued.*

	When Qualified.
ROOKE, GEORGE, Moorside, Sale	15th Oct., 1883
SIDEBOTHAM, J. W. (M.P.), The Thorns, Bowdon	4th Jan., 1888
SIDEBOTHAM, ED. JOHN, Erlesdene, Bowdon	7th April, 1896
STUBS, PETER, Newnham, Gloucestershire	1st Jan., 1872
TATTON, T. EGERTON, Wythenshawe, Northenden	13th Aug., 1868
THORNBER, HARRY, Rookfield Avenue, Sale	4th April, 1893
WATKIN, ALFRED, Dane Bank, Lymm	20th Jan., 1894
WORTHINGTON, HENRY HUGO, Feinton Court, Honiton	1st Jan., 1890

CHAIRMEN OF DISTRICT COUNCILS QUALIFIED TO ACT AS JUSTICES.

ALTRINCHAM	Vacant at time of going to press
BOWDON	H. T. GADDUM, ESQ.
SALE	J. E. DAVIES, ESQ.
ASHTON-ON-MERSEY	H. V. KILVERT, ESQ.
LYMM	G. L. WELFORD, ESQ.

MEMBERS OF THE ALTRINCHAM LOCAL BOARD SINCE ITS FORMATION IN 1851.

1851.

R. BROADBENT (Chairman)

THOMAS MARSDEN	W. MILNES MILLINGTON
JOHN MORT	EDWARD JOYNSON
SAMUEL BARRATT	ROBERT WILLIAM BENNETT
WILLIAM WARREN	JESSE BLEW

Officials :
ISAAC TURTON, Surveyor ;
NICHOLLS and WORTHINGTON, Legal Advisers.

1852.
R. BROADBENT (Chairman)

JAMES GRANGE	J. MORT
T. MARSDEN	S. BARRATT
E. JOYNSON	W. WARREN
R. W. BENNETT	W. M. MILLINGTON

1853.
R. BROADBENT (Chairman)

E. JOYNSON	T. MARSDEN
W. WARREN	R. W. BENNETT
JOHN DAVENPORT	J. GRANGE
S. BARRATT	J. MORT

1854.
R. BROADBENT (Chairman)

ALEXANDER H. PATERSON	T. MARSDEN
J. DAVENPORT	WILLIAM WARREN
JOHN MORT	JAMES GRANGE
S. BARRATT	R. W. BENNETT

1855.
R. BROADBENT (Chairman)

SAMUEL BARRATT	R. W. BENNETT
A. H. PATERSON	GEORGE BOWDEN
THOMAS KNIGHT	W. WARREN
J. DAVENPORT	J. MORT

1856.
R. BROADBENT (Chairman)

A. H. PATERSON	W. WARREN
THOMAS KNIGHT	R. W. BENNETT
J. DAVENPORT	GEORGE BOWDEN
J. MORT	S. BARRATT

1857.
R. BROADBENT (Chairman)

JOHN HETHORN	T. KNIGHT
G BOWDEN	WILLIAM WARREN
JOHN MORT	J. DAVENPORT
R. W. BENNETT	S. BARRATT

1858.
R. BROADBENT (Chairman)

GEORGE BOWDEN	R. W. BENNETT
W. WARREN	THOMAS KNIGHT
SAMUEL BARRATT	J. HETHORN
ISAAC GASKARTH	J. MORT

1859.
R. BROADBENT (Chairman)

J. MORT	G. BOWDEN
S. BARRATT	JAMES STREET
R. W. BENNETT	THOMAS KNIGHT
J. HETHORN	W. WARREN

1860.
R. BROADBENT (Chairman)

JOHN ASTLE KELSALL	S. BARRATT
JAMES STREET	JOHN HETHORN
JOHN MORT	G. BOWDEN
THOMAS KNIGHT	R. W. BENNETT

1861.
R. BROADBENT (Chairman)

J. HETHORN	J. A. KELSALL
J. MORT	SAMUEL BARRATT
THOMAS KNIGHT	J. STREET
G. BOWDEN	R. W. BENNETT

1862.
THOMAS KNIGHT (Chairman)

JAMES SOUTHERN	J. HETHORN
J. MORT	JOHN DAVENPORT
JAMES STREET	J. A. KELSALL
G. BOWDEN	S. BARRATT

1863.
THOMAS KNIGHT (Chairman)

JOHN HETHORN	JAMES STREET
S. BARRATT	JOHN ASTLE KELSALL
JOHN MORT	JAMES SOUTHERN
JOHN DAVENPORT	G. BOWDEN

1864.

THOMAS KNIGHT (Chairman)

JOHN DAVENPORT	S. BARRATT
J. A. KELSALL	*SAMUEL HOLKER NORRIS
GEORGE BOWDEN	JAMES SOUTHERN
JAMES STREET	J. HETHORN

1865.

THOMAS KNIGHT (Chairman)

JOSEPH GASKARTH	J. A. KELSALL
JAMES SOUTHERN	S. H. NORRIS
S BARRATT	GEORGE BOWDEN
ROBERT BURGESS	J. HETHORN

1866.

SAMUEL BARRATT (Chairman)

J. GASKARTH	JAMES SOUTHERN
G. BOWDEN	J. A. KELSALL
THOMAS DYSON	†M. FOWDEN
WILLIAM ARMITAGE	R. BURGESS

1867.

S. BARRATT (Chairman)

R. BURGESS	J. A. KELSALL
G. BOWDEN	T. DYSON
J. SOUTHERN	J. GASKARTH
W. ARMITAGE	M. FOWDEN

1868.

S. BARRATT (Chairman)

M. FOWDEN	W. ARMITAGE
JOHN SHELMERDINE MORT	T. DYSON
J. SOUTHERN	J. A. KELSALL
J. GASKARTH	G. BOWDEN

* In place of the late J. Mort.
† Solely nominated in place of Thomas Knight, resigned.

xx 3

1869.
S. BARRATT (Chairman)

ROBERT BURGESS	M. FOWDEN
J. GASKARTH	J. A. KELSALL
W. ARMITAGE	G. BOWDEN
J. SOUTHERN	J. S. MORT

1870.
W. ARMITAGE (Chairman)

J. A. KELSALL	J. S. MORT
S. BARRATT	J. GASKARTH
R. BURGESS	H. DAVIES
J. AMBLER	J. SOUTHERN

1871.
J. GASKARTH (Chairman)

R. BURGESS	J. BYROM
P. PONS	W. ARMITAGE
S. BARRATT	W. H. HOLT
J. AMBLER	J. A. KELSALL

1872.
Number increased to Twelve.)

J. GASKARTH (Chairman)	J. BYROM
R. BURGESS	J. S. MORT
W. H. HOLT	W. ARMITAGE
H. BALSHAW	P. PONS
S. BARRATT	THOMAS WARRINGTON
J. AMBLER	J. DAVENPORT

1873.

J. GASKARTH (Chairman)	H. BALSHAW
R. BURGESS	S. DELVES
J. BYROM	W. ARMITAGE
J. S. MORT	W. H. HOLT
S. BARRATT	THOMAS WARRINGTON
J. AMBLER	THOMAS TIMPERLEY

1874.

J. Gaskarth (Chairman)	T. Timperley
J. Ambler	J. Davenport
H. Balshaw	S. Barratt
S Delves	J. S. Mort
W. Armitage	T. Warrington
J. Byrom	P. Kinsey

1875.

J. Gaskarth (Chairman)	P. Kinsey
J. Davenport	W. Armitage
H. Balshaw	J. Ambler
T. Timperley	T. Warrington
S. Barratt	S. Delves
J. Byrom	J. S. Mort

1876.

J. Gaskarth (Chairman)	H. Balshaw
J. Byrom	S. Barratt
T. Timperley	R. Burgess
H. Kenyon	P. Kinsey
J. Ambler	G. Smith
J. Davenport	*S. Delves

1877.

J. Gaskarth (Chairman)	G. Smith
R. Burgess	J Hamilton
J. Byrom	J. Ambler
G. Wood	H. Kenyon
J. Davenport	H. Balshaw
P. Kinsey	William Smith

1878.

John Ambler (Chairman)	G. Wood
R. Burgess	W. Armitage, Jun.
G. Smith	P. Kinsey
H. Kenyon	J. Byrom
J. Davenport	W. Smith
J. Hamilton	H. Balshaw

(* James Cowsill from September, 1876, vice Delves deceased.)

1879.

JOSEPH GASKARTH (Chairman)	G. SMITH
J. AMBLER	GEORGE WOOD
R. BURGESS	JAMES HAMILTON
JAMES BYROM	WILLIAM SMITH
T. DAVENPORT	WILLIAM ARMITAGE, JUN.
P. KINSEY	JOHN SIDDELEY

1880.

JOSEPH GASKARTH (Chairman)	R BURGESS
JOHN AMBLER	GEORGE SMITH
WILLIAM GRIFFIN	WILLIAM ARMITAGE, JUN.
JOHN NEWTON	JOHN SIDDELEY
GEORGE WOOD	JAMES HAMILTON

1881.

JOSEPH GASKARTH (Chairman)	JOHN SIDDELEY
JOHN AMBLER	JOHN NEWTON
ROBERT BURGESS	WILLIAM GRIFFIN
GEORGE SMITH	JAMES HAMILTON
GEORGE WOOD	GEORGE BOWEN
WILLIAM ARMITAGE, JUN.	HENRY KENYON

1882.

JOHN AMBLER (Chairman)	WILLIAM GRIFFIN
WILLIAM ARMITAGE, JUN.	JAMES HAMILTON
GEORGE BOWEN	JOHN NEWTON
W. E. CAVE	JAMES PERCIVAL
CHARLES ESTCOURT	E. WHITNEY
A. L. TATE	GEORGE WOOD

1883.

J. AMBLER (Chairman)

WILLIAM ARMITAGE, JUN.	WILLIAM GRIFFIN
GEORGE BOWEN	JAMES HAMILTON
JAMES BOYD	JOHN NEWTON
W. E. CAVE	JAMES PERCIVAL
CHARLES ESTCOURT	E. WHITNEY

1884.

J. AMBLER (Chairman)	CHARLES ESTCOURT
WILLIAM ARMITAGE, JUN.	ENOCH FARR
GEORGE BOWEN	WILLIAM GRIFFIN
JAMES BOYD	JAMES HAMILTON
GEORGE BRETT	JOHN NEWTON
W. E. CAVE	JAMES PERCIVAL

1885.

JOHN AMBLER (Chairman)	WILLIAM GRIFFIN
S. R. ARMITAGE	JAMES HAMILTON
GEORGE BOWEN	THOMAS LEWIS
JAMES BOYD	JOHN NEWTON
GEORGE BRETT	JAMES PERCIVAL
W. E. CAVE	JOHN ROBSON

1886.

JOHN NEWTON, C.E. (Chairman)	W. E. CAVE
JOHN AMBLER	WILLIAM GRIFFIN
S. R. ARMITAGE	JAMES HAMILTON
GEORGE BOWEN	THOMAS LEWIS
JAMES BOYD	JAMES PERCIVAL
GEORGE BRETT	JAMES STEEN

1887.

JOHN NEWTON, C.E. (Chairman)	WILLIAM GRIFFIN
JOHN AMBLER	JAMES HAMILTON
S. R. ARMITAGE	THOMAS LEWIS
GEORGE BOWEN	E. G. PARKER
JAMES BOYD	JAMES PERCIVAL
W. E. CAVE	JAMES STEEN

1888.

J. HAMILTON (Chairman)	WILLIAM GRIFFIN
S. R. ARMITAGE	THOMAS LEWIS
GEORGE BOWEN	JOHN NEWTON
J. BOYD	E. G. PARKER
GEORGE BRETT	JAMES PERCIVAL
W. E. CAVE	JAMES STEEN

1889.

J. Hamilton (Chairman)	J. Percival
S. R. Armitage	T. Lewis
S. Arnold	E. Neild
G. Bowen	J. Newton
B. Goodall	E. G. Parker
W. Griffin	J. Steen

1890.

W. Griffin (Chairman)	J. Hamilton
S. R. Armitage	E. Neild
S. Arnold	J. Newton
G. Bowen	E. G. Parker
B. Goodall	J. Percival
J. Gott	J. Steen

1891.

William Griffin (Chairman)	J. Hamilton
S. Arnold	J. Hill
G. Bowen	J. Newton
T. J. Farrell	E. G. Parker
B. Goodall	J. Percival
J. Gott	J. Steen

1892.

George Bowen (Chairman)	J. Hamilton
S. Arnold	J. Hill
T. J. Farrell	J. Newton
R. Gatley	E. G. Parker
J. Gott	J. Percival
W. Griffin	J. Steen

1893.

George Bowen (Chairman)

Samuel Arnold	Joseph Hill
Thomas J. Farrell	John Newton
R. Gatley	James Steen
James Gott	J. N. Sidebotham
William Griffin	E. Yarwood

APPENDIX. 311

1894.

GEORGE BOWEN (Chairman)
SAMUEL ARNOLD
GEORGE BOWEN
THOMAS J. FARRELL
R. GATLEY
JAMES GOTT

WILLIAM GRIFFIN
JOSEPH HILL
JOHN NEWTON
JAMES STEEN
J. N. SIDEBOTHAM
E. YARWOOD

CONTESTED ELECTIONS, WITH NUMBER OF VOTES RECORDED FOR EACH CANDIDATE.

(Those marked with an asterisk (*) declared elected ; those marked (†) refused to serve.)

1851

*SAMUEL BARRATT 482
*WILLIAM WARREN 414
*JOHN MORT 270
JAMES GRANGE 150
GEORGE BOWDEN 98
*EDWARD JOYNSON 466
*ROBERT WM. BENNETT .. 351

*W. MILNES MILLINGTON 185
JOHN DAVENPORT 135
†JOHN WOOLLAM 36
*THOMAS MARSDEN 419
*RICHARD BROADBENT... 332
*JESSE BLEW............... 171
JOHN BARROW......... ... 124

1852.

*EDWARD JOYNSON   169
JESSE BLEW 114
*THOMAS MARSDEN 119

*JAMES GRANGE 122
*SAMUEL BARRATT 135
CHARLES BALSHAW......

1853.

*RICHARD BROADBENT ... 180
*ROBERT WM. BENNETT... 151
*JOHN DAVENPORT 170
WILLIAM DAVIES 137

CHARLES HOUTT 120
HENRY SERVICE 137
†WILLIAM BADCOCK......

1854.

WILLIAM DAVIES	110	*JOHN MORT	205
JOHN BRADFORD	114	*WILLIAM WARREN	196
HENRY SERVICE	110	*ALEX. HY. PATERSON	171

1855.

HENRY SERVICE	81	*THOMAS KNIGHT	210
JOHN BRADFORD	70	*GEORGE BOWDEN	193
*SAMUEL BARRATT	230		

1856.

HENRY SERVICE	72	*JOHN DAVENPORT	242
JOSEPH SMITH	34	*ROBT. WM. BENNETT	215
*RICHARD BROADBENT	247		

1857.
(No Contest).

1858.
(No Contest).

1859.
(No Contest, Mark Pierson refusing to serve).

1860.
(No Contest).

1861.
(No Contest).

1862.

*JAMES STREET	287	WILLIAM ARMITAGE	213
*JOHN DAVENPORT	219	*JAMES SOUTHERN	214
†HUMPHRY DAVIES			

1863.
(No Contest).

1864.
(No Contest).

1865.

*James Southern	322	*Robert Burgess	229
*Joseph Gaskarth	242	John Davenport	221
James Street	206		

1866.

John Hethorn	204	*William Armitage	341
James Street	121	*Thomas Dyson	378
*John Astle Kelsall	242	a*Matthew Fowden	241

a Nominated solely in the place of Mr. Thomas Knight, resigned.

1867.

*Samuel Barratt	315	*Matthew Fowden	260
William Paulden	103	Henry Hough	151
*George Bowden	247	Thomas Partington	202
John Ambler	239		

1868.

*James Southern	420	*J. Shelmerdine Mort.	314
*Joseph Gaskarth	407	Robert Burgess	310

1869.

*William Armitage	605	*Robert Burgess	413
*John Astle Kelsall	398	John Newton	237
Thomas Dyson	371		

1870.

*Samuel Barratt	386	James Byrom	279
Samuel Delves	375	*John Ambler	411
Matthew Fowden	375	*Humphry Davies	433

1871.

Thomas Partington	328	*James Byrom	573
*Joseph Gaskarth	679	James Pearson	307
*Peter Pons	676	Thomas Davison	263
Samuel Delves	455	*Wm. Henry Holt	619

1872.

*John Davenport...	895	Samuel Delves...	862
*Henry Balshaw...	960	John Siddeley	842
*William Armitage...	990	Samuel Arnold...	792
†Wm. Tudor Mabley	5	*Robert Burgess	932
*J. Shelmerdine Mort...	957	Peter Colliver...	700
*Thomas Warrington...	966	George Hodgkinson...	635
John Astle Kelsall...	522		

1873.

*John Ambler	984	Henry Dean, Jun...	826
John Davenport	808	*Thomas Timperley	856
Peter Pons	688	*Samuel Delves	984
*Samuel Barratt	850	Peter Kinsey	739

1874.

*Joseph Gaskarth	970	*John Davenport	830
*Peter Kinsey	927	James Pearson	659
*James Byrom	963	Wm. Hill Parkes	602
Robert Burgess	700		

1875.

No Election, owing to the passing of a new Act of Parliament relating to Local Boards

1876.

*H. Balshaw	803	James Percival	429
†Thomas Davison	3	James Cowsill	714
*Henry Kenyon	719	Thomas Jackson	617
*Robert Burgess	1175	*George Smith	938
Enoch Farr	366		

1877.

*John Ambler	1143	*William Smith	795
*James Hamilton	1001	Thomas Davison	492
James Cowsill	686	*George Wood	1129

APPENDIX. 315

1878.

*Wm. Armitage, Jun.	968	Joseph Gaskarth	857
*John Davenport	947	William Clegg	720
*James Byrom	958	*Peter Kinsey	895

1879.

*Robert Burgess	987	Henry Kenyon	555
George Bowen	747	*George Smith	924
Thomas Davison	341	*John Siddeley	1049
*Jos. Gaskarth	1109	A. L. Tate	442

1880.

*John Ambler	1255	John A. Kelsall	385
George Bowen	653	Henry Kenyon	633
James Cowsill	733	*John Newton	843
*William Griffin	829	*George Wood	1234

1881.

*Wm. Armitage, Jun.	1258	*James Hamilton	1323
*George Bowen	1214	*Henry Kenyon	1060
James Byrom	890	Peter Kinsey	672

1882.
(No Contest).

1883.

*John Ambler	1374	Enoch Farr	911
*James Boyd	1218	*William Griffin	1004
*John Newton	1405		

1884.
(No Contest).

1885.
(No Contest).

1886.

*John Ambler	813	John Newton	773
Wm. T. Ascroft	73	*George Richards	1070
*James Boyd	894	George Smith	680
Matt. Fowden	656	James Steen	701
*William Griffin	777	Peter Williamson	619

1887.

*George Bowen	968	John Milnes	536
George Brett	730	*E. G. Parker	903
Thos James Farrell	451	*James Percival	965
*James Hamilton	1192	Peter Williamson	653

1888.
(No Contest).

1889.

*S. Arnold	1154	T. B. Parkes	926
J Boyd	1044	W. Shuttleworth	994
J. Fletcher	998	*B. Goodall	1097
*W. Griffin	1131	*J. Steen	1145

1890.
(No Contest).

1891.

*Thos. James Farrell	1125	*Jos. Hill	1122
*James Gott	1205	Edward Neild	1067
	*John Newton	1454	

1892.

*S. Arnold	984	*J. Steen	1075
W. Collins	970	J. Drinkwater	889
*R. Gatley	996	*W. Griffin	1034

1893.

G. Arrowsmith	741	*G. Bowen	1047
*J. Percival	821	W. Collins	733
W. Brooks	463	S. Birtles	496
T. B. Parkes	527	*J. N. Sidebotham	866
	*E. Yarwood	790	

1894.

No Contest—Members retaining office until election of Urban District Council.

ALTRINCHAM URBAN DISTRICT COUNCIL.

FIRST ELECTION, 1895.

NORTH WARD.

George Allan...............	115	†William Griffin.......	101
†Samuel Rigby Armitage	56	Herbert Congreve ...	42
George Arrowsmith ...	34	†*John Newton	129
J. G. B. Barber	105	*Charles Pierson......	127
*Thomas Henry Vernon......... 148			

SOUTH WARD.

Williamson Atkinson..	58	William Pearson ...	94
*George Drinkwater...	287	Wm. Hy. Pendlebury	55
†*Joseph Hill...............	183	†James Percival	105
John Edward Meakin..	101	Thomas Turner	153
*Isaac Watts 164			

EAST WARD.

†Samuel Arnold	82	William Hulme	100
*Alfred Barker	215	William Okell..........	61
*Thomas Henry Caine..	130	*John Palmer	214
James Gregson	67	Chas. Henry Skipper..	61
Thomas Hildage.........	23	†James Steen	99

WEST WARD.

†*James Boyd...............	108	John Robinson	48
John Gibbon	71	†J. Nasmyth Sidebotham	90
†*James Gott	96	John Smith	71
William S. Mainprice..	93	John Richard Ward..	46
Wm. Agar Renshaw ...	74	†*Every Yarwood	118

ALTRINCHAM URBAN DISTRICT COUNCIL.

FIRST ELECTION, 1895.- *Continued.*

CENTRAL WARD.

Samuel Birtles	81	*Josiah Drinkwater	131
†*George Bowen	105	†*Robert Gatley	165
John Brierley	84	Walter Sydney Scott	50
Joseph Brooks	67	Jonathan Wood	72

In North Ward Mr. Charles Pierson retired through ill health, and was succeeded by Mr. George Allan.

ELECTION 1896.

NORTH WARD.

George Allan............ 98   *Samuel Thompson 185

SOUTH WARD.

John Edward Meakin.. 79   Reuben Pearson............ 72
*Isaac Watts 200

EAST WARD.

Thomas Henry Caine (withdrew) 3
William Hulme 118   *Mark Pearson 194

WEST WARD.

Joseph Brooks (Unopposed).

CENTRAL WARD.

Samuel Birtles 123   *George Bowen 155

Members marked thus * elected.
Members marked thus † members of Altrincham Local Board.

ALTRINCHAM URBAN DISTRICT COUNCIL.

Statement of Loans, &c., on taking over the affairs of the late Local Board.

SEWERAGE.

Date of Loan.	No. of Years.	Amount borrowed. £	Balance owing. £ s. d.	Paid off. £ s. d.	Annual payment. £ s. d.	When payments cease.
1871	30	4000	1505 14 0	2494 6 0	260 4 1	1901
1871	30	2500	941 3 2	1558 16 10	162 12 6	1901
1874	30	2300	1033 8 2	1266 11 10	125 1 3	1904
1878	30	1300	704 10 11	595 9 1	70 13 9	1908
1881	30	2500	1416 13 4	1083 6 8	136 8 8	1901
1882	30	1750	1020 16 8	729 3 4	96 10 8	1912

£7727 13 9

STREET IMPROVEMENT.

1881	20	1000	441 12 10	558 7 2	73 11 8	1901
1893	13	1400	1313 2 3	86 17 9	135 17 9	1906
1894	20	3500	3500 0 0	0 0 0	246 5 4	1914

£645 4 11

RECREATION GROUND.

1879	30	4000	2604 16 11	1395 3 1	238 7 10	1909
1883	30	791	600 16 7	190 3 5	45 14 10	1913
1883	10	2296	0 0 0	2296 0 0	0 0 0	
1883	10	500	0 0 0	500 0 0	0 0 0	

£4381 6 6

MARKET.

1878	30	4500	2779 17 8	1720 2 4	268 10 0	1908
1882	30	653	478 0 3	174 19 9	37 15 4	1912

£1895 2 1

FARM.

1890	50	10125	9810 15 5	314 4 7	411 8 11	1940
1890	30	875	804 17 9	70 2 3	48 6 6	1920

£348 6 10

CEMETERY.

1893	50	3300	3274 16 2	25 3 10	140 13 10	1943
1893	30	5350	5246 7 3	103 12 9	290 17 9	1923

£128 16 7

LIBRARY AND TECHNICAL INSTRUCTION.

1893	30	4000	3922 10 2	77 9 10	217 9 10	1923
1894	30	1100	1100 0 0	0 0 0	59 16 4	1924

£77 9 10

£57,740 £42,499 19 6 £15,240 0 6 £3,096 6 10

NOTE:—The Loan taken up during the year (1894) which will cause an increase in the rate is £3,500 for street improvements, the annual payment being equal to a rate of 1·07 pence in the £.

ALTRINCHAM URBAN DISTRICT COUNCIL.

BOUNDARIES OF WARDS.

Boundaries of North Ward.

Commencing at the most northerly point of the district, at the junction with the Township of Dunham Massey, at Washway, continuing along Timperley Brook (the boundary line with Timperley), to its intersection with the Manchester, South Junction, and Altrincham Railway, then continuing in a southerly direction along the centre line of such railway to Stockport Road, then continuing in a Westerly direction across Stockport Road, to the centre of Barrington Road, then continuing in a northerly direction along the centre line of Barrington Road to Woodlands Road, otherwise called Bank Street, then continuing in a westerly direction along the centre line of Woodlands Road to Church Street, then continuing in a northerly direction along the centre line of Church Street and Manchester Road to Oldfield Road, then continuing in a westerly direction along the centre line of Oldfield Road to its junction with the Township boundary with Dunham Massey, then continuing such boundary line in a northerly direction to the before-named most northerly point at Washway.—**ELECTORATE, 454 (1895).**

Boundaries of South Ward.

The north boundary commences at the end of Ashley Road, continuing in an easterly direction along the centre line of Lloyd Street to the centre of the Cheshire Lines Railway, then continuing in a southerly direction along the centre line of the said railway to Long Lane Bridge, then continuing along the boundary line with the Township of Hale to near Bath Street, then continuing in a westerly direction along the boundary line with the said Township of Hale, then along the centre line of a portion of Peel Causeway, being the boundary line with the Township of Bowdon,

then continuing along the boundary line of the said Township of Bowdon in a northerly direction, and also in an easterly direction, to the centre of Ashley Road, then continuing in a northerly direction along the centre line of the said Ashley Road to its junction with the commencement of the north boundary line.—
ELECTORATE, 675 (1895).

Boundaries of East Ward.

The most northerly boundary commences at the junction of the Manchester, South Junction, and Altrincham Railway and Timperley Brook, then continuing along Timperley Brook and the boundary line of the Township of Timperley, then continuing along the boundary line of the Township of Hale to Long Lane Bridge, then continuing in a northerly direction along the centre line of the Cheshire Lines Railway, and the centre line of the Manchester, South Junction, and Altrincham Railway to the junction with the most northerly boundary.— **ELECTORATE, 559 (1895).**

NOTE.—This Ward consists of the whole of that portion of the District situate on the east side of the centre line of the above named railways.

Boundaries of West Ward.

The most northerly boundary commences at the Township boundary with Dunham Massey, continuing easterly along the centre line of Oldfield Road to Manchester Road, then continuing in a southerly direction along the centre line of Manchester Road and Church Street, the Market Place and Market Street to Regent Road, then continuing in a south-easterly direction along the centre line of Regent Road to Railway Street, then continuing in a southerly line along the centre line of Railway Street and the centre line of Ashley Road to the boundary with the Township of Bowdon at Albert Square, then continuing in a westerly direction along the said boundary to its junction with the Township of Dunham Massey, then continuing in a westerly and northerly direction along the boundary line with the said Township of Dunham Massey to the northerly boundary in Oldfield Road.—**ELECTORATE, 527 (1895).**

Boundaries of Central Ward.

The most northerly boundary commences at Church Street, then continuing easterly along the centre line of Woodlands Road, otherwise called Bank Street, to Barrington Road, then continuing in a southerly direction along the centre of Barrington Road to Stockport Road, then continuing along the centre line of the Manchester, South Junction, and Altrincham Railway and the Cheshire Lines Railway to Lloyd Street, then continuing in a westerly direction along the centre line of Lloyd Street to Railway Street, then continuing along the centre line of Railway Street, the centre line of Regent Road, and then continuing in a northerly direction along the centre line of Market Street, the centre line of the Market Place, and the centre line of Church Street to the first-named boundary line in Woodlands Road.—**ELECTORATE, 488 (1895).**

APPENDIX. 323

LIST OF TOWNS AND VILLAGES
IN THE NEIGHBOURHOOD: ALSO
POPULATION, ACREAGE, DISTANCES FROM CHESTER AND ALTRINCHAM,
AND
RATEABLE VALUE OF EACH TOWNSHIP.

TOWNSHIPS	POPULATION							Acreage (Statute Measure)	Distance in miles from Chester	Distance from Altrincham	RATEABLE VALUE					
	1831	1841	1851	1861	1871	1881	1891				1861	1871	1872	1873	1877	1885	1890
Agden	80	113	76	98	109	104	100	572	25	4	184	1,540	1,540	1,540	1,618	1,576	66,208
Altrincham	2,708	3,372	4,488	6,623	8,478	11249	12424	457	30	—	4,932	31,308	34,226	36,044	49,024	64,315	4,725
Ashley	379	377	379	373	389	385	412	2,173	28	2	2,540	3,984	3,984	3,984	4,180	4,700	29,183
Ashton	974	1,105	1,174	1,170	2,359	3,225	4,254	1,611	35	4	3,743	13,968	16,075	17,333	20,531	27,933	8,457
Baguley	403	500	570	611	634	736	814	1,760	33	3	2,434	5,306	5,429	5,408	6,990	8,376	1,789
Bollington	268	297	300	277	253	272	253	507	57	3	1,245	1,629	1,629	1,629	1,771	1,780	20,706
Bowdon	458	549	1,164	1,857	2,262	2,559	2,702	828	30	1	1,823	21,317	21,164	22,251	25,252	26,139	4,396
Carrington	552	650	530	521	409	438	568	2,286	30	5	2,571	3,645	3,645	3,710	4,054	4,767	28,000
Dunham Massey	1,105	1,553	1,255	1,535	1,790	1,977	2,070	3,470	30	2	5,674	17,402	17,963	18,768	24,168	28,382	23,400
Hale	942	974	925	1,169	1,711	2,221	3,128	3,679	31	2	3,767	11,002	11,002	11,660	12,683	23,048	3,031
Partington	406	457	455	445	511	438	576	754	28	3	1,303	2,955	2,949	2,957	3,346	3,822	2,022
Rostherne	376	386	388	393	391	382	407	1,312	35	4	1,843	2,658	2,658	2,644	2,897	3,043	67,495
Sale	1,194	1,307	1,720	3,031	5,673	7,916	9,644	1,981	33	3	5,954	24,652	26,023	27,405	40,293	65,155	19,420
Timperley	752	943	1,088	1,571	2,132	2,241	2,461	1,628	31	2	2,559	13,581	13,006	13,857	15,921	18,911	

Total Rateable Value of Altrincham Union 1885, £466,391 ; 1895, £475,352.

ALTRINCHAM PARLIAMENTARY DIVISION.

November 1885.

Result of Poll :—

Mr. John Brooks	4798
Mr. Isaac Saunders Leadam............	4046
Majority	752

Bye-election, March, 1886.

Vice, Mr. John Brooks, died March 8th, 1886.

Sir W. C. Brooks	4508
Mr. I. S. Leadam	3925
Majority.........	538

General Election, July, 1886.

Sir Wm. Brooks returned unopposed.

Bye-election, July 13th, 1892.

Mr. Coningsby Ralph Disraeli.........	5056
Mr. I. S. Leadam	4258
Majority.........	798

General Election, July 22nd, 1895.

Mr. Coningsby Ralph Disraeli....... ..	5264
Mr. Alexander Mere Latham	3889
Majority..........	1375

LOCAL GOVERNMENT ACT, 1888.

(County Council Election, January 29th, 1889.)

Mr. Wm. Armitage, J.P.	841
Mr. John Newton, C.E.	723
Majority	118

Bye-election, vice Mr. Wm. Armitage elected Alderman at the first meeting of the Cheshire County Council.

Mr. T. W. Killick, J.P.	961
Mr. John Newton, C E.	879
Majority....... ..	82

LOCAL MEMBERS, 1889.

Bowdon Division	Mr. J. Davies, Hollinfare, nr. Warrington.
Timperley ,,	Mr. T. E. Tatton, Wythenshaw.
Knutsford ,,	Lord Egerton of Tatton.
Sale ,,	Mr. A. K. Dyson.
Lymm ,,	Mr. Charles Lister.

Election, March, 1892.

Altrincham	Mr. T. W. Killick, J.P. (unopposed).
Bowdon	Dr. E. J. Sidebotham (Vice, Jas. Davies).
Sale	Mr. H. Thornber.

SALE LOCAL BOARD.

List of Members of First Board, elected 1867:

WM JOYNSON (Chairman).
JOSEPH CLARKE
WILLIAM BUTTERFIELD
JAMES HODGSON
WILLIAM THORNBER
JOHN HENRY STOREY
ALFRED WATKIN
JAMES WORTHINGTON
ISAAC HOYLE
WILLIAM WILSON
JOHN MORLEY
JOSEPH CORDINGLEY

SALE URBAN DISTRICT COUNCIL.

List of Members of First Council, elected 1895:

JOHN EDWARD DAVIES (Chairman).

HARRY THORNBER
WILLIAM CRITCHLEY
SAMUEL SMITH FAULKNER
WILLIAM TAYLOR
MATTHEW WELLS
THOMAS KIRKLEY
JOHN CAMPBELL
JOHN MORLEY
THOMAS FOSTER WAINWRIGHT
HENRY BROWNHILL
JOHN BATTERSBY
JOSEPH WILLIAM LLOYD
ROBERT WRIGHT
WILLIAM SPEED COPPOCK

BOWDON URBAN DISTRICT COUNCIL.

List of Members of Council 1895-96:

H. T. GADDUM (Chairman).

J. HALL
E. J. SIDEBOTHAM
F. G. WHITTALL
J. ALDERLEY
R. A. WARBURTON
R. W. TRENBATH
S. W. GILLETT
D. SENIOR
A. HAWORTH
J. FERGUSON

ASHTON URBAN DISTRICT COUNCIL.

Members elected June, 1895:

St. Mary's Ward.

ALEXANDER LAWSON   WILLIAM HALL   JOHN EDWARD DEAN

Mersey Ward.

JOS. HUGHES SLATER   WM. HY. WALMSLEY   ENOS WALLWORK

St. Martin's.

HARRY VERNON KILVERT (Elected Chairman).
RICHARD READ   JOHN ARTHUR GILBODY CHADWICK

LIST OF SUBSCRIBERS
TO
HISTORY OF ALTRINCHAM & BOWDON
AT ONE GUINEA.

ADAMS, W. SALKELD, ESQ., Ellersdene, Hale.
ALEXANDER, A. H., ESQ., The Hermitage, Hale.
ALLEN, BULKLEY, ESQ., West Lynn, Dunham Massey.
ARMITAGE, J. FRED, ESQ., Heathside, Knutsford.
ASHTON, T. W. H., ESQ., Norwood, Altrincham.
ATKINSON, JAMES H., ESQ., Glentwood, South Downs Drive, Hale.
ATKINSON, REV. C. CHETWYND, M.A., Fairfield House, Ashton-on-Mersey.

BARKER, JOHN LEES, ESQ., Dunham Road, Bowdon.
BARTON, EDWARD W., ESQ., Holly Bank, Sale.
BOWLAND, JACOB, ESQ., The Limes, Norman's Place, Altrincham.
BOWLAND, JAMES, ESQ, 48, Chesterfield Road, Montpelier, Bristol.
BOWLAND, JOHN, ESQ.,
BOYDELL, JOSHUA H. ESQ., Dinglehurst, Arthog Road, Hale.
BRAGA, A., ESQ., Raby Mount, Ashley Heath, Hale.
BROGDEN, HENRY, ESQ., Hale Lodge, Hale.
BROOKES, WM, ESQ., Albert Square, Bowdon.
BURGESS, MRS., Bowness Villa, Altrincham.
BURGESS, H. M., ESQ., Stamford Street, Altrincham.
BURNS, JOHN, ESQ., 3, Arrow Street, Lower Broughton, Manchester.
BUSH, SAMUEL, ESQ., Columbia Villa, Burlington Street, Altrincham.

CLANAHAN, HUGH C., ESQ., Oakfield, Ashley Road, Hale.
COURTNEY, MRS., The Rookery, Manchester Road, Altrincham.
COUPE, JAMES, ESQ., Central Stores, George Street, Altrincham.
COWAN, WILLIAM ROBERT, ESQ., 5, Laurel Mount, Rose Hill, Bowdon.
COY, DR., Sale.

DARBYSHIRE, JOHN, ESQ., 5, Railway Street, Altrincham.
DISRAELI, C., ESQ., M.P., Hughendon Manor, Bucks.
DONALD, JAMES, ESQ., M.B.C.M., Sutton Lea, Ashley Road, Hale.

EARNSHAW, JACOB, ESQ., Lindhum House, Ashton-on-Mersey.
EGERTON, HON. TATTON, Rostherne Manor, Knutsford.

FARRELL, JOHN, ESQ., Holly Bush, Market Street, Altrincham.
FODEN, JOEL, ESQ., Church Street, Altrincham.
FORREST, REV. JAMES, M.A., 3, Cromwell Terrace, Ashton-on-Mersey.
FOX, REV. A., M.A., Albion House, The Downs, Bowdon.

GADDUM, CHARLES E., ESQ., Hale Carr, Hale.
GADDUM, HENRY J., ESQ., J.P., Oakley, Green Walk, Bowdon.
GALLOWAY, EDWARD N, ESQ., Normanby, Altrincham.
GIBB, JAMES, ESQ., Heyscroft, Bowdon.
GOLLAND, DR., Church Street, Altrincham.
GREY, W., ESQ., Albert Road, Hale.
GROVES, JAMES GRIMBLE, ESQ., J.P., Oldfield Hall, Altrincham.

HALL, JOSEPH E., Weston Villa, The Firs, Bowdon.
HAMPSON, H. J., ESQ., The Gorse, Priory Road, Bowdon.
HARDY, THOMAS, ESQ., Mere Hall Farm, Mere, near Knutsford.
HARRISON, JAMES, ESQ., Hope Cottage, Ashley Road, Hale.
HARRIS, J., ESQ., The Downs, Bowdon.
HARSFORD, J., ESQ., Addison Villas, Timperley.
HAWORTH, A. W., ESQ., Ecclesfield Park Road, Bowdon.
HAWORTH, JESSE, ESQ., J.P., Woodside, Bowdon.
HAWORTH, JOHN F., ESQ., Oldfield House, Altrincham.
HERTZBERG, REV. A. M., St. Martin's Rectory, Ashton-on-Mersey.
HIGHAM, A. MARSHALL, ESQ., Dunham Town, Altrincham.
HILL, JOSEPH, ESQ., Fernside, Broomfield Lane, Hale.
HOLMES-POULTON, MAJOR JAMES V. D., The Elms, Vale Road, Bowdon.
HOLT, OLIVER S., ESQ., Sidcot, South Downs Road, Hale.
HOMAN, HAROLD, ESQ., Claremont, Hazel Road, Altrincham.
HOWORTH, GEORGE, ESQ., Woodthorpe, South Downs Road, Hale.

HUGHES, J. TAYLOR, ESQ., Surgeon Dentist, Thorleymoor, Ashley Road, Altrincham.
JOHNSON, FREDK., ESQ., Railway Street, Altrincham.
JONES, WM. OWEN, ESQ., Surgeon, 32, The Downs, Altrincham.
JOYNSON, E. WALTER, ESQ., J.P., Ashfield, Sale.
JOYNSON, R. H., ESQ., Chasefield, Bowdon.

KERSHAW, G., ESQ., Holm Side, Dunham Massey.
KENNERLEY, HARRY, ESQ., Woodcote, South Downs Road, Hale.
KILLICK, T. W., ESQ., J.P., Gracemount, Altrincham.
KILVERT, H. V., ESQ., J.P., The Lodge, Ashton-on-Mersey.

LEATHER, J. B., ESQ., The Nag's Head Hotel, Bollington, near Altrincham.
LEECH, SIR BOSDIN T., J.P., Oak Mount, Timperley.
LEES, JAMES, ESQ., Westfield, Chesham Place, Bowdon.
LINDSELL, F. R. B., ESQ., Cotswold, Groby Road, Altrincham.
LORD, MISS, Oakleigh, Ashton-on-Mersey.

McBEATH, ROBERT J., ESQ., M.S.A., Birnam House, Sale.
MACKENNAL, ALEXANDER, ESQ., Beechwood, Bowdon.
MASON, FREDK. WM., ESQ., Homehill, Groby Road, Altrincham.
MOFFAT, ARTHUR, ESQ., Belmont Park Road, Bowdon.
MORLEY, JAMES S., ESQ., V.D., Stamford Street, Altrincham (Two copies).
MOTHERSILL, H. J., ESQ., Heathside, Knutsford.
MOTHERSILL, MAJOR, Knutsford.
MUNRO, A., ESQ., M.R.C.V.S., Stockport Road, Altrincham.

NEWHOUSE, RICHARD, ESQ., 4, Ash Terrace, Vicarage Lane, Bowdon.
NEWTON, JAMES W., ESQ., 2, St Peter's Square, Manchester.

O'BRIEN, REV. FATHER, New Street, Altrincham.
OXLEY, ARTHUR, ESQ., The Griffin Hotel, Bowdon.
OWEN, WILLIAM, ESQ., A.J.B.A., Ferny Lea, Ashley Road, Hale.

PARKER, EUSTACE G., ESQ., Broomfield Lane, Altrincham.
PATERSON, D. R., ESQ., Green Bank House, Langham Road, Bowdon.
PIERSON, CHARLES, ESQ., 18, Tib Street, Manchester.
PIERSON, CHARLES, ESQ., Woodlands Road, Altrincham.
PODMORE, G., ESQ., Dunham Road, Altrincham.
PROCTOR, J., ESQ., Northenden Road, Sale.

RENSHAW, ADOLPH, ESQ., M.A., L.R.C.P., Lindenholme, Sale.
RENSHAW, CHARLES J., ESQ., M.D., Beech Hurst, Ashton-on-Mersey.
RIGG, SIBSON S., ESQ., Motley Bank, South Downs Road, Hale.
ROGERSON, THOMAS, ESQ., 53, Ashfield Road, Altrincham.

SCHWABE, EDWARD, ESQ., Claremont House, Cambridge Road, Hale.
SHAW, CHARLES, ESQ., Devonshire Cottage, Ashley Road, Hale.
SHAW, JOHN, ESQ., F.R.H.S., Landscape Gardener, Ashley Road, Altrincham.
SHERWIN, CHARLES, ESQ., The Hall, Ashley.
SHIERS, R. HERBERT, ESQ., Moss Side, Queen's Road, Altrincham.
SIDEBOTHAM, J. N., ESQ.,
SMITH, MRS. FORD, Harrington Road, Bowdon.
SOUTHERN, JAS., ESQ., Booth Hurst, Dunham Road, Altrincham.
SOWLER, HARRY, ESQ., The Manor House, Hale.
STAMFORD, EARL OF, 2, Whitehall Court, London, S.W. (Two copies).
STAFFORD, J. H., ESQ., Oak Hill, Groby Road, Bowdon.
STEEL, JAMES, JR., ESQ., 2, Hawthorn Bank, Stamford Road, Altrincham.

TAYLOR, WILLIAM, ESQ., Devon Villas, Irlam Road, Sale.
THORNTON, J. E., ESQ., Rokeby, Oldfield Road, Bowdon.

VALENTINE, MISS ANNE, The Elms, Hale.

WALKDEN, WM., ESQ., The Hall, Carrington.
WALMSLEY, W. H., ESQ., Magdala House, Ashton-on-Mersey.
WALTHAM, W. H., ESQ., Waltham Lodge, Stretford.
WARBURTON, WM., ESQ., South Holme, Bowdon.
WARBURTON, H. A., ESQ., The Grove, Hale.
WARBURTON, JOHN, ESQ., Greenbank, Bowdon.
WARE, HIBBERT, ESQ., Hall Bank, Bowdon.
WATERS, ESQ., Hawthorn Lea, Langham Road, Bowdon.
WILLIAMS, FRANK V., ESQ., Braeside, Altrincham.
WILLSHAW, THOS., ESQ., Holmrook, Dunham Massey.
WOODHEAD, DR. A. MIALL, M.B.C.M., Chisholme, Ashton-on-Mersey.
WRIGHT, RICHARD, Earlsleigh, Groby Road, Altrincham.

www.ingramcontent.com/pod-product-compliance
Lightning Source LLC
Chambersburg PA
CBHW031427230426
43668CB00007B/473